God, Pain, and Evil

Abingdon Press • Nashville • New York

George Arthur Buttrick

God
Pain
and Evil

GOD, PAIN, AND EVIL

Copyright © 1966 by Abingdon Press

Library of Congress Catalog Card Number: 66-16020

Scripture quotations unless otherwise noted are from the
Revised Standard Version of the Bible, copyrighted 1946 and
1952 by the Division of Christian Education, National Council
of Churches, and are used by permission.

For our friends
in Garrett Theological Seminary
—students, faculty, and staff—
with gladness and gratitude

Preface

This book is by no
sudden impulse. It has been twelve years aborning, and that is a
long time for labor pains. It is written because I am fool enough to believe that a new word can now be spoken about the agelong enigma of
pain and evil. Twelve years ago I tried to give a series of lectures on
God and Suffering, first as the Earl Lectures in Berkeley, California;
next as the Emory Lectures in Emory University, Atlanta, Georgia; and
then as the Lowell Lectures in Boston, Massachusetts. During that time
span I endeavored to improve on each earlier attempt. The hearers were
kind in comment, and Abingdon Press offered to publish the manuscript.
People can be cruel, but sometimes they are too kind. So the lectures
might even now be in print had I not sent an S.O.S. to the publishers:
"Help, help! I want them back!" I knew the manuscript had not jelled;
it was not yet "right."

So in these last twelve years I have read any book that promised
guidance. A few kindled in the reading; more of them left me in
dismay. Of these latter some argued that in a world of natural law
we must expect pain, good men and bad alike, if we break the law. I
rebelled. Is life an unthinking legalism? Is God more concerned with law
than with people? Besides, I was not sure that natural law is a tenable
belief. Others in the group offered answers which did not answer: they
refused to confess the Mystery in which our good and evil, our life and
death are always held. Others were drunk in an incredible optimism:

they alleged that science will soon conquer all pain. Once more I rebelled. For one thing, I could find no evidence in our pain-racked world for the coming victory, and for another thing the optimism seemed callously unconcerned about those who had died in the struggle: are they only manure for our bright(?) garden? Still others undertook to explain suffering, and they introduced religion (e.g., the Christian faith) only as a coping stone to a house built mainly by confident rationalisms; meanwhile they were unaware of the pride or the blasphemy. Year by year my wife kept saying, "If you'll only take that manuscript from that bottom drawer and read it as if you had not written it, you'll see what's wrong with it." In the last shreds of husbandly independence I ignored her. I *had* written it. Besides, I thought I might be "on the road," even though far from home.

Then one day light struck. I was wont to carry the "problem of pain" on my mind (or on what for the sake of comic relief I call my mind) wherever I went—in the study, on the street, wading a trout stream; and one day I addressed myself (an unpromising congregation) as follows: If pain were a problem, there might be an answer in philosophy or theology; and if pain were a concern in medicine only, there might be an explanation and even a cure in science; but since pain is existential, an event, even if it be no more than a toothache, the only possible answer is another Event set over against it. So now I make confession: I, a preacher of sorts, had never outrightly confronted in regard to pain the focal Event of the New Testament or dared to expose myself to the light shed by that Event on the enigma of man's suffering. I laid aside the books and read and reread the Bible. The light that had pierced a dull mind now broadened into day. Still I found no neat answer: there is none. But I no longer cared about an answer. Why waste time on rationalistic "reasons" when you have been "surprised by joy"?

So this last summer I began to write, not as a task, but in a Gladness; and I have written for four hours each day for a hundred days. Now I am writing the preface which is really a postlude. This book has deliberately avoided Greek and Hebrew terms because I am an indifferent scholar in these languages, and because a book intended for the general reader should not be cluttered with these linguistics, the more so because they easily become pride in the author and a barrier to the reader. Scripture quotations are from the Revised Standard Version of the Bible except in instances indicated in the notes. In an age in which the children bring up their parents in the way they should walk, my sons tell me that my writing has been too compact, even to the point of a perfectionism. So I have tried to "loosen" the style, not to a colloquialism, but on an I-thou line with the reader. My sons are probably right, just as they were in their youth when they came home from the movies and said: "It is not the kind of picture mother and you should see."

How to give thanks to those who have helped me when there are no words wide and deep enough to hold the gratitude? My two preacher-sons have helped in many a conversation; Robert from his parish in Monmouth, Illinois, and David from his post on the faculty of Pittsburgh Seminary. Their older brother, John, would have made his decidedly unministerial comments if he had not been in the University of the Andes, trying to establish there an AID program in the field of economics. The leaders in Berkeley, Atlanta, and Boston, where the original partly blind lectures were given, were more than gracious: it is pain that my correspondence file no longer yields all the names. Marilyn Butt has again typed the manuscript at short notice, in two weeks after the hours of her regular work, yet with great accuracy, overcoming my original script which though in type was sprinkled with corrections in my minuscule handwriting, of which one of my students said: "You write with the left hind leg of a centipede." Cecil Jones, Emory Bucke, and Paul Pettit of Abingdon Press are excellent craftsmen, but also friends in a friendship that any man might covet. My wife has prepared the notes and the three indexes. The latter have been tedious yet straightforward work, but the notes have involved endless labor in library stacks. If a quote "gets" me I remember it, but not always the source. This book could not have been written without her help. It is hers more than mine.

I still think these pages speak a new word. Is this brash self-confidence? No, for the book is new only as the New Testament is new in every new age. The newness could never be mine: it is gift from him who gives new songs in every new night, and who leads his human flock by mountain and desert, by storm and sunlight of this world to a new city. To whom be all praise!

George A. Buttrick

Evanston, Illinois,
Friday, October 29, 1965.

Contents

1. Soundings

Many books on the problem of suffering—there are thirty of them standing in a row on my desk as I write—are somber and at times even morbid. They are preoccupied with the theme. Preoccupied means occupied ahead of time so that nothing else finds houseroom. But there is no need to write of pain in whispers, as if we were "viewing the remains" in a funeral parlor. We would not know sorrow except for prior joy. Even cancer, a fact which dramatizes what we call "natural evil," presupposes a healthy body. If everything were cancer, there could be no cancer, and there could be no life. The modern cult of despair is either play-acting or undue pessimism or a mixture of the two, for the very word "despair" comes from *de spero:* absence of hope. That is, the very word testifies to an earlier gladness. A little girl told me how she was caught in a rainstorm on the way home from school and was soaked to the skin, and ran crying; and how on reaching home she took a hot bath "on her own" and went to bed (as her mother might have proposed), and kept on crying. When I asked, "Why did you keep on crying?" she answered, "I was enjoying it now." It is possible to take a dark delight in misery to the forgetting of life's goodness. So the title of this book perhaps should have been *God, Joy, and Pain.* Too bad that the real joy is often refused, or that life is lived as if the joy had not been offered!

Our culture is not notable for gratitude. It is so *un*grateful that we have a special day in the year, 1 day in 365, to remind us of Thanksgiving. Modern journalism is no help, for it is an ellipse with two foci—sensation and conflict. Murder and rape would not be "news" if most people were not living neighborly lives. Divorce, though it is tragically prevalent, is still "news" because far more homes are unbroken. The "eternal triangle" is not eternal: it is marked out either for wise change or for destruction. The "fourth estate" may one day reexamine its definition of "news." It *is* news if a dog bites a man, especially if we know the dog and the man, and it is *not* news if a man bites a dog, for that is a case for the psychopathic ward. Some of our journals read like bulletins from that ward. Psychologically they hurt our nation. We went round the world and finally reached Geneva, there to taste white bread for the first time in months. We had not dreamed that one day we would give thanks for pure water from a faucet and white bread on the table. We came on another Thanksgiving Day! Surely every day gives some cause for gratitude, the deepest cause if only we would open eyes and hearts. Sartre's "nothingness" [1] testifies to a prior "somethingness," and the "somethingness" makes the alleged "nothingness" an act of *un*faith.

I

Yet, as first sounding, we must still confront the fact that

Man is born to trouble
as the sparks fly upward. [2]

It is the nature of sparks to fly upward. It is the nature of man to suffer. So far, so good; or, rather, not so good, for then the questions throng. *Is* man so born? Maybe science can get rid of pain. If so, why has science come so late in the day? What of the millions who, their pilgrimage now ended, have been denied the blessing? But perhaps science is not a magic wand. As to that, we shall say "no," rather than "yes." Suppose it is true that man *is* "born to trouble," then why? Does the trouble come altogether from his own folly and self-will? That is what the original

14

author believed. He contended that we bring all sorrows on ourselves:

> For affliction does not come from the dust,
>   nor does trouble sprout from the ground;
> but man is born to trouble
>   as the sparks fly upward.[3]

Is he right, or is there a plus of undeserved pain? No final answer can be found to these agelong questions, for our minds are finite. Perhaps the demand on our part for final answer is blind and almost blasphemous —blind because it is blind to our human limitations, and blasphemous because it presumes to a Godlike understanding. But our minds are given to us for some good purpose, and so we may rightly seek some answer. Else how can we rightly act?

So in this first sounding we confront the fact of pain. Every reader can supply the bill of particulars. Indeed, if everybody in any city were to bring his ills to the city square, and if they were visible, the black mountain would seem to darken the sky. Matthew Prior's Solomon has given his verdict:

> Who breathes must suffer, and who thinks must mourn;
> And he alone is bless'd who ne'er was born.[4]

That is an overdrawn conclusion. It forgets the joy without which we might not recognize the sadness. Yet it is true that "who breathes must suffer," in the mother's breath when the child is born, in the child's breath in many a sickness and in final death; and it is true that "who thinks must mourn," for thinking provokes many an agonized "why?" As for the second line of the quotation, it makes little sense, for how could anybody be "bless'd" if he were never born? Most people cling to life despite its dark side. But the questions multiply. Is pain constitutional both in the world and in us? Why must we suffer?

We continue the confrontation, while refusing any morbid forgetting of life's goodness. Pain is legion, as if some devil with a genius for sadism had spent half an eternity concocting torments. Recently I went in the late evening to the home of one of my former students. He and his wife are fine people who daily enrich our land, yet they have suffered. They

15

told of losing their two-year-old son through cancer, though their word
was faith rather than bitterness. When we went to the car the kitten
with which I had been playing five minutes earlier was crushed under
the wheel, and when I reached my hotel room I read in the newspaper
of the avalanche which killed a hundred people in Switzerland. So there
are nature's evils to which that avalanche is only a tiny footnote. There
is "man's inhumanity to man" [5] with its midnight at Buchenwald.[6] There
is the sheer wantonness of events: a father with his lawnmower throwing
up from the grass a small piece of wire which pierced his child's head
and killed him.[7] There are multitudinous pains of body, and worse
pains of mind which seem to multiply as the body's pains are conquered
or anesthetized. There are pains of memory and pains of futile longing,
for it is our nature to

> Look before and after,
> And pine for what is not.[8]

That fact involves pain with the whole mystery of time. There are vast
corporate ills such as plague and war.

The questions are compounded when we contemplate the sufferings of
worthy people. Human love brings pain. Social compassion is target for
the darts of sadness. Just to think of the thousands of men in prison
opens the door to grief. Jesus told his followers that they would meet
persecution—for being his followers. Now the inevitable "Why?" is seen
in black silhouette against martyr fires. The prayers of the saints do not
bring instant peace; they go through "the dark night of the soul." [9] The
pains of guilt we can partly understand, though we must still ask how
and why guilt came into our world. But what of the sufferings of the great
hearts of our race?

The multifarious and multitudinous facts of pain must be faced. In
this book we shall not dodge the shock. Indeed, we can never fully
escape, however fast we run. Pollyanna,[10] who looked for "the silver
lining" until she convinced herself that we can have the lining without
the black cloud, is a nasty little girl. She is a liar, and she peddles a mirage.
Imagine her in a bombed city or the city morgue! There is no dodging
the "problem of pain," and there is no easy answer. The Buddha's father

tried to shield his son from the sight of man's misfortunes, even to giving him a palace for each season of the year, but when the youth ventured into the streets he saw an old man, a sick man, a dead man, and a man who had renounced the world. So sounding number one is realism.

II

Now for sounding number two: We drop the lead in the channel to ask if pain *is* constitutional? My answer is, "Yes, for we cannot escape it in our mortal life." Now I have "taken on" the confident humanism of our time, for modern hope answers: "But is not science conquering pain?" What to reply? There has been blessing through science. Even so, it is not easy to leave friends and submit to anesthesia, and not easy to wake to dull pain after surgery, to say nothing of exile from home and work. Pains of body and pains of mind are strangely interfused.[11] In any event the surgeon who skilfully amputates a man's leg cannot give him a new leg. The psychiatrist may help the man to "adjust," but the psychiatrist and surgeon together cannot remove the limitation. Meanwhile, kittens are crushed under cars, children die of cancer, and avalanches crash down on unsuspecting towns. As long as accidents happen, and as long as men cannot guess and forefend against every contingency, pain is constitutional.

That is to say, we fall short in wisdom as well as in skill. Statesmanship takes its calculated risks, but the calculations have often blundered with worse than schoolboy mistakes. Our Western world and the Communist world have in foreign policy lately staged a competition in blunders. So with our science itself. I would not know if the book, *The Silent Spring*,[12] has proved its case, namely, that our spraying to get rid of agricultural blights has killed the birds as well as the weeds. But history is filled with such miscarriages of human hopes and plans. The failure of technology is an instance. We resolve by means of the machine to overcome drudgery (and encourage laziness?), and we brag about our "gre-a-a-t technological progress," when suddenly we meet not only the threat of automation, but the worse threat of a society in which creative thought is imprisoned by technic, so that the cult of know-how blinds us to know-what and know-why. In any event, and supposing we were all

17

wise, our memory trips us, as when we forget to watch the road while driving a car. The Bible laughs at the pretensions of human wisdom: "Has not God made foolish the wisdom of the world?" [13] But we are not yet ready to return to the Bible's much deeper wisdom. Pain is constitutional because man's mind is by no measure infallible.

There is a worse enemy than unwisdom: our overreaching pride, our resolve to be our own god. The suburban home is lovely with trees, but because the parents are intent on suburban status the children "go wrong," with attendant suffering for that home and for society. Nice people flee the slums, and the hopeless slums breed delinquency, and neither the nice people nor the delinquents are free from blame; and then there is violence in the city. Nations covet the spotlight or refuse to be pushed into the shadows, so the fields of Picardy hardly look like fields when modern war has finished with them. The church seeks its own life, and therefore while it is against war, speaking piously about "the Prince of Peace," it always justifies any present war. In short our egocentricities splinter our world into capsuled groups and selfish people, and the world cannot be splintered without pain. Until men are angels pain is constitutional. Pain goes down to the roots of our human nature. It is not removed by our spraying the leaves. That may bring a worse "silent spring." So pain is constitutional. That is why we "feel it in our bones."

III

Sounding number three brings us again to the bright side. Man is born to *joy* as the sparks *dance* upward. Can we really appreciate our usual good health except for times when we are sick? Not really. So joy and pain are perhaps the two sides of a shield, though that metaphor should not be pressed. Perhaps every dark word has its bright twin brother. Thus *mortal* implies *immortal,* and *time* as well as

> Life, like a dome of many-coloured glass,
> Stains the white radiance of *Eternity.*[14]

Our trite saying about smiles and tears being close neighbors is more true than trite. Without suffering life might be an unending glare, and without joy it might be an unrelieved midnight. So we set a face of sorrow and a face of laughter at either side of the theater's proscenium arch, for on the stage of life there is always comedy-tragedy.

Comedy is better than satire or wit, for satire is a venomed dart thrown at the whole world, and wit impales some fellow man, while comedy is a wry smile at our human dilemma. Why do we smile at man's predicament? Perhaps because we secretly know that life is held in Grace. Sartre is not only an unreconstructed rationalist despite his existential pose: he is learnedly sullen, even with all his talk about courage. Courage is of the heart by the very meaning of the word. Stoicism of a kind may walk blindly into an alleged "nothingness," [15] but courage could never play that role. A lovable clown is always the butt of the joke; he deals in comedy, not satire or wit, as when Emmett Kelly, his very bearing a sadness, tries to sweep sawdust over a spotlight circle on the circus floor.[16] Modern atheism is suspect because it has so little power to laugh at itself. Our joy is pain because we know it must soon pass; our pain can hide a rapture, for the saints have cried: "Count it all joy . . . when you meet various trials." [17] A profound book on laughter might be almost a final theology.

To pursue this fact of kinship between joy and pain: pain is linked not only with joy, but with God. The believer in God makes that connection, for he asks of sudden misfortune, "Why has God done this to me?" The skeptic makes it, as in Archibald MacLeish's *J. B.*:

> If God is God He is not good;
> If God is good He is not God.[18]

If God has power to save us from pain and doesn't use the power, he is devil rather than God; conversely if he lacks the power, he is a tinpot monarch who is vassal to some demonism. We shall confront that jingle, which theology rather than drama first posed. Here we are content only to show that for believer and skeptic alike, for faith or unfaith, the fact of pain gets linked with God. That is a strange conjunction. C. S. Lewis in his *The Problem of Pain* [19] comments on it to the effect that pain is so rife in our world that nobody should believe in God, yet awareness of God seems to be even more persistent than the awareness of pain. The two confessions—of God and of pain—are joined, for good and evil

19

are somehow joined, and joy and sorrow; and in such a world we must look to One greater than the world.

The word "God" in our Anglo-Saxon speech comes from the same root as the word "good." The "proof" of God is given in subtle ways, not by an onrush of theological armies. It comes in our thankfulness for a fine summer day, for we do not then thank trees and soil (that would be ludicrous), but we are grateful to—Whom? Thankfulness is a person-to-Person call. In the same subtle way pain reminds us of a Good in the past and bids us hope for the same Good when pain shall have passed. Perhaps that is why people go to church more when war darkens over us, that and our uneasy awareness that every war is our denial of the Good. We are not now saying that joy and pain, good and evil, are alternates. It is true, as sermons are apt to tell us, that if we cleave to joy pain becomes our agonized "problem," but that if we cleave to pain as our clue we have on our hands the "problem" of joy. But such sermons do not say enough. Good and evil are not balanced options: good in some sense resolves the evil, but evil cannot resolve the good. Here is the simple instance: The ambitious man in the office with his attempts to "take over" easily disrupts the place, while the quiet man accepting whatever misfortune may come and doing his work cheerfully brings a comradeship, perhaps without knowing it.

This strange conjunction, joy-pain, Good-evil, throws light on another quirk, namely, that noble people are always risking pain rather than live untroubled lives. We blame God for the suffering in our world, and then we deliberately add to the burden, at least in our finer moments. We are now discussing not any kind of masochism, but heroism. There was no need for the first sailor to dare the ocean: he could have stayed on shore. There was no need for the Wright brothers to build an airplane: they could have kept head and feet on the ground. No need for a high-school boy to play football, and perhaps he would not play if there were no risk of his getting hurt. On a higher level, no need for Socrates to drink the hemlock for an unidentified "truth": he could have gone on breathing. No need for Christ to die on the cross: he could have died in his bed, and why not when there were sick folk to heal and followers to train? Perhaps human nature needs danger more than bread. Perhaps a cause transforms pain. Perhaps the highest cause brings amazing transmutation. But as to that we must bide our time. Let us here and now

be content to notice that we blame God for risks, and then add to them
—for a cause. What cause?

IV

We have already hinted another sounding: Men are silent before
the cross of Christ. If that picture should be flung suddenly on any movie
screen the chattering would cease. But why in a world disfigured by pain
should we stand silent at the very place where pain is most outrageous
because most undeserved? Even the cynic cannot scoff at Calvary unless
his life has altogether curdled. At the lagoon entrance of the landfill
by which Northwestern University is extending its campus into Lake
Michigan, a large crane with its crossbeam stood high on a mound of
sand, dark against the morning sky. "Look!" I said to a fine-spirited
agnostic. That word came of itself. He understood, for he instantly replied: "Yes, it's a rotten world!" I did not answer, "Maybe it's a redeemed
world," for faith does not proselyte, and there are right times and wrong
times. I did say, "Well, it's still there, and it's empty." Then I marveled
again that at Calvary, where history seems bereft of both pity and conscience, men worship.

We should take a pencil, a red pencil, and underline that fact. What
we call "natural evil" darkens over Calvary—pierced hands and feet,
the ebb of blood bringing cramps, flies buzzing round a helpless head,
the sun striking down like a sword. Isn't it strange that the story hardly
hints this evil? Yet it is there. And a worse evil, for our outright selfishness darkens over Calvary in a blacker sky. Our fashionable sins there
converge: the greed of traders whose tables he had overturned, the
trampling might of empire, the perfidy of the temple, the taunts of
enemies, the treachery of friends, and the bloodlust of the crowd. Then
why should we be silent there, as if there we might find some solving
word in the "problem of pain"? Why there? We postpone answer. Meanwhile we may think of that valley in the Tyrol of which H. Wheeler
Robinson has told us. It was deep in snow and moonlight, a haunt of
peace. Yet there he came on a wayside crucifix, and he makes his fine
comment: "The Sufferer seemed to say, 'O foolish men, to think that
peace is ever found in seclusion from the world, or in flight from its
suffering. Here, on the Cross, is My peace." [20]

21

V

One other sounding, and then we can begin our journey into deeper waters: The "problem of pain" is always more than a problem, for all of us must meet pain even if we have no convincing answer. We must live in some kind of risked faith. The word "problem" has become a snare. Our age sees only the outside of life. The world for us is like Peer Gynt's onion: he peeled it and peeled it and could find no core: it was "all outsides." [21] We accept thus only scientific tests. We look for some answer which is as instant as a vending machine and as clear as a conclusion in geometry. But life never yields to these simplicities, and never waits: pain strikes before we have reached what we please to call "a philosophy of life." Nay, since pain goes to the roots of human nature and the core of creation, our minds can never find a complete answer. Of necessity we live by faith.

Here we pause, because the very word "faith" is in disrepute. It is more caught in confusion even than the word "freedom." And what misunderstandings have been heaped upon that latter word! A man cannot be free except in his constituted nature. Yet few people ever seriously ask what kind of a creature is man. The word "faith" suffers worse slander. Millions of people construe it to mean "what I choose to believe." Even philosophers fall into that snare. Thus Louis Lavelle in his *Evil and Suffering,* which probes as deeply as philosophy can, and which almost becomes a deeper theology, keeps saying that faith is a meaning which *we* impart to life: "I must give suffering itself a meaning that penetrates and transfigures it." [22] But in actuality faith never begins with us. There is always a prior beckoning. We read in American history of men such as Lincoln and Lee, and, thus beckoned, we respond, pledging our allegiance. It is a notable fact that we feel this obligation to the bright omens, to Lincoln, not to Benedict Arnold. So once more we must note that good and evil are not balanced options: there is a creative beckoning in the good. Thus the deep implications of such a word as, "looking to Jesus the pioneer and perfecter of our faith." [23]

Why do we bridle at the word "faith"? Science rests on it. The physical world beckons, and science then says at risk: "This is worth studying." That faith implies another: "Mind and matter have some communalty, so that mind can at least partly understand matter." That faith goes still

22

further back: "Time is a straight line of purposeful change, so that time will not travel in a circle to bring me always back to the beginning of this experiment." At each step there is beckoning, but no proof except by an act of faith.

So the "problem of pain" is not merely a problem on the mind-level: we must needs act in patience or impatience, in compassion or despair. Where is the beckoning? We do not decide it: it finds us. When and where? These questions we shall not evade. Meanwhile we may have begun to understand William Blake's lines:

> Joy and woe are woven fine,
> A clothing for the soul divine.
> It is right it should be so;
> Man was made for joy and woe;
> And when this we rightly know,
> Thro' the world we safely go.[24]

Of course the lines make no sense if we lack his faith. What *is* life "made for"? We must dare an answer, in response to some beckoning. Here is a hint which we shall later follow: We go through life while seeing ourselves go through life, and pain is the event which traces as with dagger point the line between the two dimensions. We are creatures living in two worlds, and suffering wrings from us a two-world cry: "I am mortal! Where is my salvation?" Therefore life is "made for" . . . ? But enough of soundings. We next look at some partial answers to "the problem of pain."

2. Some Answers Fall Short

We sell out nowadays to a wretched account of reason in relation to faith, namely, that reason "goes as far as it can," and that then we must "simply believe." The church has not been blameless: "Only believe!" Believe what? This wretchedness downgrades both reason and faith. The facts are these: faith of some sort is basic, for even the man who reasons *trusts* his reason (which may easily become unreason as in a lunatic asylum); and faith is always response to some prior beckoning, for even science is the response of the senses and the analytic mind to the beckonings of the cosmos. A true faith both instigates the life of reason and provides it a home. That is why the great discoveries of science come not from reason alone, but from the deeps of the subconscious.[1] But a true faith does not break the life of reason, though always it provokes reason to the next adventure. There have been various faiths about suffering. Some of them we now discuss.

Always we meet life in some faith. The botanist, first beckoned by flowers and trees, says at risk: "These are worth studying!" He says it though he may be aware that our planet may one day suffer an ice-age. He says it though he knows his little years are numbered. Why does he say it? Any worthy faith is a star-studded mystery, or would be if our eyes were not sealed. Perhaps there is a Faith that gathers in all our vocational faiths. Such is the tremendous claim of the Bible. To that issue we shall come, and without any under-the-table assumptions.

The "problem of pain" is no little problem. Some problems are not immediately vital, such as, "What is the height of that mill chimney?" or "Do new galaxies come from cosmic explosions of hydrogen?" Of course, even these questions may move to the quick center: the chimney may hazard the plane in which we travel, and distant galaxies always make us wonder about our own place in the scheme of things. But the puzzle of pain is always at the center. We cannot leave it solved or unsolved. It is not like a puzzle bought in a toy shop. It is like the ancient puzzle of the Sphinx, which the pilgrim had to solve or else forfeit his life. So we come to some answers in faith which, though they have some show of reason, do not answer the enigma of pain, but rather darken and confuse the issue.

I

A few people have believed that pain is good in itself. They have taken pleasure in pain. The outright form of this faith is called masochism. Psychology finds many an instance, but reckons masochism a perversion. It is life unhealthily turned in on itself. If we are honest we shall admit that it has had some place on the biblical scene: the priests of Baal, in their contest and encounter with the prophet Elijah, cut themselves with knives in the hope that the blood so shed would win the favor of their God. But again we should note that the great prophets of Israel turned from such excess. Elijah taunted the priests for their bloodmarked idolatry.[2] Some mystery cults in the time of the early church offered higher bliss as reward for self-emasculation, but the faith of the church shone bright against such self-mutilation. Masochism in many a modern form *enjoys* pain without any good cause. This is a topic for textbooks in psychiatry. Incidentally, the textbooks disagree as to the cause, but they agree that the masochist is sick. Honesty obliges us to confess that a martyr-role, bereft of the noble cause that might justify it, has its attractions. Have we not all been tempted? The business man "works himself to death," the minister hasn't "had three evenings at home this month,"

25

and the dowager stays endlessly in bed "because I'm a great sufferer." But, once more, common sense looks askance at these "martyrs" and knows that they have a "complex." That is to say, life in its beckonings calls us to a finer and happier faith.

But masochism, such as that of Heinrich Suso[3] who wore a hair shirt with straps fitted on the inside with one hundred and fifty sharp metal points, and who whipped himself until the blood flowed, all for the sake of "discipline," has this virtue: it provokes a blunt word: pain *of itself* is *not* good. On the contrary, it is *incipient death.* This verdict applies even to asceticism. There is need for a gladly accepted discipline, the pruning of the vine that fruit may be more abundant, but no need for monks to scatter ashes on plain food in the fear that the food might be "too tasty"! Simeon Stylites,[4] living in cold and heat, night and day, on top of his pillar for thirty years, that he might mortify the flesh and "save his soul alive," apparently forgot that other people had to bring him food; and, that, by his own faith and practice, he was therefore cheating them of salvation. The Bible holds that God made the earth and looked on it, "and saw that it was good."[5] Joy, without which we would not know pain, is the basic word: pain is incipient death.

To speak thus about pain sharpens the question "Why?" "Why, then, should pain invade our life?" But the fact that all pain *of itself* is ultimately fatal must be faced. The doctor asks, "Where is the pain?" He looks for the place where incipient death has breached the wall. Sudden pain distorts our face, and wrings from us a cry of astonishment. Pain of mind destroys or threatens our powers of concentration, and sets us aloof from our neighbors. The Bible never sentimentalizes on this issue. Books on pain may fall into emotional stickiness: "The leopard's claw gave to the antelope its surpassing grace."[6] "Gave"? Many a time the leopard has killed the antelope! As for animal suffering, we do not know, and presumably we must guard against attributing our acute sensibilities and self-awareness to animals. But there is no doubt that animals also suffer pain. Had I been tempted to nature worship, I would have turned my back on the seduction forever on a certain day when I saw bare trees filled with vultures looking down, there in north India, on a sick cow about to fall in final weakness. Both realism and compassion forbid us to deify nature.

So we stress the fact, even though it may compound the enigma, that pain *of itself* is not good. The two Old Testament words for suffering mean respectively devaluation and outright hurt. The New Testament words have an even darker cast.[7] The Bible, the most clear-eyed book, the only one not taken by surprise by our present world, never sentimentalizes over pain, evil, and death. Jesus healed men both in body and mind. He refused to spend his life thus, and that fact makes for deep ponderings, but he was against pain. The Bible describes heaven in moving language: "God himself will be with them; he will wipe away every tear from their eyes, and death shall be no more, neither shall there be mourning nor crying nor pain any more, for the former things have passed away." [8] Pain is not in heaven: it belongs to the other place, or to a disfigured earth waiting for redemption. Pain may be useful as a warning-bell: suppose fire did not burn as it destroyed. Pain may by its very pain cry out for some catalyst that can transform it into gain. But *in itself* it is no boon: it is the encroachment of death. That fact must be scored deeply even though it sharpens our recurrent "Why?"

II

A few people have believed or tried to believe that pain has no real existence. The philosophic ancestor of this notion is solipsism, the doctrine that the outer world has no reality except to our senses. This theory says that a tree would not be green except for my sense of color, nor hard but for my sense of touch, and indeed would not be "there" at all but for my sense of sight. But the tree refuses to cooperate with this theory. It stays in the same place even though my senses and my convenience might wish to remove it to a distant field. Moreover all my neighbors see it in the same place, which means either that we all have mass-production senses, or that the tree insists on being "difficult." Moreover the tree, when I bumped into it on a recent dark night, seemed to me to have its own stubborn "will." The Buddhist, when his faith is thoroughgoing, declares that both nature and history are illusion: the only pain is the pain of desire, which pain we can slowly or swiftly negate until we enter the oblivion of Nirvana. But common sense, the response of average men to the beckonings of nature and history, will reply that the death of

27

desire is the death of the person: the operation is successful, but the patient dies. As for me, the image of the Buddha spells not peace, but complacent dessication.

Our Western version of the belief that pain has no real existence is centrally set forth by Christian Science: Suffering is simply the "error of mortal mind." We pause here to make clear that these pages are not written in contrariness: no man should wish to disparage his neighbor's faith. So no harsh criticism, even though I could cite instances of people dear to me who seemed to me to die of Christian Science. Rather let tribute be paid to the utmost limit. This tribute: Our attitude of "mind" *does* influence the intensity of pain: a cheerful person with a weak heart stands a better chance in a serious operation than a fear-stricken person with a weak heart. An Indian fakir can train himself to sleep on spikes without discomfort. This tribute also: The way we "think" either stays or invites many bodily ills: worry thus brings asthma and ulcers which trust in life avoids. Pain is not of the body only: its centers are in the mystery of self-consciousness. This even better tribute: There is worthy argument "behind" Christian Science as follows—pain is so agelong, so cruel and so rife that any decent-minded man shrinks from saying that God "sends" it. If God did not "send" it, a promising alternative belief is that it does not exist: it is an "illusion" from which the mind can be freed. This other tribute: Prayer and meditation, even meditation which, as in Christian Science, is constantly guilty of *mis*translation of the Bible, may nurture a faith by which pain for a time may be alleviated.

But when every tribute has been paid, sharp questions riddle the doctrine. Yes, the mind can alleviate pains of the body, but by the same token pains of the body, or even an injection of alcohol into the veins, can influence the mind. Commonly, when we do not tinker with either body or mind, we find it hard to dismiss even a toothache, much less the desolation which fell with a bomb on Hiroshima. The fakir may master the spikes, but the spikes remain, and to me they are still spikes, for I have neither time nor wish to master them. Furthermore, if suffering is only error, so is courage, unless a man must struggle just as hard against the "illusion," in which case only the language has changed.[9] Furthermore, if we cannot trust the instant reaction of our life to a knife entering our flesh or an accident summoning our compassion, what

28

can we trust? Not any postmortem rationalizing that the pain has not happened! Furthermore, and this is momentous, the theory of "illusion" and "error" leaves the "problem of God" still unsolved, for a God who victimizes his children with "error" and "illusion" is no more attractive than a God who "sends" pain.

Even deeper questions are involved, namely, those that concern the constitution of human nature. Man is a psychosomatic unity: there are *two* terms to the paradox, body and psyche, even though they still comprise one unity, but "mortal mind" is still inescapable: it is *in measure* the only mind that a man can use. Yes, there is a paradox of mind: the discursive mind is caught in everyday affairs, while the meditative mind "sees" the man traveling on the commuter train. But perhaps pain is felt in both minds. In any event, we cannot escape mortal mind, at least not this side of death. So perhaps the theory that pain is only illusion is itself an "error of mortal mind." The whole question of "truth" is now raised. We shall not evade the question. Here and now, meanwhile asking patience of the reader, we make what may seem a fiat statement: Truth is *not* the mind's "reasoning." Let us reiterate: Jesus on his cross was not victim of an "error." He was not agonizing over an illusion. Such a pretension mocks his hard and joyous life and is not far from sacrilege.

III

So to another doctrine of pain which, while it has some measure of truth, still leaves us with short rations: Many people have believed that present *pain comes from our sin in a prior incarnation.* Clearly the doctrine has *some* truth. Pain *does* come in part from the past, from our own past in this mortal life and from the history of our race. And pain *does* come of sin, man's pride as he tries to stand at the center of the world. The tragedy of wrong choice, "man's inhumanity to man," [10] is too rife and bitter to be denied. The question of our culpable pride with its dark entail will soon engage this book.[11] But we here and now confront a distinct and separate version of the fact that suffering comes from sin, namely, that it comes from our personal sin in *our prior incarnations.* The theory has a certain appeal, even a romantic appeal, as in the John Masefield poem:

I hold that when a person dies
   His soul returns again to earth;
Arrayed in some new flesh-disguise
   Another mother gives him birth.
With sturdier limbs and brighter brain
   The old soul takes the roads again.

Such is my own belief and trust;
   This hand, this hand that holds the pen,
Has many a hundred times been dust
   And turned, as dust, to dust again;
These eyes of mine have blinked and shone
   In Thebes, in Troy, in Babylon.[12]

There are finer poems by Masefield, such as "The Widow in the Bye Street," for this poem, despite its lilt and a certain loveliness, affronts both mind and heart.

The outright Hindu doctrine holds that the "eyes" that "have blinked and shone in Thebes" may have been those of a gnat or a crocodile in an African swamp, and that my present sin, far from giving me "sturdier limbs and brighter brain," may return me to that animal estate. Moreover, love is outraged by the idea that one and the same child can have successive mothers. The whole poem sells out to the notion that the body (which Christian faith exalts under God) is evil or unreal, while the "soul" (a vague something temporarily inhabiting an unfortunate body) can somehow be transferred, a notion which the vivid psychosomatic unity of our human life flatly gainsays.

There are more painful difficulties to a theory which tries by a doctrine of reincarnation to explain pain. This, for instance: Most of us have no memory of having been here before, either as a camel in Manchuria or a king in Egypt. Some men have claimed such a memory. John Buchan tells of walking in an African veld for the first time in the conviction that it was not for the first time, even though he had never before been in that part of Africa;[13] and Nicholas Berdyaev in his autobiography writes, "Throughout my life, whenever I entered a Gothic church, I was overwhelmed by a strange sensation of reliving an experience in some previous existence." [14] But these instances could be explained fairly easily as subconscious memory—of a picture of the veld or of entering a church during early childhood. Meanwhile the vast majority of us have no clear recollection of prior life, though we are aware mysteriously of a prior wonder:

> Trailing clouds of glory do we come
> From God, who is our home.[15]

So why should we imagine that we can explain pain by retreating into the unknown, or at best into conjecture? A Hindu priest once assured me that I would remember all my prior incarnations if I would practice yoga. It was a safe claim, for yoga and I do not agree. When I replied that "pure" Hindu doctrine allowed that such prior lives may or may not be recalled, he answered that I could not remember much of my present life. True, but I am still sure that I am presently alive and that any memory of present life may return.

Actually the doctrine of reincarnation is a philosophy rather than a faith. Sin *does* have entail, and some suffering *does* come from sin. Present pain is so prodigious that present act does not account for it. So why not push back the explanation into prior life? But such life for most of us is a vast unknown. Besides, the theory assumes that every man must work out his own salvation. *Can* he? Do we not suffer infirmity of will as well as "infirmity of mind"? It assumes that if God is, he is a cold-blooded taskmaster: history is governed by cold justice. *Is* it? It assumes that we can cleanse our own memory. *Can* we? If we thought we could, would we not fall into the deeper sin of self-righteousness? It has too little care for the other man's sufferings: it lacks compassion and, therefore, leaves unexplained the fact of pardon in human story, unless by our compassions we cleanse our prior life. But then we must ask if any of us *can* cleanse history, e.g., send back into the sky the bomb that fell on Hiroshima and bring the dead back to life. In short, the doctrine raises far more questions than it settles. Interestingly enough India, with wonderful courage, is now resolved to get rid of poverty, ignorance, and sickness—on the tacit assumption that these ills are not inevitable and must not be uncritically accepted.

IV

But there is a much more formidable version of the doctrine that suffering comes from sin, namely, an Old Testament version. It is outright:

31

all pain comes from sin, from either our present sin or from somebody's sin in the past. The doctrine, called by theologians the Deuteronomic doctrine because it is set forth most boldly by the book of Deuteronomy, is formidable because it is so largely true. As for the present entail of past sin, who could doubt it? Our world is darkened by the pride of our forefathers. There is a mess in Vietnam as I write, and it comes in some measure from French colonialism, which white men rationalized as "the white man's burden," but which actually was the white man's greed and aggression. As for individual entail, "the sins of the fathers" *are* visited "on the children," through syphilis for example, "to" more than "the third and the fourth generation." [16]

We cannot excuse ourselves or our forefathers on the plea that "human nature cannot help it." Why evil entices us is partly, though not wholly, a mystery. Sometimes the enticement is so sudden and sharp that we seem to have no chance. We are then tempted to say that God has let children play with matches. But we are still free and therefore responsible to the measure of our freedom. The freedom is limited—we cannot grow cabbages from bacon fat, or wage war without instigating further war—but it is genuine freedom. Admittedly freedom is hard to prove. Conversely it seems easy to prove that every act is the inevitable outcome of all our previous acts, and that therefore life is only a straw on a vast stream. But we have no right to play with such plausibilities, for when all arguments are ended we instantly reassume our freedom. Every injunction, such as "No Trespassing," assumes our freedom. So does every condemnation: "He should be ashamed of himself." So does every praise: "That is very kind of you." The man who argues against freedom does not doubt that his argument is free! [17] Austin Farrer has rightly written that if I decide as I drive a car that I do not have time to pass before the approaching car arrives, it makes nonsense of life to propose that my foot was stayed on the accelerator by every prior happening.[18] Our unassailable assumption of freedom is better evidence than clever abstract rationalizing, which always assumes that *it* is free. We are responsible, and we culpably fail. That failure is the black fountain of countless pains. The Bible, with its unfailing realism, almost tells us that we could well endure other pain if sin could be overcome. Thus our chapter five.

But our present question nudges us: Does *all* suffering come from sin? We write of *responsible* pride which tramples on our neighbor: there *is*

32

psychotic guilt, but the very adjective implies real guilt. Is guilt guilty of *all* sin? The answer is "No." We must say that all sin brings suffering, but we cannot turn the words inside out and say that all suffering comes from sin, even though that latter judgment dies a hard death. Time after time a preacher is asked by people struck down by tragedy: "What crime have I committed?" Thus the Deuteronomic doctrine still darkens over our world. The book of Job makes its brave protest, to prove again that a heresy is sometimes truer than a creed. Job suffered every calamity, loss of property, loss of health, loss of children, loss of his wife's love (for she told him to "Curse God, and die" [19]), but he still refused the explanation offered by his "comforters": that all his pain came from his sin: "Though he slay me yet will I plead my case against him!" [20] Job knew he was not innocent, but he could see no just proportion between his sin and his disasters.

We must defend Job's heresy while admitting the "sea of troubles" that comes of man's agelong transgressions. Polio does not make a detour round the doorstep of the relatively righteous man. Dietrich Bonhoeffer is killed by the Nazis.[21] The peasants of Korea, their farms devastated by napalm bombs during the Korean war, were not necessarily more wicked than peasants in Thailand whose peaceful farms brought forth abundance. Final and sufficient item: Jesus on Calvary did not "get just what he deserved." Indeed, we must confess that conversely the wicked sometimes tower "like a cedar of Lebanon." [22] They may have secret griefs, but we cannot see them, and they may not feel them. If we could peer deep enough into life and far enough into the future we might know that justice never miscarries, or that justice alone is not the end of creation. But we do not have such Godlike eyes. So far as we can judge, not all suffering comes from sin, though all sin brings suffering, unless we must believe that both the cruelties of nature and corruption of human nature are the legacy

> Of man's first disobedience, and the fruit
> Of that forbidden tree, whose mortal taste
> Brought death into the world, and all our woe.[23]

The part that Adam played we shall consider, though the resolve to try to be honest is not making our task any easier! But since the rule of life is one thing at a time, we are here facing the fact that, so far as we can trace, there is a plus of pain beyond that which sin brings. Jesus here confirms us, for he said of the man born blind, when his enemies, clinging to the Deuteronomic doctrine, asked him who had sinned, the man himself or his parents, "it was not that this man sinned, or his parents, but that the works of God should be made manifest in him." [24] That last phrase compounds our "why?" But one thing at a time! In like vein Jesus said of men who died by the collapse of a tower, when the Deuteronomic people (who are always looking for other people's sins) asked him if the dead men had been greater sinners, "I tell you, No; but unless you repent you will all likewise perish." [25] Again the accompanying phrase sprouts questions as a porcupine sprouts quills. But one thing at a time! There is a *plus* of pain. The Bible discounts it over against sin's nemesis, but it is there. It is called by books on suffering "the enigma of natural and historical evil." Thus our next two chapters. Meanwhile we have reached a way station on our journey: all sin brings suffering soon or late, but not all suffering (so far as we can judge) comes of sin.

Must we say, therefore, that the justice of God is impeached? A Harvard student, when I was there as professor and preacher, echoed Eugene O'Neill: "I can partly understand how God can forgive us. But how can he forgive himself?" [26] Modern skepticism has the merit of honesty, or at least of knowing the "hot spots" of our baffled mind. We shall not dodge the question of the origin of evil.[27] But two tentative comments are now in order. First, could we endure a God of strict justice? Do we not hope for more than justice? Imagine him keeping a million celestial ledgers, his world filled with millions of invisible detective-accountants! Could we love God on those terms? Could he love us? Would there be any courage of faith in such a world, or even kindness? Would not goodness vanish in a prudential resolve to keep on the right side of the ledger? Thus one comment. The second is sharper: Where would we be if justice were the rule? If

> Justice be thy plea, consider this,
> That, in the course of justice, none of us
> Should see salvation: we do pray for mercy;
> And that same prayer doth teach us all to render
> The deeds of mercy.[28]

34

We glimpse below the surface of our life a deeper justice. If we are free from pain, and if we sidestep our neighbor's pain and thus become hard of heart, *are* we blest? Conversely if a man wracked with pain thus becomes aware of his neighbor's pain, and in love casts himself on the Mystery, and thus finds peace (yes, there *is* that witness), is he cursed? Job made protest against God's injustice. But a breakthrough of Light found Job.[29] Then he knew that no man has any righteousness in God's sight—or any wisdom. But these deeps are not our present task, we shall come to them and shall need more than a diver's apparatus.

V

We have examined some fractional answers to the puzzle of pain and found them thin rations. Pain is not good *in itself:* it is incipient death for both flesh and psyche, even though by some alchemy of Presence we may win blessing from pain. Pain is not *unreal:* it is too sharp and sudden, and, in any event, if it were banished, its twin brother, joy, together with all courage and compassion, might vanish with it. Pain is not *a legacy from prior incarnations:* a man has no clear memory of such earlier pilgrimages, and such a treadmill universe contradicts certain innate hopes and, indeed, the love we already know. *Not all suffering comes from sin.* The proposal that sin brings all our pain "comes close," but there is an *excess* of pain from nature's blights and from history's dark entail. These are our conclusions. We have not gone beyond them at this stage of our journey, though we can begin to understand or appreciate Milton's proposal that rebellious angels, expelled from heaven, deliberately disfigured man and his world;[30] but we have not settled for that account.

We have seen that Jesus, whose cross brings us to silence as we ponder the mystery of pain, has underwritten our conclusions. He never hinted that pain is *good in itself:* he healed the sick in body and mind, deeming pain a handicap or curse from which men should be delivered. He never dismissed pain as *unreal:* he broke the agelong law of the Sabbath rather than leave a man in afflictions, and he described our pain as "tribulation"[31]: the Latin word means a threshing flail. As for the theory that we have sinned, each of us in some prior incarnation, there is no echo of such doctrine in the Bible: the Book does speak of a legacy of sin from generation to generation, as witness the "dark saying" from the lips of

Jesus spoken to people of his time (and our time?): "That upon you may come all the righteous blood shed on earth" [32]; but Jesus and the Bible describe our life not as one of a series of lives, but rather as a momentous once-for-all encounter which holds the issues of heaven and hell. Doesn't our pilgrimage have precisely that "feel"? As for the doctrine that every man "gets what he deserves," Jesus flatly contradicted that proposal, even while he insisted that no man "gets away with" a low self-concern. We turn to Jesus with no wish to beg a question which we must soon face. This book is written, not for believers only, but for our skeptical time, and in the awareness that every man is believer-doubter even though he be a church member. We make appeal to Jesus at this point because his realism again and again wins assent from our experience. Doctrines are true not simply because they are in the Bible: they are in the Bible because they are true, and because the beckonings of our daily life validate them. Therefore the conclusions of this chapter.

The mystery of pain is always a mystery. But we can rightly hope for some beams of light across the abyss: else we would be doomed to dark bafflement. Perhaps what we need is not final explanation. Perhaps we do not covet any such word, for it is joy as well as necessity to venture on faith. Perhaps our need and wish asks a sign and a path for our feet. When Frederic H. W. Myers was eight years of age his father died, and his mother was so inconsolable as to declare that she now despaired of any happiness. Then the child, with an instinct given to children, said to her: "You know that God can do everything, and He might give us just once a vision of Himself to make us happy all our lives after." [33] Yes, of a truth; and more than a vision, for truth may be an Event, not a theory or a "vision." Suppose that the total Event of Jesus Christ *is* Truth! Suppose that he, whom Bonhoeffer rightly called "the Man for others," [34] is the disclosure of God in the midst of the years: he, not the thin formulas of science or the abstract reasonings of philosophy! Such is the outright daring of the New Testament.

Old Siward questioned Ross about the death of young Siward slain in the duel with the wicked Macbeth:

> Siward: "Had he his hurts before?"
> Ross: "Ay, on the front."
> Siward: "Why then God's soldier be he." [35]

Many a lowly warrior, fighting tyranny or accepting death in martyrdom rather than shed a brother's blood, has so died, proving himself thus God's soldier. His wounds have been "on the front," facing a Cross, a now-empty Cross. Perhaps there we may find the central answer. But that is not yet written. When we come to it, we shall give no "pious" reasons, and we shall not offer some answer because it is "in the back of the book" where answers to geometry are given. The problem of pain is a problem for momentous life. There are no neat prefabricated answers, but there is an Answer.

3. On Natural Evil

Why Are There Snakes and Earthquakes?

The very title repels us, and the fact itself brings shock and dismay. Why should people lose their homes and their lives in the Alaskan earthquake, on Good Friday of all days? If the order of nature were altogether outside us, like stage scenery come to life, natural evil would be no worse than ugliness. But it is not outside us: it is outside and inside us. Our bodies are *within* the natural world, and our brains are part of our bodies; and, whatever be the bond between thought and brain, there is some kind of concomitance; and cancer strikes both body and brain, making no distinction so far as we can see between a doctor and a gangster. So we have a not-so-pretty problem on our hands—and hearts.

I

The Bible is almost an unknown book in our time. So its view of natural evil is unknown. Even if we knew the view, we would find it

38

hard to accept. For though natural evil is not discounted in the Scriptures, it is pushed into the background by the evil of human irresponsibility. Indeed, human evil is said to have occasioned natural evil. Adam and Eve presumed to try to steal the secret of the knowledge of good and evil: they played their own god. Therefore the pains of childbirth came on Eve, and Adam's garden was cursed with thorns and thistles.[1] A worse punishment came on them: they thought they *did* know the deeps of good and evil, but then they had no power in themselves of real goodness or even of discernment. But our age laughs off such an account. We do not believe "ancient myths." We forget that the time of a myth is always now, and that its "heroes" are always ourselves. It is much easier to confront the neutral formulas of science than the piercing truth of "myth." So we must think through the problem of drought and tidal wave on our own terms, until we find the terms are false. We shall start from where we stand in our skeptical time.

The Bible, linking natural and culpable evil, natural evil being always the sign of God's "no" and of man's alienation from God, links also the redemption of nature and the redemption of man. As we fly over the planet (biblical man could not have conceived of that skill and might have called it impious had such an imagining disturbed him), we see that most of it is desert, salt sea, and frowning mountain. The Genesis word returns on us, though we may not know that it is from Genesis: man lives "by the sweat of his face." [2] When, we cry, shall the earth become a garden? The Bible replies that there shall be a double salvation: "The desert shall rejoice and blossom; like the crocus. . . . Then the eyes of the blind shall be opened." [3] The "whole creation" groans "in travail," waiting until we ourselves are redeemed.[4]

But all this is in a "strange tongue." In any event the outlandish biblical view does not answer the agonized questions, even for the Bible. Why did fire burn up Job's sheep and his servants? Why did tempest strike "the four corners" of Job's house and destroy both his house and his children? [5] Why was Job himself afflicted with "loathsome sores from the sole of his foot to the crown of his head"? [6] So the Bible confronts the "problem" and chooses the thorniest instance, for it tells us that Job was a man "blameless and upright, one who feared God, and turned away from evil." [7] Why was a man "born blind"? This is a

New Testament instance of the Old Testament problem. We can partly understand blindness if it comes from human folly. But in this man's case neither he nor his parents had sinned.[8] That we know on the word of Jesus. Then why was the man *born* blind? Why from his birth was he denied sight of sunset and human faces? These questions are compounded for us because we belong to the "scientific generation." We see nature as something "out there": we have split life into subject and object. The wisdom or unwisdom of such a deliberate lesion we do not here argue. We are concerned to show that when we make the natural order an object, natural evil seems to be an instance of broken law, or of sheer unreason, or of wanton cruelty. *Our* thinking must start from *our* stance. What other point of departure? When we walk from New York City to Yonkers, we start from New York City. In our present journey there is no swift subway to help us. Maybe there *is* help from *above* us. So to *our* journey.

II

We should note that the natural order brings joy as well as blight, a fact which we forget in our sometimes morbid involvement with the "problem" of pain. Most people cling to life despite its floods and plagues: they cling because they find life good. We repeat what has already been written: The basic term is "joy." Our planet is trustworthy, and the promise has been fulfilled: "While the earth remains, seedtime and harvest, cold and heat, summer and winter, day and night, shall not cease." [9] Thus the rainbow was set in the cloud. We could not know the shadow but for the light. Despair is *de spero,* lack of hope; we could not despair had we not known glad expectation. Suppose summer lasted until all the fields were parched, or winter until food failed. Suppose day continued until we wearied of garishness, or night until we hopelessly longed for day. There are more terrible supposings. For what if rivers ceased to run, or if the same seed one day grew raspberries and the next day poisonberries, or stairs disappeared, or gravitation stopped? A library of gratitude could be written on the fidelities of nature. We speak of "natural law," but it is so geared-in with human need and gladness that we would be wise to cling to biblical language and talk about the faithfulness of God. The split between subject and object, though it may

40

be intended as a convenience of mind, is in this instance a lesion in life.

Nature's hand is filled with many another bounty. There is provocative *challenge,* secrets hidden in every flower and star to quicken and excite the mind. There is *healing* as well as pain, for any wise doctor knows that he is only nurse to nature's medical skill. There is *mercy* even in the time of crisis: in an automobile accident consciousness blacks out just *before* the impact, and the pain itself when it becomes too hard to bear is overcome in unconsciousness. There is *beauty* in nature in such prodigality and poignancy as to steal the soul. What right have we to wave aside such benedictions in a few beggarly sentences? As these words are being written, and eyes are lifted from the typewriter to the window, the grass is so green, the lake so glad in dancing light, the sky so clear after rain that I also know the poet's "fear":

> Lord, I do fear
> Thou'st made the world too beautiful this year;
> My soul is all but out of me,—let fall
> No burning leaf; prithee, let no bird call.[10]

Our normal consciousness confirms the Bible in this conviction: *The natural order is essentially good.* God made it, and "God saw that it was good." [11] Christian faith has rightly resisted the Greek doctrine that the world about us and in our bodies is evil, a prison for the soul. World and flesh are constitutionally and originally good. Certain questions should, therefore, spring to our lips. If life can be lived only in a dependable world, what right have we to ask God to break his fidelities for our private comfort? If shadows are of the texture of beauty, if we could see nothing without shadows, not even the faces of our friends, why should we ask that shadows be banished in favor of a flat nothingness? If we remember joy more quickly than we remember sorrow, or if we remember sorrow only "against" the prior joy, why should we doubt that the ground of life is joy? Why, when we can joke about outward disaster, as in the case of the man who fished from his roof while the flood carried his house down the stream, should we mistrust laughter in favor of gloom? The natural order in origin and purpose is good. That word is the prime guideline.

41

III

But no guideline, not even the conviction that the natural order is in essence and intention good, gives us any right to blink the fact of natural evil. For nature seems both cruel and callous. The callousness is harder to "take" than the cruelty, for cruelty at least keeps a man in sight, whereas earthquake and tidal wave treat him as if he had never been born. That wire flung up by a lawnmower to pierce a child's temple seems sheer wantonness.[12] And what of leukemia? It is not enough to say that soon we may find the cure: millions have already been killed. Our phrase, "the progress of the race," hides a brutality. For what of the multitudes who have died? Are they only manure for some future human harvest? Are God's fields "dung'd with rotten death"?[13] Many of our slogans, such as "the progress of the race," are not summations of truth but ways for evading truth. Does "progress" mean that a hundred generations must be cursed that one generation may flourish in a brief paradise which itself is doomed by time? What monstrosities are proposed in the name of "progress"!

What then shall we say? The man in the street says, "Things have somehow gone wrong." His straightforward realism is sometimes a better theology than theologians offer us. A tornado tearing through the village to topple homes and kill people is grotesque and cruel: "Things have somehow gone wrong." A nation, the land of Goethe and Bach, selling out to a megalomaniac paperhanger with his ranting diatribes, killing Jews, bringing down on itself the answering violence of an incredulous world, is not merely wicked, but possessed: "Things have somehow gone wrong" in human nature as well as in nature, and the incredulous world has the same virus in its blood. Our planet appears to have run off the track. It keeps going, but slowly, through rough country, with many a jolt, instead of running on the right rails. That is precisely what the Bible says. It traces our tragic disorder to Adam and Eve. The origin of Adam as a name may or may not be linked with a word meaning earth—the man made from dust. The derivation of Eve as a name is even more uncertain. Adam in most instances in the Bible is a generic rather than a proper name: it stands for man or mankind. Man and his wife presumed to a knowledge not given to human beings. Pride blinded

42

them to the fact that to be human is to be free yet dependent—on God. So the curse fell on both man and his world.

Such an account does not explain, if by explanation we mean a scientific answer. Does science itself explain? It is ironic that science in its explanation of matter has reduced it and reduced it until nothing is left but the thin wraith of a mathematical formula, which hardly gives a true picture of the ground on which we walk! Genesis does not explain how temptation came on Adam and Eve. It tells us that a snake insinuated the seduction into the mind of Eve.[14] But we are not told how the snake was created, or why it is a venomous creature with slimy ways. We shall probe further in chapter four into this "mystery of evil." Perhaps we can find only a partial answer. Perhaps to probe too far would be our own falling into pride, our own eating of the forbidden tree of the knowledge of good and evil. But it is worth noting that modern literature is returning to the ancient-modern answer: "Things have somehow gone wrong." William Golding's *Lord of the Flies* [15] is a study in "original sin," as he himself has told us. Albert Camus' *The Fall* [16] describes an urbane modern man as instance of "the fall" of Adam. Robert Penn Warren says outrightly, in a poem that flatly contradicts Jeffersonian hopes,

> There's no forgiveness for our being human.
> It is the inexpugnable error. It is
> . . . the one thing we have overlooked
> In our outrageous dreams and cunningest contrivances.[17]

The Bible cancels that first line in joy but refuses to "overlook" either the tragedy of man's colossal presumption or the fact of natural evil.

Our skeptic world now announces that "God is dead." Perhaps we must reach that point of despair before we can return to the courage of a realistic faith. Perhaps we have invited the despair because it is *we* who are dead while we live. However that may be, humanism is dead—from the diabetes of a false optimism. The chaos of our world has come only in part from the failure of the church, for the prevailing "religion" ever since the Enlightenment has been humanism. The cult of "the brotherhood of man" marching along the highroad of "scientific intelligence" has marched straight into the slaughterhouse of war because it refuses to confront the human predicament. It closes its eyes to the fact that "things have somehow gone wrong," that there is a fatal flaw both in nature and in history, and that man, however attempt be made to deify him, has only a finite freedom. One of my students told of a gentle-spirited parishioner who, when he had purged his own garden of thistles, thought it his neighborly duty to do as much for his neighbors' gardens. So he dug up their thistles. But on his way home he saw a whole hillside filled with thistles and began to weep; he could not cleanse his world of thistles. On the next Sunday, when he arrived at church early, he found a woman arranging the altar flowers: they were Scotch thistles. The blight had now invaded the church. There we let the matter rest, or might, if it could ever rest.

IV

But the Bible, rigorously confronting the flaw in nature and man, never doubts that God is in control. Often it traces the threats of nature to God's direct act:

> The Lord also thundered in the heavens,
>   and the Most High uttered his voice,
>   hailstones and coals of fire.[18]

He can turn the sun "black as sackcloth," so that "the full moon" becomes "like blood." [19] If there is a malign spirit in man, that spirit is still subject to God. If there is a devil perverting nature, he also, whatever hopes he may cherish, is agent of God's ultimate will. Even Cyrus, boasting his conquest of proud Babylon and its armies, is fulfilling God's predetermined purpose:

> I surname you, though you do not know me.
> I am the Lord, and there is no other,
>   besides me there is no God.[20]

So emphatic is this proclamation of God's sovereignty that almost it says that God sends the tornado. Does he? To that in a moment. But let us first interject: Our own awareness of God, the Mystery from whom we come without our having any control over our birth, to whom we go without our having any final control over our death, tells us that God *is* sovereign; he is "over against" our transience, our self-deceptions, and our blunderings. He is God, and there is no other.

Then *does* God *send* natural evil? Does he deliberately plant cancer cells in the flesh of that man in the next street? Does he single out that Indiana village, rather than some nearby village, to level it by a tornado which also is deliberately summoned? Does he paint a mirage on the desert sky that the traveler, crazed by thirst, may more surely die? Here we grope in mystery, but both mind and heart rebel. We would not so deal with one another, unless some excess of despair drove us to the demonism. Jesus confirms us in that protest, "If you then, who are evil, know how to give good gifts to your children, how much more will your Father who is in heaven give good things to those who ask him?" [21] God, being "over against" our transience is "over against" our evil and our pain. To say that God planned and executed the sinking of the Titantic [22] would be tantamount to calling God the "author of confusion" and "the father of lies." [23] "God is not a God of confusion but of peace." [24] As for "the father of lies," Jesus himself gave that title to the devil: "He is a liar and the father of lies." We have to say that God *allows* pain from natural evil. We cannot say that he *inflicts* it. Soon we shall say that in Christ he suffers our pain: he is "afflicted with our affliction." [25] Admittedly the distinction between *inflicting* natural evil and *allowing* it is not complete. But it is clear, and we must make it, under guidance of the Bible, lest we ourselves confuse darkness and light. Yet it does not resolve the mystery.

The fact of natural evil, which God allows, assuredly means that no hedonism, however refined, can be the purpose of our pilgrimage. Pain and pleasure are foil and counterfoil: neither is our true end. Jeremy Bentham described the slogan "the greatest happiness of the greatest number," as a "sacred truth" and "the foundation of morals and legislation," [26] but the motto is neither sacred nor the truth nor the foundation of anything worthy until "happiness" has been truly defined. Such a definition comes by gift and in person. Jesus bequeathed his joy to his disciples,[27] but the legacy was by means of a Cross. In his Beatitudes [28] he offered his congratulations to the lowly, the gentle, the mourners, and the persecuted. Yes, the word "congratulations" is nearer the Greek word than the customary, "Blessed are those who." Thus we may surmise that natural evil *can* be an *ingredient* of real life *if* there is a touchstone

45

to transform it. Meanwhile it obscures our view of God's glory and invites our unbelief. How hard it is to trust Providence when famine and drought curse the fields! How pitiably we then cry out for the redemption of both nature and men!

V

But *need* we say that there is a flaw in nature, that "things have somehow gone wrong"? Must we thus compound man's agelong "Why?" Surely we can find some nearer and clearer explanation. Such is the modern proposal. So we look, not in any dogmatic denial but in hope, to see if the modern hope is sound. If it is not sound, we must once more probe the mystery. We may have finally to confess mystery, but we should not make it an "out." The modern explanation is, "We live in a world of natural law." Does this line lead to an answer? Many theologians follow the "line." Charles Cuthbert Hall, writing at the turn of the century, says: "Bodily calamities are only the results of natural laws. Every one of them can be traced to natural causes." [29] Charles F. D'Arcy writes, "We can see that pain has its place, and a very important place, in evolution." [30] Even John Whale tells us that "necessary 'laws' like these are necessarily inexorable," [31] and that there "is continuity in the evolutionary process from the lowest brute creation up to man." In like manner B. H. Streeter speaks (rather sententiously) of "an Intelligence which itself upholds the great interconnected system of cause and effect that we call nature," [32] and on that ground tries to find a solving word—for cancer.

Here I must be frank with the reader: I simply cannot follow this line of argument. It seems doubtful if the great scientists themselves could follow it. In a book written over twenty years ago [33] I pleaded that we must choose between a then-dominant theory of natural law on the one hand and the reality of prayer on the other and affirmed that our doctrine of natural law would change, because prayer has the tang of both instant time and an implied eternity. That avowal came partly from seeing that the assumptions of science were even then being eroded, and partly, I suppose, from an "invincible surmise." [34] I did not dream that conjecture would be so quickly justified—by the rigorous honesty of science itself. The "laws" which science may posit (or used to posit) are only for science; they do not cover the give and take, the instancy and urgency of our daily life. They have their place, for the scientist is entitled to his own categories, but when they are given totalitarian sway they break —into fragments of abstraction. If a schoolhouse is carried away by a tornado and the children are killed, we do not say: "This is all explained by the laws of meteorology," for it is not "explained" (it is only abstractly described), and to offer the explanation is an insult to human sorrow. When a friend dies of cancer, we find no comfort if someone should say, "Bodily calamities are only the result of natural laws." The geological description of the Alaskan earthquake, if we have nothing more to say, is an affront to both the courage and the grief of the Anchorage community. Science in these instances may win our gratitude by helping us establish safeguards for coming days, but it is no "answer" to the agelong "Why?"

The very categories of science are now in question from science itself. "Law" itself is under attack, for there can hardly be "inexorable" patterns in quantum physics, because the play of the quanta is now in measure unpredictable. In any event, how can "law" be an agent? Perhaps these laws are patterns *we* trace in events when they are past and therefore "fixed." Thus "objectivity" is now under attack, for things are objective *to us,* and thus infected with subjectivity. "Evolution" is now under attack, for the important item is the strange mutation, not the broad continuity; the new instancy and man's power to wreck the continuity. "Cause and effect" is now under attack, for no new event can be fully explained by its antecedents: it is a *new* event. Gabriel Marcel has an important essay in which he proposes that we must now think in new terms because the question about "God causing" our life is not only out of style, but out of truth.[35] Life is still lived in the event, not in the artificial samenesses by which our science tries to cover up the piercingness of the event. Perhaps existentialism is right in its proposal that the abstractions of philosophy and the laws of science are both a form of escape, and therefore unauthentic, because life is an ever new dialogue between the event and the person. Science is an affair on only one level of mind (the sense-analytic level) addressed to only one aspect of the world (the quantitative aspect). Therefore, it can give only fragmentary answers. As a world view, though not as a fine endeavor and vocation, science is bankrupt.

This "natural law" approach to the problem of natural evil raises

47

still more urgent questions. Has God set a neutral belt of "inexorable necessity" between himself and his human creatures, a no-man's-land which even he cannot or will not cross? Does he say, "I am here in celestial bliss, while over there are men, and in between us there is a self-regulating system which may slay them, but cannot touch me"? Surely it would be more honest to rebel against God, or to confess a mystery than to believe in such a God! Besides, if all is law, and if our duty is simply to obey "causal laws," how can either God or we escape a new legalism? Besides, our life and our world alike, when we look at them with clear eyes, do *not* wear the aspect of iron necessity. Both seem to have a strange freedom. Paul Tillich has almost proposed that God has given nature its freedom as he has given us our freedom.[36] The proposal raises problems: the two freedoms are obviously not of the same order. But it would seem truer to say of the world of nature that its fidelities are enfolded in a certain liberty, than that its unpredictable surprises are imprisoned in an iron necessity. But this "natural law" gambit dies hard. In scattered notes from my reading there is this as yet untraced quote: "The Bible makes it quite clear that the moral structure of history is objective and impersonal." But I, for one, cannot find any such clarity in the Bible. I do not see how morals can ever be impersonal. They are always personal. The sexual act, for instance, is not an act of biologies, but of persons, and morality by my conviction always rests back on an inescapable sense of obligation and responsibility. That is, persons find themselves under a constraint personal enough to make demands on persons. Explanation by natural law is simply a blind alley, with walls so high that we are denied even a view.

VI

Other "explanations" of natural evil also fail to explain—those, for instance, which use metaphors drawn from our daily life, such as, "You would not blame a father if he allowed his son to play high-school football, and the lad broke a leg." There is some merit in this line of argument. Jesus used it: the prayer he taught us begins with the word "Father." There may be further merit, namely, in the implication that for God and man courage spells danger, and that it is hard to conceive of a danger that is not dangerous: God may have set limits to his own freedom for the sake of our freedom in this planet-school. But there are no parallels for God, and therefore all our metaphors fail at last. An earthly father *cannot* avoid every "accident," but presumptively God ordains all the conditions of our life on earth, or God would not be God, and therefore *he could* have made a world in which a child does not break a leg.

All metaphors die before this mystery. We cannot imagine how courage were possible without danger, or sympathy without suffering, for our life is a strange linking of contradictories. But we can hardly build a complete theology on what "we cannot imagine." It is far from enough, therefore, to say that pain from the natural world is for our "discipline." When a parent is killed by lightning, who is being disciplined? The small orphans? Nor can we argue that natural evil is sent to "teach us compassion." When a fire occurs (only partly from human blame, for accidents will happen) and children die in the flames, there is no guarantee that the neighborhood will "learn compassion"; there may be a run on fire extinguishers because most neighbors continue to think mainly of their own safety. So if discipline and compassion are intended, God's method fails. Besides, what kind of a God would choose a tidal wave for our "education"?

The other metaphors likewise fail. We say, "God knows the role we play in life's drama: we know only our own part, whereas he sees the whole play from end to end." But how could we ever fulfill any sensible role on such terms? Besides, life is not play-acting, unless in our felt urgency of life God is toying with our grief. We say again, in a metaphor so cruel that it should long ago have been silenced, "There must be sepia if there is to be any picture." Now we have turned people into pigments, and the cosmos into a large palette, and God into a devil who pours lava on Pompeii so as to throw Capri into bright relief! Perhaps only sentimentalists who have never really shared the poignancy of our human lot could ever have proposed such a simile. I am not disparaging our figures of speech, for they are far better carriers of truth than the dreary formulas of science or the far-too-wide abstractions of philosophy. No, the trouble is that there are neither formulas nor metaphors for the Mystery of God. Nature is God's garment: we think we have lost him in the shadowed folds when suddenly he touches us with his hand. That is a better "figure," but—how to trust the hand when the folds are cancer or a swarm of locusts? Perhaps we can and must trust, but not in our own poor power, not without. . . . That sentence we shall soon complete. Meanwhile we are thinking through these issues, as far as we can, from the strange "God-is-dead" stance of our skeptical generation.

All explanations fail us. They all raise as many questions as they answer. Thus even H. Wheeler Robinson gets trapped, despite the fact that his book is a wonderful affair. For he writes: "We must not blame God for it" (natural evil), "as though there were not a host of secondary causes, a network of Nature and history." [37] That first clause must stand: "We must not blame God for it," for if we do, the immemorial constraint which men have called God would disappear, and it does not disappear. But the second clause cannot stand, for if God is God no "network" of "secondary causes," not even a "host" of them, is beyond his control. This Dr. Robinson sees, for he promptly contradicts himself: "The casual ought not to present any greater difficulty than the causal, since the small things are not less in His hand than the great." [38] Agreed. But then the prior explanation does not explain and the problem remains. There are no neat answers. We may add that there are no neat answers to any "why?" dark or bright. My small granddaughter pointed to an object in a field, asking, "What is that?" I answered in adult self-sufficiency, "That is a cow." She replied, "Why?" I refer the question to the reader.

> Why grasse is greene, or why our blood is red,
> Are mysteries which none have reach'd unto.[39]

The only reason why we cannot say of natural evil that "God sends it" is that evil is evil, and we cannot make God the author of confusion or commit suicide by saying, "Evil be thou my Good." [40]

VII

Nevertheless we can hardly doubt that God has found some people *through pain* from the natural world. That is their clear testimony won at cost. For myself, I find it worthier of acceptance than the rationalizing of some merely spectator-mind who talks glibly of "illusion" and "projection." These modern accounts savor of the childishness that would

50

say of the stars: "They are only lights from distant airplanes." Behold a paradox: We rightly shrink from saying of cancer, "God sends it," yet God finds people in and through cancer. Not soon shall I forget the words of a parishioner as he died from that scourge. He was as realistic a man as I have known. His churchgoing was not the kind which clamors for some "religious emotion." Yet his last words were almost rapture: "If only you could see the Plan!" I trust that man rather than some lecturer in psychology theorizing about "projection." Projection—on what? H. G. Wells has written, through the voice of "Mr. Britling," "If I thought there was an omnipotent God who looked down on battles and death . . . able to prevent these things . . . I would spit in his empty face." [41] Mr. Britling's diatribe does him more credit than our "natural law" gambit gives us. But the fact remains despite him that tragedy has again and again been apocalypse. Shakespeare's greatest plays are not his comedies. We cannot say that "God sends natural evil," but we can say, "Natural evil has often been God's door." This saying saves us from the proposal that there is a neutral belt of natural law which God (who is then not God) has set between himself and us.

Need we marshall instances? There are two at strange opposites. William James wrote of the California earthquake: "I personified the earthquake as a permanent individual entity. . . . Animus and intent were never more present in any human action. . . . But what was this 'It'? To some, apparently, a vague, demonic power; to me an individualized thing." [42] Notice how the questions throng: Can "It" have "intent . . . never more present in any human action"? Can a "thing" thus "act"? These questions also we shall not sidestep! Meanwhile to the opposite instance: Stanton Coit told of the sinking of the "Titantic" (partly due to culpable human blame, partly to "natural evil"), quoting one of the survivors to the effect that she and others were all one, not only with one another, but with the cosmic being that for the time had seemed so cruel." [43] Again the questions throng—a "being *that*"? Should he not have written, "a being *who*"? But why quote other people? Have we not all known in tragedy that we now have dealings not with one another only, but with the Mystery who controls our birth and death? Perhaps we could not know God piercingly except in those times when another Will cuts clean across our human will. Perhaps when pain strikes we

51

confront a choice: to rebel in our poor finiteness or to agree with God silently.

So we confront another contradiction: The pain of natural evil seems to come from an uncaring scheme of things but may by its inward thrust bring tidings of God. An American soldier in the Korean war who knew that the signal for the armistice would soon sound was fatally wounded in the last hour and died as the signal sounded, saying, "Isn't this just like God?" [44] All the bitterness of our human lot is in the exclamation. But he used the word "God." Fénelon, without bitterness, read the word "God" into the sickness of the Dauphin: "If God be no longer enraged against France, he will recover. . . . Yet there is a fear at the bottom of my heart that God's anger against France is not appeased." [45] If we look at history objectively, whether in the Korean war or the course of events in France in 1711, and if we judge the wounded soldier or the ailing Dauphin by medical science, neither the soldier's exclamation nor Fénelon's comment makes any sense. But we cannot judge history with pure objectivity, and the scientific view is so limited as almost to impose blinders. So events have an outer shallow meaning which tempts us to say, "That's the way things are!" and an inner secret meaning of which we confess, "There God found me!"

There are no parallels or parables for this experience, for God is alone and there is no other. Thus the Assyrian conquest of Israel could be "explained" in any number of ways from any number of strictly limited angles: by sociology or military strategy or politics. But Israel still knew that the disaster was a judgment of God. Not that Assyria had any merit: Assyria was but a scourge in God's hand—God who at will could cast away the scourge. This typically biblical view is no "blinders" view: it testifies to the sovereignty of God finding creature-man through the secrecy and mystery of events. The tapping of the Morse code gives us a poor analogy, poor because all analogies are poor. You hear it in a telegraph office, and it seems only a tapping of sounds which over a sufficiently long span of time could be reduced to patterns quite comparable with those of "natural law." So with the apparently meaningless tapping-out of events in "objective" history:

> "Tomorrow, and tomorrow, and tomorrow, . . .
> To the last syllable of recorded time." [46]

But the telegraph clerk understands: the tapping to him is as if someone were speaking. So in the events of life every man has his private code. Do we not read even the newspaper by that inward light? "So he got caught, while I, guilty of the same folly . . . ," or, "Jim died yesterday, and I did not even phone to inquire about him, and he has been my friend for years."

Perhaps we thus have a clue to our incorrigible belief in "special Providence." The outward fashion of events makes nonsense of such a doctrine, and we say, "God, if we are foolish enough to believe in him, cannot play fast and loose with the laws of his universe, sending fine weather for this man, and foul weather for his neighbor in the next street." But the inwardness of events asks another verdict, for in that secrecy we are in dialogue with the Will speaking *through* events. Then the sun's rising speaks a mercy which overcomes our gloom. Then prayer "makes sense":

> "God answers sharp and sudden on some prayers,
>   And thrusts the thing we have prayed for in our face,
>   A gauntlet with a gift in 't." [47]

There are strange coincidences between outward event and our secret will. Someday soon we may learn to cast off the tyranny of science. Then we shall say, "What a fool I was to accept those blinders, as if I were a mule, as if I *had* to go down only that narrow lane!"

All this may explain in some measure the phrase which our common law uses of events beyond our control: "An act of God." I am not pleading that every disaster is or can be clearly understood. Again and again we are baffled to the point of blank dismay. I have confessed in this chapter that there are no neat explanations. My only plea is that we may find through inwardness what can never be understood in an impossible "objectivity." A magazine article describes how the victim of a train wreck, with all the signs of serious brain injury, recovered at the very moment when prayers were offered for him in church. We must and should admit that the questions throng. This question, for instance, must be asked in any honesty of mind: Why did other men die from that wreck even though prayers equally heartfelt were offered for them? If we sidestep that question we may avoid agony of mind, but we surrender any claim to truth.

But we can still say that every man has his secret code which he honors or violates. Tragedy or a "happy ending" has a meaning for you or me which is hidden from our neighbors. The tapping is just that and no more to the man in another city as he reads about us in the newspaper, but for you and me the event has a private message.

> This poor man cried, and the Lord heard him,
> and saved him out of all his troubles.[48]

That poor man cried, and the Lord heard him, and saved him from earth's bondage and welcomed him into "the eternal habitations." [49]

VIII

What has this chapter proposed about the mystery of natural evil? That it *is* a mystery which our neat "explanations" never explain, least of all the shallow and limited answers offered by science; that "something *has* gone wrong" both with our world and with us, and that the Adam and Eve account, though it is a "strange tongue" to our skeptical time, finds echo in us; that we rightly shrink from saying that God sends cancer or drought or earthquake, though we are driven to the verdict that he allows this far-flung suffering; that though there are no neat answers God has found us *through* natural calamity, thus proving both his presence and his power; that events have both an outward and an inward fashion, and that though they may *outwardly* defy any attempt to find a good meaning in them, *inwardly* they may find *us* through our own private code; and that we—most of us—cling to life, despite natural evil, deeming the suicide either desperate or deranged, because life is essentially good. These are tentative judgments in a resolve on as full honesty as is given to us: we are not obsequious before them. Perhaps we may add that tragedy and joy alike open doors into the Mystery, if we are willing to enter at risk, not distrusting joy and not shrinking from pain. The Niagara River offers joy at Grand Isle, for there people have summer homes. The same river has brought many a tragedy at Niagara Falls, for there it breaks into cataracts and plunges into a gulf. Yet more people visit the Falls than go to Grand Isle, for the Falls have majesty and a rainbow mist and power to supplement our toil and to light our homes. No, that simile, like any other, is not enough. It raises questions even though it may suggest answers.

But the Cross is not metaphor: it is dark and bloody Event. Yet it brings us to silence, and it is now more than curse and midnight. To that fact these pages must return and return, for that may be the clue. Christ's words about nature are hard for us to construe, for often they seem to be unaware of nature's blight. He bids us "be sons of your Father who is in heaven; for he makes his sun rise on the evil and on the good, and sends rain on the just and on the unjust." [50] Surely, we exclaim, Christ did not forget that the sun sometimes spells drought, and that rain too sudden and full brings floods! No, he did not forget. He knew our dire need of water, as witness his conversation with the woman at the well [51]; and he told of a spate that swept away the house which a foolish man had built on the dry river bed.[52] Yet he knew that the strong and steady undertone of life is joy, and told us again and again that we should not fear to make this world our "home away from home" (that hotel slogan suggests more then it has guessed), because all its dark mysteries are held in love.

We shall return also, though presently only in hint, to our provisional description: Pain of any kind traces the line between the transience in which we must live, and the eternity which we dimly know and without which we could not say, "Time is swift." Pain wrings from us therefore a double cry: "I am mortal! Where is my salvation?" It turns our eyes from time to the Mystery beyond time. So what we need is not an explanation, but a salvation. The explanation of mystery is not possible to mortal minds, and in our more profound moments we realize that mystery is a better gift than any poor explanation. For without mystery our life would lack the dimension of depth, and we would be strangers to the joy that flows only from the springs of faith. What salvation? What faith? Under what beckoning? Perhaps we are on our way to a better answer than an explanation.

4. On Historical Evil

Why Should We Pay
for Dead Men's Sins?

This chapter is about history's dark entail, the suffering that falls on any generation because of natural evil and man's transgression in the past. To take a single instance: Why should the "iniquities of the fathers"—by sexual promiscuity and syphilis, for example—be "visited on the children," and why to "the third and fourth generation"? If you and I were in control of the world, would we blind a baby by the pox? To take a multiple instance: Why should the children of our generation suffer from the political blindness that brought two world wars? Why should hate and disillusion, taxation and new wars be our portion because of the childish pride of power politics? Of course *we* hand on the dark legacy to *our* progeny. So perhaps we have no right to ask "Why?" But we cannot help asking, for historical evil is a vast reservoir of pain.

Natural evil is linked with historical evil, as when men greedily cut down forests and so invite dust storms, or make slum dwellings which invite rats. Both evils fall on the relatively innocent. Our children are not responsible for the quagmire of the Vietnamese war, but the war has already left many a home desolate, especially in the relatively ignorant and innocent villages of Vietnam. We speak of "the dead hand of the past," but it is not dead: it is very much alive, to our gain and loss. Yes, there is gain, to which we must attend, for at times the hand is like a mother's hand laid on a child's fevered brow. But at other times the hand is more like a claw. Why isn't each generation given a clean start and an unmarked page? But we write our lives on paper that in its very texture has the strife, the groping, and the prayers of all history.

"*Dead* hand": yes, death is involved, from both natural evil and historical evil. The Bible says that death came through Adam's sin.[1] However it came, we must meet it. In one sense it is the prime fact of life, though our humanisms refuse to confront it. That is why humanism has grown thin, through a kind of cancer, and become a pessimism which exclaims that "God is dead." According to many a textbook in psychology sin is not really sin: it is recoil from frustration. The theory is obviously partly true, and therefore worth offering, but the real questions are still unanswered: Why should parents frustrate their children? Is the frustration on their part due to their being frustrated, back to some original frustration, some "original sin"? How can we help being frustrated, and therefore violent, when all of us must meet the final frustration of death?

> Last scene of all,
> That ends this strange eventful history,
> Is second childishness and mere oblivion,
> Sans teeth, sans eyes, sans taste, sans every thing.[2]

What of "progress" in such a world? Skeptic diatribes are more honest than luncheon-club prattlings about "peace, prosperity, and progress." Thus the problem of historical evil.

I

Of course, there is joy through history. That fact also we should gladly confess. Once again it must be written: We would hardly know the pain except for prior blessing. Look around your room. By what labor other men, our unknown friends of past generations, fashioned furniture, invented clocks, wove rugs, tamed fire to bring us light and heat, grew wheat and ground flour and baked bread! Nay, the very walls and windows of the room to make shelter from the storm, yet with a view of the earth and sky, are our inheritance, a vast legacy of wealth beyond reckoning by any computer. And those books on the shelf—what blood of heart and brain has brought them to the birth! That gift alone should bring tears of gratitude. The Bible is among the books. It should be: the only Book not taken by surprise by our present world. It looks at us now, asking, "What did you expect?" Genesis is more profound than our sciences, the Psalms more vital than our philosophies, and the Gospels when compared with our overheated novels are "star-fire and immortal tears."

Now look beyond the window. The fields begin to turn yellow-gold with harvest: other men taught us how to till the ground. That path outside the door and that paved road were once a trail through the forest or a long trek across the plains. You can see, if you have eyes, a pilgrim-ship crossing an endless ocean, and covered wagons swaying and rattling across the prairies, with Indians (it was *their* land) opposing the journey. If you have real eyes, you can see mothers burying their children in nameless graves, and then on and on toward an unknown West; and men being buried in snow in Donner Pass. These pioneers beckon the mind toward more precious gifts: our systems of law, which, while in their clumsiness they can never transmit full justice and can never read our secret heart, are yet the girding of our daily life. Laws have come a long way, through the Decalogue, Roman jurisprudence, and British common law. And what of our liberties of vote and speech? Every one of them is bought with a price which cannot be reckoned in any currency of earth, for of these heroes "the world was not worthy." [3] Furthermore and furthermore: Jesus comes as living legacy. He taught us glad thankfulness for the past: "Others have labored, and you have entered into their labor." [4] Let us here keep ourselves on the right road: historical joy is a deeper term than historical evil. Nay, joy is the ultimate term. William James has rightly said: "There is a problem of evil, there is no problem of good." [5]

But in this book we are trying to relate good and evil. Therefore we should try to be realistic: there is a dark line in history's face, nay, a grinning skull that can be seen through the flesh. Why should there be an evil bias in our human nature? Why should it give bent to the very stuff of history? Why should hate beget hate, ignorance beget ignorance, violence beget violence down all the years? Why should machines bring hope of surcease from toil and end by binding creative thought in a prison of technic? Why should revolutions miscarry, at least in part, so that they are well named: They revolve? Nicholas Berdyaev tells in a footnote of a man transported to an ecstasy by the success of the Bolshevik revolution, crying: "I have seen him, him, Kerensky . . . a crowd of thousands . . . ecstasy . . . prophecy . . . I saw how a ray of light fell on him. I saw the birth of New, Eternal Man!" Note the capital letters: the ultimate humanism. A friend burst out laughing. Then the transported man shot a glance at the critic and rushed from the room. He had suddenly realised "the predicament of man"! [6] To drive our questions to deeper ground: Why does the church grow hard with the years, measuring success by market standards, yielding to "suburban captivity," forgetting the poor, echoing government, so that the church must again and again be reborn in all the pains of rebirth? We think that the course of history will save us: "Give the race another million years!" Meanwhile man's guilty violence may cheat us even of a million hours, and in any event we die. When shall we meet the fact that history itself is infected? It never occurs to the Bible that history has any necessary permanence. To the Bible, history cries aloud not for continuance or mere renewal, but for total change and redemption.

Our humanisms will probably cling for a time to their empty hopes. There is much about them to win our gratitude. They sometimes serve man's need, at least on the surface level, more instantly and with less parade than a half-recalcitrant church. But they shy away from the fact that "something has gone wrong," which fact the church within the churches still confronts. They think that nothing has gone wrong which science, governmental reform, and the new economics cannot cure. We need all three agencies, but not in a blind hope. The humanists are by and large a noble company. I live among them with a "lively sense of favors," and feel more at home than in the "little churchinesses" [7] of many a church. But I know—as who does not in his realistic moments? —that they are painting over with white paint the flaw in the marble in the hope that thus the architecture of our life will become pure, the noble habitation of noble men, who nevertheless are not noble, until and unless. . . .

II

So what has gone wrong, and how, and why? There is no full answer, but we have the right to ask and seek understanding. Yes, history brings joy, and joy is the basic term, but the legacy is also the nameless poor and the slain prophet. What we call modern optimism is often more like practical and greedy shrewdness, or not "sense" at all. Carlyle said with his customary gruffness, which yet carried truth, "The Public is an old woman. Let her maunder and mumble." [8] The trouble is that she also murders. But most men share a deeper common sense: "Something has gone wrong." They add, "Surely this world is not what was intended." Then was God half asleep, or talking to the angels, and did he drop a stitch in the cosmic tapestry? Or did one of the angels deceive him, or even try to usurp the throne? Yet how can angels go wrong? But the Bible knows that something has gone wrong. That is a recurrent strain, though the dominant theme is hope. So, for the Bible, "We know that we are of God, and the whole world is in the power of the evil one." [9] What a conjunction of phrases! Is there then a personal devil, who is yet subject to God?

Two answers, both partial but both pertinent, can now be given. This first, we cannot get rid of human responsibility whatever be the origin of evil and its pain. This we know. Is there not a story of Dr. Johnson's reply to a woman who asked him how we know that we are sinners? "Everyman knows his own sins." [10] We do know. That is why we judge by praise or blame. That is why we are indignant when a man steals money from a child. Humanism has a deep verity, even though it is unexamined. There is a certain value (poor word: too mercenary and too polygamous!) in every man, or, rather, an ultimate worth: he must not be made a means, for he is an end. Yet we treat one another as stepping-stones to *our* fancied good. This book does not argue that case: it is an axiom. To argue it only gets it "sicklied o'er with the pale cast of thought." [11] Jesus was quite clear: "Hear me, all of you, and understand: there is nothing outside a man which by going into him can defile him; but the things which come out of a man are what defile him." [12] The words are urgent and blunt. Then this: "For from within, out of

60

the heart of man, come evil thoughts, fornication, theft, murder, adultery, coveting, wickedness, deceit, licentiousness, envy, slander, pride, foolishness. All these evil things come from within, and they defile a man." [13] The list appalls us! The "heart" (nearer to our word "will") is a black, black fountain! Yet we know that Jesus is speaking about us. No, we are not guilty on every count, but we know that our excuses are just that: the very word means the attempt to dodge a true case. Such is the biblical emphasis. We shall return to it in the next chapter, for we must ask the meaning and cure of wrong choice. So much, for the present, about our first verity.

The second is this: though we are responsible, evil does not originate with us or with "Adam." The actuality may be our blame, but what of the potency? Theologians shy away from this mystery. So E. F. Sutcliffe concerning Adam and Eve: "Their sin is thus represented as a sin of disobedience rooted in pride and accompanied by a credulous adherence to a most unworthy insinuation against their divine benefactor." [14] Yes, but whence the "insinuation" or even the credulity? And were they, meaning any man and wife, altogether "credulous"? Yet evil is often plausible, for it come tricked out in the clothes of goodness. The same writer says again, "The origin of all hardship and misery in the world is explained in Genesis. None of it was in God's original plan. Its presence and prevalence are the fruit of sin." [15] Now who is being "credulous"? The *origin* will never be explained until we know the whence and why of the snake, and that item Genesis does *not* explain. Eve did not create the snake. Yet, in the wise and witty title of a modern book, we must often say, "The snake has all the lines"! [16] Furthermore, if the snake was not in God's original plan, God was taken by surprise. He had to patch up an unforeseen emergency: he was fooled and, therefore, is not God. Loring W. Batten likewise evades the mystery of evil: "One of the greatest evils man has to face is ignorance." [17] True. But whence the ignorance?

So we must hold together two facts: We are responsible for evil choice, but evil does not originate with human nature. These two cannot be held together in theory, but they *are* held together in daily life. Adam and Eve were guilty of disobedience and presumption, yet they did not create the snake. All this is in the wisdom of the Bible; it is found also in our deeper kind of common sense. We never get rid of responsibility: if we could our world would dwindle to a nastiness of what happens, and it does not wear that cast. Thus Hitler and his evil crew were guilty, and to believe otherwise would rob life of any worth or meaning. Yet we must also say that the land of Goethe and Bach was "possessed." In fact, we say that of one another: "He is not himself today." Even Freud said it: "Dark, unfeeling and unloving powers determine human destiny." [18] He is wrong in that word "determine," but he is right about "dark, unfeeling and unloving powers." At least he is right insofar as our eyes and knowledge can pierce. Of course, he thus falsifies his own philosophy, for he is in effect now denying that the "id" is the blind, impalpable, amoral base of the "ego" and the "superego." Unbelief always contradicts itself. Freud is usually truer in his flashing asides than in his system, though the system gives some measure of staunch truth, as for example in his not-yet-explored fact of the subconscious and in his not-yet-carried-to-fulfillment doctrine of the shaping of children by the home. The latter doctrine carried to fulfillment would join our two facts: Parents are responsible, yet there are "dark, unfeeling and unloving powers" in all parents and in their parents and in all our ancestry.

It is hard in our *thinking* to hold together the two facts, yet not hard in *life* for in life we simply confront them already joined. Omar Khayyam has some reason for his diatribe:

> O Thou, who Man of baser Earth didst make,
> And who with Eden didst devise the Snake,
>   For all the Sin wherewith the Face of Man
> Is blacken'd,—Man's Forgiveness give—and take! [19]

But the diatribe is still just that, for it shies away from the totality of fact. If God is God he cannot at the same time be "the father of lies," [20] and it would be blasphemy or nonsense for man to try to forgive God, *and* Omar himself is still responsible—guilty like Adam and Eve of pride and presumption. By cleaving to these two facts we may be compounding our problem, but we are trying to be honest to what we know both in Scripture and "in our bones."

III

Now the question is: Whence came the snake, and why does it sometimes have "all the lines"? Perhaps in answer we may have to confess with the New Testament that iniquity in its origin is a "mystery of lawlessness." [21] But there is help in the partial answers which have enlisted men's minds. What of the myth of fallen angels? Did they rebel against God, and, being cast out of heaven, corrupt men on earth? That is the mighty theme of Milton's *Paradise Lost*. There are echoes of this belief in early Scripture: "The sons of God saw that the daughters of men were fair; and they took to wife such of them as they chose," [22] presumably by coercion of their freedom. I would hold, while admitting that there can be no final proof, that there is another echo, about Christ himself: "Who, though he was in the form of God, did not count equality with God a thing to be grasped, but emptied himself, taking the form of a servant, being born in the likeness of men." [23] Perhaps this means that he refused to join the angelic rebellion. Paul Tillich once said to me in conversation that the myth of the fallen angels only pushed the question further back. Yes, indeed, but perhaps it does more: it does some justice to our awareness that evil did not originate with man, but *entered* both nature and human nature. Yet, he was right: the question is now only "further back," for we must now ask how evil could seduce angels, and whence that presumptuous insinuation. Nevertheless such a story has more pungency than our merely philosophical "explanations" such as this: Concretion, the entity-existence of men and the cosmos, always spells limitedness and, therefore, implies a fall from perfection. Yes, but the questions now gather: Is evil mere limitedness, or is it evil? Is our awareness of perfection, without which we would not know concretion, a blank infinity? Milton grips us more than finespun theories. Drama quickens us, while abstraction leaves us still dull in mind.

Then what of the doctrine of a personal devil? Modern man laughs at it. He paints a picture of a sinister intruder with horns, dressed in crimson tights, and then asks, "Is this the childishness proclaimed in churches?" Then modern man, if he is a broker, rigs the market; or, if he is a professor, parades his degrees. Meanwhile broker or professor is urbanely unaware that a seduction personal enough to exercise a personal constraint has captured him! The doctrine has had a history in Scripture: the devil or Satan was at first the testing angel, and then the adversary who incited men to unbelief, but in both characters he was an acknowledged servant of God and attached to God's court. But in later writings of the Old Testament the word "devil" means one who evilly seduces men, seeking to destroy the vital bond between God and men. That is to say, devil came to mean the adversary both of God and men. Jesus underscored this meaning: "He [the devil] was a murderer from the beginning, and has nothing to do with the truth, because there is no truth in him. When he lies, he speaks according to his own nature, for he is a liar and the father of lies." [24] Jesus, we are told, was "tempted by the devil" [25]: the struggle was not shadowboxing. An "enemy" sowed weeds in the farmer's field.[26] The "devil had already put it into the heart of Judas . . . to betray him." [27]

We cannot honorably get rid of this belief by talking about the "thought-forms of an ancient time." We have a few scientific thought-forms of our own at which later generations may laugh aloud. In any event the conviction about a personal devil has outlived the years. It reappears in our time. *The Screwtape Letters* tells how a senior devil in hell ("The Lowerarchy") briefs a junior devil on earth in ways of corrupting the faith of a Christian, and the book wins quick popularity among thoughtful people.[28] Or, to notice another instance, we spin neat psychological theories about "frustration" and then go to the theater to see a play named *Damn Yankees*,[29] which tells of a downtrodden Washington fan receiving almost supernatural batting powers against the Yankees—from the devil, for a price! Or, even while we dismiss with a sophisticated smile "crude doctrines about a personal devil," we pay large money to see *Will Success Spoil Rock Hunter?* [30] a comedy-drama which shows the devil (dressed not in crimson tights but in a well-fitting, expensive business suit) tempting a would-be writer to trade his literary integrity for a cheap success. We watch there in the darkness of the theater, and laugh—uneasily. Truth does not come by logic or by a kindergarten mind that keeps insisting, "Define your terms." Logic itself rests back on axioms, and cannot move an inch without them, and —how do we *know* an axiom? Besides, definition (the word means to bring to a finish, to bind within clearly traced lines) is possible only in science, that is to say, in the study of things, and it is not final even in that realm. Meanwhile we ask, *Will Success Spoil Rock Hunter?* the devil's success. That play certainly cannot be dismissed as unsophisticated.

Why we continue to believe in a personal devil is clear: temptation either seems to come or actually comes with a personal seduction. We ourselves may contrive the seduction, but that is not how life strikes us. On a fair day when our thoughts are fair suddenly the tempter's voice (voice, not vague feeling): "Brother, can you spare a—self?" Moreover the devil has an impressive wardrobe: he matches his wiles to our weakness, promising "romance" to the teenager, academic preferment to the professor, money and a suburban house to the broker, a large church to the ambitious preacher, and continued youth to the man who is actually getting old. Ponder that list of disguises! Moreover the devil (or somebody or some baleful "spirit") *organizes* evil. The refusal to "get involved" in regard to civil rights or the overcoming of delinquency is not a decision only of this or that individual: it becomes "the pattern of the age," dope-peddling soon flourishes as "the drug traffic," and corrupt politics goes beyond this or that politician to emerge as "the political machine." No, individual responsibility is *not* cancelled. That we have already written, and we must soon come to closer grips with the matter of man's outright sin. But we are also "possessed" by an "evil spirit," so that we cry with Paul: "I do not understand my own actions. For I do not do what I want, but I do the very thing I hate." [31] We try to be sophisticated, and then ask if the devil will succeed with "Rock Hunter," for Rock Hunter is our name, and the sophistication itself is a devil tempting.

Yet we must not dogmatize about a personal devil, for we do not know. We have never seen him, and the whole mystery of evil eludes us. Good and evil alike are in their origin hidden in the mystery of creation. We cannot understand how anything (our explosive cosmos, for example) can come from nothing, or why anything is as it is. Our minds are both finite and fallible: they falter and fail before the ultimate mystery. It is worth noting that the Lord's Prayer says, "deliver us from evil" [32] while Paul, who is true to the teaching given him by the apostles of Christ, speaks of "the flaming darts of the evil *one*." [33] He speaks again (for if Paul did not write Ephesians, as we may well surmise, somebody even more "Pauline" than Paul wrote it) of "the prince of the power of the air," an invisible "personal" onset, "the spirit that is now at work in the sons of disobedience." [34] We shall probably go on talking about the devil, with sharp and tragic cause, because the instant seduction, personal enough to be addressed to persons, *is* sharper than our modern theorizings. Yet we should not pretend that we know. That pretension—mark this fact clearly—would be to commit again the sin of Adam and Eve: to presume to eat of the forbidden tree,[35] to claim what belongs only to God, who alone is above and beyond our good and evil, our life and death. Meanwhile we have a battle on our hands which we cannot win by ourselves, a fight, not a gymnasium exercise. I shall not forget the day when, in morning prayers at Harvard, a professor said to the surprise of the Harvard mind that we had better keep the word "devil": otherwise the battle that we know, should we succeed in evaporating it by our theories, would carry away with it the tang and verity of our whole life!

IV

Now another important word: Just as we must hold together personal responsibility *and* an awareness that evil does not originate with man, so must we hold together a conviction well expressed by the word "devil" *and* an avowal of the sovereignty of God. Joy is a deeper term than pain, good than evil, and God than the devil. On this issue the New Testament, indeed the whole Bible, is forthright. The writer of I Peter, for instance, is aware of the destroying power of the devil: "Be sober. Be watchful." A drunken man has his guard down! "Your adversary the devil prowls around like a roaring lion, seeking someone to devour." [36] The devil's power involves suffering, but it is transient power: "And after you have suffered a little while, the God of all grace, who has called you to his eternal glory in Christ, will himself restore, establish, and strengthen you. To him be the dominion for ever and ever. Amen." [37] There is no shadow of doubt in the Bible about that "dominion." There is confession that God's ways are mysterious, even bewildering and dismaying, but God—is God. The presence of an evil spirit is acknowledged: "This is the spirit of antichrist, of which you heard that it was coming, and now it is in the world already." [38] But it is inconceivable that wrong can triumph: "Little children, you are of God, and have overcome them; for he who is in you is greater than he who is in the world." [39]

What we have called deeper common sense has this same conviction, though not with biblical assurance. It assumes what it calls "the supremacy of truth." The ground of life is not a rubble of lies or a morass. Come to think of it, that is a tremendous assumption. Perhaps we should not say assumption, but necessity of thought and life. Why haven't lies overcome truth—social lies, political lies, white lies, ecclesiastical lies, sophisticated lies? But truth stands, and must stand, because truth is truth. The modern mind laughs at what it calls the "pious optimism" of

> God's in his heaven—
> All's right with the world.[40]

For the modern mind forgets that the clear-minded peasant girl, Pippa, sang the song, and that Sebald and Ottima heard it in the morning as they woke from a guilty liaison: Pippa in her poverty, they in their wealth. They knew her song was true—as judgment; she knew it was true—as joy. Perhaps this conviction lives in our Western world because the Bible is in our blood, and because we have not yet spent our patrimony; perhaps it is in every man's blood, as Paul proposes: "They [the Gentiles who do not believe in God] show that what the law requires is written on their hearts." [41] In any event we *do* believe that truth is truth and that lies cannot prevail. Not soon shall I forget seeing a flower box with bright flowers set outside a window ledge in a bombed city. Ultimately flowers are stronger than bombs!

The Bible says much more: God will make an end of evils and suffering, yes, has already made an end: "Then comes the end, when he [Christ] delivers the kingdom to God the Father after destroying every rule and every authority and power. For he must reign until he has put all his enemies under his feet. The last enemy to be destroyed is death." [42] "Must": It is in the very grain of creation, "since the foundation of the world." [43] Evil can destroy for a time, but cannot redeem: Beelzebub cannot cast out Beelzebub.[44] That word seems merely obvious, but hides great deeps: evil has no creative power. It is deceitful; that is, it must pose as good to get anywhere. Nay, it must ape the good within its own bounds: the Brink robbers must be honorable in the sharing of the loot, and when one breaks that rule and another squeals, the robber-band is broken. So evil, with its suffering, is always *inferior*. The very word "Belial" means the worthless one. We must move with caution at this point. We still cannot say that "evil is null, is nought, is silence implying sound," [45] for evil is evil with brokenness as its heavy fee. Nor can we say with Nels Ferré that "evil is ever an aspect of becoming more than of being," [46] unless we remember (he himself would underscore the re-minder) that evil with its suffering is incipient death. But we can say that evil lives only by imitating the good,[47] and that God has it in control and is indeed leading evil itself to the death chamber. So we reiterate: God in his goodness is the vital term: there are no other gods beside him.

V

Toward the end of each chapter thus far we have hinted at a solving word in "the problem of pain." I would have preferred for my part to have begun the book with that avowal in outright proclamation. But I am trying to write for the mind of our skeptical time and with acknowledgment of my own debt to the skepticism: it is better than the half-belief, the shabby compromise between the New Testament and a "successful" humanism which marks many a church. Our path is from honest doubt to the solving word. So we close this chapter in a further surmise.

As we consider historical evil with its progeny of pains, what is truth? We assume that truth is something we say, as when in a law court we swear (on a Bible!) to "speak the truth, the whole truth, and nothing but the truth" in a preposterous temerity. Truth is by this as-sumption a strict accord between our words and what has happened. Yet we know that truth has a deeper thrust and far wider bounds. Or we assume that truth is the end of a journey in philosophy: the college student pathetically believes that he may come upon "a true philosophy of life." If he has no better hope, he will find only a maze, for philos-ophy is a mind-affair which too easily gets exiled from the actualities which beset John Smith on Main Street.

> Myself when young did eagerly frequent
> Doctor and Saint, and heard great Argument
> About it and about: but evermore
> Came out by the same Door as in I went.[48]

Or we assume that truth is a scientific formula, as if truth could be any-thing so small as the findings of a fractional mind analyzing a frac-tional world. The Bible never doubts that truth is speaking to us through events, and through an Event which gathers all other events into its light and power and love. If our time asks, "Why such a faith?" the answer may be, "Why not? What does your life say?"

Jesus, as the Event, never minimized what we have called historical evil. He knew that our world is flawed: "If you then, *who are evil*," yet have sufficient goodness to love "your children. . . ."[49] There is no hint in the Gospels of a sellout to our empty doctrines of "progress." He was not starry-eyed about human nature, yet he never despaired, for in him was the solving Word. As to that, more as we travel. Meanwhile he said of historical evil, in a phrase that is very darkness, "the blood of all the prophets, shed from the foundation of the world, may be required of this generation."[50] Whatever may be the contextual explication of that appalling word (that exegesis is not our present task), it certainly testifies to Christ's concern about the terrible entail of history's sins. The same concern appears in his sharp-edged forecast about the place of his own coming death: "For it cannot be that a prophet should perish away from Jerusalem."[51] He knew how the devil pretends goodness: the time was coming when those who killed his followers "will think he is offering service to God"![52]

Yet he was sure that historical evil with its swarm of pains could be redeemed, nay, was already redeemed: "Now is the judgment of this world, now shall the ruler of this world be cast out, and I, when I am lifted up from the earth, will draw all men to myself."[53] What happens to us when we read that word? Do we dismiss it with, "Religious vaporizings! The messianic complex"? But he did not indulge in vaporizings: he is "the true Son of Fact."[54] As for the messianic complex, students of the Gospels doubt more and more if he claimed messiahship. Certainly he did not claim to fulfill the nationalistic, military hopes that attached to the messiah-expectation in his time. What *does* happen to us as we read? The words "lifted up" have a double meaning in the Fourth Gospel: "lifted up" on a Cross, and "lifted up" beyond the Cross to that "dominion" that rules all evil and all pain. The words "all men" mean what they say: all human beings. Incredible claim! But suppose he is *the* Event! The future, he told us, would justify the claim: "What I am doing you do not know now, but afterward you will understand."[55] What he was doing was taking the part of a slave to wash the disciples' feet: history is under God's sovereignty and, therefore, would bring interpretations—of a life and death that conquered death by the death of all pride. Unbelievable, but suppose again . . . ! The strange bond between present and future is there hinted: life is never a "now" only, for if it is very life it is also "tomorrow." This item also shall engage us. But we are here and now content to hint: Is he the Event and the solving Word?

As for those who have died in the past, whom our age appallingly dismisses as the manure of the field of *our* dubious "progress," the New Testament has an astonishing conviction-hope which makes fitting end to this still tentative discussion of historical evil. It says of the heroes of the past, known and unknown, that "all these, though well attested by their faith, did not receive what was promised, since God had foreseen something better for us, that apart from us they should not be made perfect." [56] The better thing for us is a thing in love: we have a share in fulfilling the lives of those who did not know Christ in the flesh, who had not reached the bright shore, yet waved to it in greeting. Or, to change the figure, since the grandeur of Scripture requires all our metaphors and then beggars all of them, history is a great symphony: every generation is a theme, every age is a movement. Soon shall come the pain of the dissonance of the penultimate chords, and then the "great Amen" when all history shall be gathered back into the Mystery of love *who* brought history to the birth. All dissonances shall thus be redeemed. Yet metaphors *do* fail, and people are not notes—they are at long last the redeemed children of the Most High God. "To him be the dominion for ever and ever." [57]

5. On Personal Evil

Sin and Pain: Now the Question Strikes Home!

Now we come to *ourselves*, to the pain that you and I bring on ourselves and others by our guilty pride. A Charles Williams novel [1] shows a woman suddenly aware that she herself is coming down the street to meet her. She steps into a doorway until she (herself) has gone past. That fiction is fact for each of us. I have been guilty, for in this book up to this point I have been mainly studying "the problem of pain" as if I were a spectator, and have invited the reader also to play that impossible role. The Bible, which is the only book of the only realism, finds us in whatever doorway. It acknowledges that *some* evil-pain cannot be ascribed, so far as our human wisdom carries, to our blame; but it keeps saying that the *weight* and *bitterness* of our suffering come from our transgressions. [2]

Obviously this Bible-stress gathers in much historical evil. People such as ourselves in days now past, yet not past, have sinned as we sin, to our dark loss. The pride of rulers aided and abetted by the

71

lethargy, violence, and national conceit of a thousand little men on a thousand little streets brings war; war brings weariness and disillusionment with longing for revenge; this complex brings a vindictive peace; this in turn brings new wars, as long as the ages roll; this invites our modern and cowardly despair by which we say,

> Raving politics, never at rest—as this poor
> earth's pale history runs,—
> What is it all but a trouble of ants in the
> gleams of a million million of suns? [3]

The Bible answers: "Don't blame the ants: it comes from the pride, unconcern, or ambition in people exactly like you." You and I have little right to blame our ancestry for sins which *we* commit against *our* posterity.

As for natural evil, we have seen that the Bible ascribes that also to man's transgression. Labor pains came on Eve and labor pains of another kind came on Adam struggling with weeds in his garden because the archetypal man and wife presumed in overreaching pride to know what only God can know. Adam and Eve are you and I, the garden is our world, and the time is our time. Elsewhere the Bible confesses "the mystery of lawlessness," [4] but still insists that the mystery could be borne, and even shot through with light, if our minds were not darkened by iniquity. Job's "comforters" were wrong in charging that all Job's ills came from his open or secret sins, but they were not wrong in the conviction that any sin and every sin has its nemesis of pain. When I fall sick what troubles me is not the physical pain (which can easily be accounted for, if I try to be content with surface explanations, on medical grounds), but the waste and failure of days when I was not sick. That "trouble" is not morbid, for the sickness reminds me also of joys which I took for granted unawares. The sense of sin is basic: it comes from the knowledge of God. That fact we must now explore.

I

We should distinguish between psychotic guilt and sin. The former has been traced by psychiatry, and the tracing is our gain. A man comes to his minister (the instance is disguised beyond recognition lest pastoral confidence be broken, but in substance it is not falsified) confessing that he had long hated his mother, she being now dead. When he had suffered back pains as a child, she had told him that he must bear with fortitude what was "God's will." The result was that he always had to wear a steel brace. Meanwhile, to compensate for a dimly realized hatred, he had indulged his mother in excessive "love." Thus there was a conflict in himself, and a tendency to rail at any kind of authority. In such an instance we see the strange mixture of sin and unreal guilt. Soon he was able to ask questions. Is it altogether wrong to hate a hateful pietism? Is the family bond beyond judgment? Is not any mother shaped in measure by her parents? Ought we not, therefore, to try to think in terms of understanding and love, yes, and of forgiveness, rather than hatred? Sometimes the psychotic element becomes so dominant that a man will charge himself with imaginary crimes. Thus the police have added trouble finding the real culprit because so many people confess to a murder in which they have had no part. The questions throng: How far was Nietzsche's alternate longing for love and his rigorous insistence on the "right," his ambivalence between fear of all things effeminate and his sense of "mission," due to his upbringing? We cannot tell. But our new knowledge of psychotic guilt is added reason why we should be slow to judge. The real reason is that people who live in glass houses should not throw stones, that and some brighter reasons.

But the adjective "psychotic" itself points to *veritable* sin. Indeed, the instance given above raises all the issues of right and wrong, for notice the words used of man's increasing realism: "Was it wrong?" . . . "under judgment" . . . "ought we not?" Then what is sin? Not merely or mainly the breach of a moral code or even the breaking of the Ten Commandments. The Decalogue is not finality in any event: the tenth commandment [5] enjoining a man not to covet his "neighbor's house" nor "his wife" nor his manslave nor his maidslave nor his "ox, nor his ass," makes scant distinction between the wife and the house, or even between the wife and the ass, and it offers no hope of freedom to the slave. House, wife, ox, slave—they are all the chattel possession of the dominant male. These comments do not mean that we can sit loose to the Ten Commandments, for a keen sense of right may give them

73

clearer interpretation and a sharper relevance. What we do mean is that the nerve of sin is not between a man and a code, but between man and God. Preachers forget that the Ten Commandments are themselves set within a covenant between God and men,[6] so the preachers preach a moralism instead of a Promise.

Then what is sin? The denial of God and the pride and presumption by which we try to play our own God. This book will not now pause to "prove God." Would we ever pause to "prove" ourselves? We know God not by "great argument," which proves nothing, but as the Bible knows him, by his "mighty acts." The evidence of God is found in history, and centrally in Bible history, not in our "learning" which is painfully slow to learn. We are here by a birth beyond our control, and soon we shall die in a death beyond our control. We are given certain gifts: we may or may not develop them, but we did not contrive them. Our children are not our children, for we can only transmit life: we cannot create life. We are under Sovereignty. The original form of the question, "Who am I?" is "Who are you?" We say "Thou" to God only because he has first said "thou" to us. Our very personhood is delineated not by our body, which, though it may in measure demark us from our neighbor, also links us with animals and things; nor by our minds which have appalling power to get lost in other and perhaps baser minds, but by the confrontation of the Mystery called God. Meanwhile he speaks to us through the Event of Christ and through the onsets of our daily life. No apology is offered for these sentences. The truth of them is not established or overthrown by debate. Life, not logic, is the testing stone. So the Bible never "proves" God: it points to "his mighty acts." [7] The classic "proofs" [8] come in part from man's mind and, therefore, hide fallacies. But they would never have been attempted if the God they try to "prove" (and inevitably assume) had not found us. That fact is their value.

So sin is the denial of God "with whom we have to do." Notice that phrase, "with whom we have to do"; not, "about whom we may choose to argue." Thus the penitential psalms:

> Against thee, thee only, have I sinned
> and done that which is evil in thy sight.[9]

74

We confess to ourself, "What a fool I've been!" and then find small help from a fool. Or we confess to our neighbor, as they do in Russia, licking each other's sores with diseased tongues. For our sin is not primarily against ourself or our neighbor (we only transmit life and cannot create it), but against the Creator. Our skepticisms have left us suspended in mid-air: there is no ultimate Reference. We have neither ground-of-life nor overarching sky. Therefore, we are not only sinners but "miserable sinners." That phrase does not mean a supine wretchedness, but what it says: "miserable" because now the main nerve, the bond between us and God, is broken, with multitudinous pains and death. So we return to our description: pain traces as with a daggerpoint the line between two dimensions of life, between God and ourselves, so that we cry in double cry: "I am mortal! Where is my salvation?" Our sin is against God, and in God is our only hope. Sin is not centrally a breach of a codified "thou shalt not," but a denial of a living "thou shalt."

Sin is legion. The forms may be new, as new as the atom bomb, but the substance is old: "Our sinful nature prone to evil and slothful in good." [10] By the way, that phrase from *The Book of Common Worship is* true, isn't it? Always sin is pride: the creature man refusing to acknowledge his creaturehood, coveting the center of the stage, front, spotlight. So sin is *disobedience,* against him who says "thou." So sin is *irresponsibility,* failure to respond to him who has found us through "his mighty acts." So sin is *baalism,* sinking into the natural order, though we know God's order is over us. So sin is *unbelief,* lack of trust in him who is our only life. Open your newspaper for the various forms, which are only one in substance. There you see a lying advertisement from the loan company telling you that you can "get rid of all your unpaid bills," if only you borrow from them at a rate of interest not specified. There the politician deliberately appeals to base motive: "Let's bomb them before they bomb us." There the newspaper editor explains that he does not make the news, he only reports it, though actually he determines the headlines, and the front page or back page, and the highlighting of sensation, sex, and violence. "Fools make a mock at sin," [11] moralists impose a code, reformers busy themselves with other people's sins, but saints confess their own—in a penitence which God alone can give, for he alone is God.

II

Our sin is linked with our freedom. All books on suffering underline that fact. Sin is an affair of the will. It is not "a vestige of our animal inheritance." That trivial notion comes from an unexamined, too-quickly swallowed doctrine of evolution. Why blame the brute creation? No self-respecting wolf would be guilty of our modern wars. We will to do evil, and we will to do good. There is a cleft in our will, and, since the bond with God is now broken, our good will has no power (there is a break in the main contact), and our evil will prevails: "For I do not do what I want, but I do the very thing I hate." [12] But we go on choosing— with a broken will. We have that much freedom: God says, "I have set before you life and death . . . therefore choose life." [13]

This fact of good or evil choice does not "explain" our sin, for we still ask why God made the world in such a way as to leave the door open to wrong or blind decision. But we cannot imagine how a man can be good without choosing good against a very possible and plausible evil. Dr. D'Arcy has written that God seems more intent on beauty than on goodness,[14] for beauty is flung across earth and sky with lavish hand, whereas the Diogenes search for an honest man continues un-fulfilled. But D'Arcy rightly adds that God can fashion beauty without our help, while goodness comes only when a man wills what God wills.[15] A compelled goodness would not be goodness, but only compulsion. We speak of a "good clock," but a thing cannot be good. Only a man can be good, and he only because God is the sole good. So we should not say, "That is a good clock," but, "That clock was made by a faithful and ef-ficient clockmaker." Omar railed against the world as a "sorry Scheme of Things," declaring that if he could take it in hand he would "shatter it to bits," and then "Remould it nearer to the Heart's Desire." [16] But if someone had asked him, "Just what do you have in mind?" he could not have answered. For no man can imagine a freedom that is not free, or a good choice without an alternative.

The freedom is limited by the constitution of the world, for we cannot wave a wand to turn pumpkins into houses. It is limited also by our own constitution, for if we try to reach the moon we must pathetically turn a capsule into a tiny earth, with earth temperatures and earth oxygen. It is limited by our earlier faulty choices, by which our will to goodness grows weak and at last helpless; and by death, which writes *finis* to the little time given us for choice. But the freedom is within limits free: we vote for goodness against the other candidate, the devil. We know our responsibility. The protest is in vain:

> Oh Thou, who didst with Pitfall and with Gin
> Beset the Road I was to wander in,
>   Thou wilt not with Predestination round
> Enmesh me, and then impute my Fall to Sin?[17]

There *is* that Mystery: we have confronted it. But there is the knowledge of our freedom and our responsibility and our wrong choice. I was lazy yesterday, or unconcerned, or blind altogether, when I ought to have helped my neighbor. Indeed, this very fact is the reverse side of a glory. A cat cannot sin, even though it may swallow the canary, for a cat does not know the difference. But a man knows evil, and therefore knows —God. Pain and death come from sinful failure.

III

The sins and the resultant sufferings are "more in number than the sand." [18] *There are sins of commission.* The mendacity that cankers all speech, so that we say: "You can't believe everything you hear," brings the pain of being deceived: who has not known that sharp agony? The false claims that pervert our processes of law bring loss: once a man walked off the sidewalk against the traffic light into the side of my car, was knocked down, though without any serious injury, and then sued me for thirty thousand dollars. The commercial greed that turns both radio and television into a cheap huckstering, so that we must look hour after hour at human beings grinning like hyenas at a glass of beer. The trampling instinct, egocentricity become brutal, all the way from the street-corner gang to any war, fills the world with agony:

> Man's inhumanity to man
> Makes countless thousands mourn.[19]

There is a chain reaction from land to land, and from generation to generation: historical evil. Antisemitism with its pogroms and ghettos

77

encouraged Zionism, and Zionism, partly with no wish and partly through the violence of the Stern group, made Arab refugees, and that whole issue now bedevils world politics. The slave trade becomes the "race issue" across the world. One book on suffering speaks in its very title of "ills unlimited." [20]

There are *sins of omission,* and they may exact a heavier price in pain. One of my sons, as we walked through Harlem when he was a child, asked, "Are they really different from us?" We know they are not, for pigmentation of skin is not a prime concern: they have the same blood-chemistry and the same tears and laughter. Then why does race prejudice persist? To satisfy the pride that is willing to believe other human beings are "inferior"? To continue an oppression which relegates some neighbors to inferior jobs? To "justify" the colonial role of the white man? Yes, but the main reason for the persistence is not active pride, but passive indifference, the sloth and fear that will not bestir themselves for an "uncomfortable" cause. This comment is not a diatribe: it is a confession and a penitence. The sin of default may be written in heaven's books in larger script than the outrightly sinful act. Nor can we blame God for what we know is our blame.

Yet we could hardly imagine another kind of world. Men who could not sin would not be men: they would be "good clocks" ticking out goodness. Then not even God would be a "good clockmaker," for he would have deceived us into believing in the reality of free choice. Suppose fire did not burn, but still destroyed? There are deeper questions: Would we know the good if we were not thus apprehended in obligation and in the pain of wrong choice? The final issue of our sin is death: "The wages of sin is death." [21] That fact does not deny that death in our present world is a biological necessity: the planet would swarm with feeble life if nobody died. Neither does it deny that death is a "natural event," whatever that may mean. It affirms what we have already written: that outer events have inner meanings. Death has appalling finality: it ends our chance and choice in this momentous world. It spells judgment. Our word "crisis" is directly from the Greek, and means judgment: death is crisis-judgment on our delinquencies which even in this world bring death. Our only hope is that He "will not leave us in the dust." [22] So sin is father of pain—pain of conscience and of body, pain of loneliness, and pain of the mind's distraction.

IV

The sharpest pain for perceptive and sensitive people is the penalty which falls on the "innocent." Sin breaks the bond between man and man, as well as that between man and God. Mark the pain of parents: "Our Bill could never have done such a thing!" Yet Bill was found guilty. Mark the crippleness of a child knocked down by a drunken driver, or the desolation of France overrun by Hitler's armies. Of course no responsible person is completely innocent. Indeed, everyone who has knowledge of good and evil is partially to blame. The custom of ancient Israel of punishing the whole family when one member sinned, as when Achan's greedy hiding of the spoils of battle brought death to his whole household,[23] was too sweeping a judgment. But it should remind us that *we* are too indulgent: we fail to see that when one man sins every other man shares the blame. Here is an instance: A bank clerk handled millions of dollars in farm mortgages, but was himself grossly underpaid. So he stole from the bank, partly under pressure to support his family while trying to pay the interest on a mortgage on his own modest home. One of the directors explained that they "had to take his home," and then added in a nasty self-righteousness, "But we did not drag him into court." Actually they were trying to avoid bad publicity for the bank, with, we hope, some admixture of human pity. But in any event they were guilty with the clerk, for they underpaid him while sticking daily temptation under his nose. The point is this: No man can shrug off his personal accountability. He is chargeable directly for his own sin, as in the case of the clerk, and chargeable indirectly for his neighbor's sin, as in the case of the directors. The further point is that the sin of the guilty is visited in pain on the relatively innocent.

Of course, the blessings of our common life are also shared. Thus we confront again gratefully the fact of joy and make again our prime comment: The joy is the basic term. The daily boon of food: Does any man deserve the toil of neighbors which gives him breakfast, the labor in the fields, the hoeing and the harvesting, the loading of ships and trucks, the packing and the selling? And what of symphonies which we could never have composed? Or freedoms which were purchased by the blood of a thousand Hampdens? Or the piercing and ever-blessed witness of Christ? This reminder does not explain why the innocent suffer with the guilty, but it draws some of the sting. We cannot imagine a world in which joy is shared and sins are a privacy. The mystery remains. But there is no surcease of sin and pain—unless God himself. . . . But that is our next concern!

It is not strange that men have surmised that some devil has seduced mankind. We can quote Andre Gide's "Journal" on that issue: "I am utterly indifferent as to whether or not this name of demon is the right name for what I mean, and I grant that I give it the name out of convenience." [24] Strange sentence! For how could he be "indifferent"? And if he were "indifferent," why should he raise the question in such urgency? And how can a "demon" be "it"? And why and how could his motive be "convenience," when clearly it came from the dimness of our mortal sight and was nearer to necessity? But Gide, confronting a mystery, did not deny our responsibility. Nor did he deny God. When we must choose, yet with a will already made weak both by historical evil and by our own sin, what help or hope have we, unless. . . . Thus our pilgrimage brings us closer to an open secret and a path of light. But there is another item in our preparation: The meaning and the dilemma of our systems of justice, with their word about righteousness and the always broken will of our righteousness, and the insufficiency of any righteousness unless it leads on to love.

V

Why do we frame systems of justice? Because if sin and evil are unchecked we could not live: thieves and murderers would make chaos of the common life. But behind this reason there are deeper reasons. There is an awareness that human nature *is* corrupt: "The whole world is in the power of the evil one." [25] Our confident humanisms speak about the "brotherhood of man" and about "the evolution of the perfect man," but our systems of justice betray the confidence: we know that for our own safety we must establish and enforce laws, lest our proud and perfidious will should destroy all human life. Note: for our *own* safety: selfishness which is sin infects even our promotion of justice. But there is a deeper reason behind even this deeper reason: we know we are under Sovereignty, that obligation rests on us, and that we must try with whatever broken powers to transcribe on earthly tablets this higher demand.[26] Because our nature is corrupt and our eyes dim, because our conscience is uneasy, we are tempted to regard God's law as punitive, but we know it is holy: "For I am the Lord your God; consecrate yourselves therefore, and be holy, for I am holy." [27] What a crisscross of motives good and bad appears within our lawcourts!

The worthier intention is never altogether lost. Therefore, we seek judges who show promise of being impartial, and pay them salaries which (we hope) may make them immune to bribery. There are lawyers for the defense and for the prosecution who honorably (we hope) will bring to light all the pertinent facts. We engage policemen who will track down the culprits, and jailors who will execute the sentence; and we inflict sentences that will not only provide some respite to the community for the wrong committed, but may by lonely silence bring the criminal to his senses. All this is a heart-shattering portent in its deeper meaning: man's attempt to transcribe by legislation and enforcement the statutes which God has written secretly not only on statute books or "on tablets of stone, but on tablets of human hearts." [28]

Yet our human justice always fails in measure and thus becomes unjust. Men emerge from jail worse men. Judges are sometimes venal: the Chicago papers have recently revealed collusion between court officers and judges to "fix" traffic "tickets" for cash. Detectives fail to detect, and it is a safe guess that most crimes are never brought to court. Lawyers may become ambulance-chasers or make it their main concern to delay justice or to find loopholes in the law: a famous tennis player, when a rule was passed forbidding tournament committees from paying large fees to amateurs, remarked, "There's nothing to stop the committee from betting me a thousand dollars that I can't jump over my racquet." Juries are prejudiced, as witness the present failure of "justice" in Mississippi to convict men clearly charged with murder in the civil rights movement. Sometimes an innocent man is found guilty, and the blunder may never be revealed. Meanwhile all who try to maintain justice are themselves guilty, though they may never have "broken the law." Brother Juniper of the Franciscan band, wrongly accused because of his facial likeness to a wanted criminal and therefore about to be hung, was rescued at the last minute; but when his comrades asked him why he did not more vigorously prove his identity, he answered that in his angry motives he had often deserved hanging, so "why should I not be hung?" [29] Meanwhile no hanging brings to life the murdered man or consoles his family.

The failure of justice thus raises questions and questions. Is any of us worthy to judge his neighbors? Are our eyes ever keen enough to trace the measure of guilt? Does the loneliness of prison life promote penitence or resentment? Is it not true that the criminal is likely to emerge from jail a more hardened man and that hanging has not discouraged murder? In any event does a man who "always keeps the law" and always insists on "law" come thus to creative manhood, to understanding and love for instance, or is he likely to become satisfied and censorious? If we "keep the law" are we not likely to become self-righteous, losing life in respectability? If we know we cannot keep the deeper law, are we not threatened with despair? Who was the jurist, more perceptive than most, who pointed to a law court and said, "There justice is dispensed— with"? The deepest question we have not yet asked: How can corrupt man keep the laws of the Eternal God? Yet we must try, or the common life will fester and break. The attempt of Israel to "keep the Law" is a moving affair. Was there ever such devotion to law, almost to the point of idolatry? They said that if a scribe even wrote the law without mistake the kingdom of God would come. But there is no such scribe, still less the perfect man who walks perfectly in the law of the Lord which is perfect. All this we write to make clear one prime fact: We ourselves by our "justice" cannot cure or even overtake our sin. Yet we must try to keep the law, knowing that we cannot keep it.

There is nowadays a more profound movement in our penal systems. People such as John Howard and Elizabeth Fry voluntarily shared the imprisonment of criminals in the endeavor to *redeem* our systems of justice. But can corrupt man be redeemer, unless. . . ? Do not methods of probation also fail, though they may show more promise than any vindictiveness or "eye for an eye" enforcement? These questions bring us nearer to our open secret. So this chapter about pain and sin closes, as with each foregoing chapter, with a hint, this time in the form of a story. It is told of the California gold rush that two sailors rowing an officer from the mainland of San Francisco to their ship's anchorage in the Bay, threw him overboard, and joined the gold rush. They were caught, tried, and sentenced to die. The gallows was set up on the main deck. But before they were hung the ship's command, under some strange compelling, thought it well to observe the service of the Sacrament. They borrowed communion silver from a San Francisco church and invited the whole ship's company, including the murderers, to partake of the bread and the wine, despite the exclusion which many a church might practice. Why the Sacrament—in front of a gallows, of all places? Was it because they knew they were all guilty, if only in the fact that the harsh life on a frigate and the lust for gold made for temptation and thus beckoned the murderous act? Was it because they sensed that only Heaven can make reparation, since the gallows could not bring back the murdered man or mend the sorrows of his family? Was it because they realized that the ultimate law is the law of holy love within the nature of God, and that only he can forgive and restore? At any rate they commemorated a Gallows before a gallows. Maybe the Gallows is set from the foundation of the world! Maybe there, before a Gallows, the "problem of pain" is pierced with Light. So, after an intermezzo, to that tremendous mystery.

6. Dawn Watch

But How Can God Suffer?

There is a solving word in the problem of pain, and better than a solving word. For merely to dissolve pain, and thus get rid of it, might rob life of its reality. If you were seeking wisdom at some crux of decision, you would not go to some smooth-faced man with a glib tongue who had spent his days dodging hardship. What we need is that God shall break through into our world of pain, so that we can see through the opened door another world, so that the very pain contributes to the new journey into joy. We repeat: that *God* shall break through. For in a world in which pain is constitutional, which is "in the power of the evil one," [1] where our own will toward God is broken, only he can save us. Yet how can God and suffering be joined? The very words seem to clash, for suffering is evil and God is good. Thus our present question, in the dawn watch, before the door opens on another Realm.

Most people, perhaps all people, believe in God, though they name him in their differences by different names. Perhaps there is no alternative, for the creature finds life only in the Creator. The atheist is devoted to

84

what he calls "truth" and may be worshiping on the other side of the altar. This belief in God comes not because "there must be a beginning to things" but because things of themselves in their strange happening proclaim his word. The Old Testament never "reasons its way" to God, but believes in him because of "his mighty acts." [2] The New Testament likewise never seeks "a philosophy of life" but is found of God in the event of Christ. We do not say, "There must be a purpose to pain," and then surmise God. No, for pain of itself brings no wisdom: God finds us in pain, and himself unfolds the purpose. Maybe the word *"man"* implies the word *"God,"* as *earth* implies *heaven.* Maybe we need not say "maybe."

But here is the question: If God enters our suffering to share it, is he not thereby limited and disfigured by evil? On the other hand, if he is lifted above our pain in an eternal Passivity, which seems to us an eternal callousness, can he be God? Certainly it would seem that in the latter event, beneath such an unapproachable heaven, our life is "solitary, poor, nasty, brutish, and short." [3] If God shares our pain, it would be "justified," or at least we could wait for the "reasons." Yet pain, we have seen, is incipient death. How can the Godhead be infected with the obscenity of death?

I

The German theologian, Baron Friedrich von Hügel, wrote a famous essay on "Suffering and God." [4] It is likely that he himself regarded it as his most important work. Surely the members of the London Society for the Study of Religion, to whom the essay was first given as a lecture, listened with great excitement. Scholars know the essay and take their bearings from it, like travelers gauging their path and their distance by a mountain. But our book is not for scholars. It has in mind the thoughtful man in the street, preachers, and other ordinary mortals such as the writer. So, for the sake of those who do not know the essay, we try to summarize the Baron's argument. He does *not* believe that suffering and God can be joined: nothing can mar God's transcendent Perfection. The essay begins by his quoting from the opposite camp, from theologians who claim that if God does not suffer he is lower than his creatures, since he then lacks the poignant insight which some people have garnered from pain, yes, and the neighborliness which comes of troubles shared: if God knows no pain, perhaps human beings courageous under affliction should pity him. The Baron chooses the most telling passages from the writings in the other camp. James Hinton, William Temple, Walter H. Moberly, R. L. Nettleship, and the others who believe that God and suffering *are* joined, could hardly quarrel with the Baron's choice, for he quotes them at their best. Then like a skillful debater, when he appears to have given his case away, he says, "But. . . ."

It is a trenchant and noble "but." Yet it is not final, for no man can speak even the first word, let alone the last word, about God. An Eastern proverb says that a camel is supercilious because though man knows ninety-nine names for God, the camel knows the hundredth. Actually there are a thousand names for God, and both man and camel are stymied. The Baron issues subpoenas for three witnesses to prove his case. The first is Plato as spokesman for Greek philosophy. Plato conceives of God as "Beauty only, absolute, separate, simple and everlasting . . ." "pure and clear and unalloyed." [5] The Baron thus has a fine witness. But the other attorney could reply that God to Greek thought was still impersonal, an archetypal Idea or Form rather than God; and that to Plato our human life was only a "broken arc" of heaven's "perfect round," [6] or at best a refracted ray of light destined for no better fate than to be drawn back into the sun and there lost. Greek culture was a pyramid: the top was an illumined intellectualism, while the base was a multitude of slaves. It is doubtful if Plato had much meaning for *them*. As for Jesus, "the great throng heard him gladly." [7]

The second witness is the Old Testament community. [8] That book is at odds with Greek thought:

> I will brandish your sons, O Zion,
> over your sons, O Greece. [9]

The Baron now coaches the testimony: he makes the witness say that the central word in the Old Testament about God is his supernal glory: he is

> the high and lofty One
> who inhabits eternity, whose name is Holy, [10]

who dwells far above the little duststorms of earth. The Baron has to admit that the Old Testament speaks also about the anger of God, his love, and even of his repenting that he ever made such an unruly creature as man. But these passages he dismisses as somewhat primitive: they are "physico-morphic." [11] It is his word, not mine. It means the attempt on man's part to print nature's weather and man's emotion on the Divine Mystery. But reply can be made. The Old Testament folk knew that God's thoughts are not as ours; his ways are as high and unreachable as the sky is high above the earth.[12] They knew it, and they said it. Yet when the psalmist spoke of God's laughing he meant something, and what he meant was tremendous and terrible:

> He who sits in the heavens laughs;
> The Lord has them in derision.[13]

That particular psalmist was not unsophisticated. On the contrary he was wide awake to the ironies of history and the orderings of God.

The third witness is the New Testament, and more particularly the Gospels.[14] To the casual spectator in court this witness offers the poorest help to the Baron's plea. The focus of the gospel is joy: such is the claim, and it is well made. The sufferings of Christ did not break the basic peace. Meanwhile God to him, though he was "Father," was yet "above the heavens." [15] Earth "is his footstool." [16] He is the "only God," and to him shall be ascribed "glory, majesty, dominion, and authority, before all time and now and for ever." [17] But there is much else in the New Testament, not least that picture of God which Jesus gave us: he is the Father, or at least like the father, who sorrowed over the prodigal in the far country and rejoiced over the lad's return.

These subpoenas fulfilled, the Baron eloquently proclaims his faith in God's untrammeled and unblemished Perfection, almost to the pitch of Platonic ecstasy. That is to say he believes in anti-Patripassianism.[18] Isn't that word a ton of bricks—falling? Split it up: *anti* means against, *Patri* means the Father, *passian* means suffering, and *ism* means school of thought; so the whole word means the doctrine which is against the proposal that there is suffering in God. The Baron is a staunch proponent of anti-Patripassianism, which is the classic teaching of his church, the Roman Catholic Church. We cannot rightly say that he is prisoner of his heritage, unless we say as much of ourselves in our heritage, for the Protestant church has traditionally believed in Patripassianism. We should confront the Baron's case on its own merits. He offers five clear reasons:

1. Suffering is intrinsically evil, and God cannot be evil.[19]

2. Suffering and sin, while not identical, are linked both in the Bible and in life: God cannot be a sinner.[20]

3. God alone is free: "He can create, and he destroy."[21] The only real freedom is freedom for goodness, as we ourselves dimly know. Real freedom therefore excludes choice. So God cannot choose, but is in himself the ultimate Goodness.[22]

4. The conviction of the Otherness of God is essential to any worthy faith. Man is man, and God is God. There is sympathy in God toward us, but not suffering: his purity is not stained by our earthbound life.[23]

5. God is Transcendence, the unblemished Joy. Our aspirations otherwise would have no ultimate goal. Only as God is Ultimate can the creature press on in obedience to the command of Christ.[24] "You, therefore, must be perfect, as your heavenly Father is perfect."[25]

This summary does no justice to the Baron. It is scant indeed compared with his richness of thought, and a dull blotch alongside his eloquence. But it represents rather than falsifies his argument.

What to say? Surely any thoughtful man is almost ready to throw in the towel: "You've got too much punch for me!" Pain *is* limitation. It cripples the body. It binds the mind, for we find it hard to think when pain strikes. The noble pains of compassion are no exception: if our child is critically sick, we cannot casually go about our daily work. There is a sense in which the sufferings of war are most deeply felt by sensitive noncombatants: the fighters are partly relieved of pain by struggle and excitement. So a heaven that only "looks down" on our human woe, instead of "comes down," would not be immune; and that anguish of the Onlooker would limit him. How can God be limited? There have been those who boldly declare that he is limited, but this doctrine has won no great following because to our groping minds a limited God seems a contradiction in terms.[26]

The limitations inflicted by pain are more crippling than we have confessed, for pain in our experience is linked with sin, though not cocentric with it, and pain is incipient death, or we would not go to the doctor. How can there be sin and death in God? An Old Testa-

88

ment story tells of a king who, in sorrow for the hunger of his besieged city, wore sackcloth beneath the crimson of his royal robes.[27] Is that God's way? But the king was only a man like us, and pain is constitutional in our world. What right have we to make "the most high God" in our own image? The Baron says [28] that two lovers may wish to be absorbed in each other, but if they were they could not each surrender in love to the other; and that we had better not blur the line between man and God, or he would be no longer God, and we could not say, "Not my will, but thine, be done." [29] The baron is trenchant in debate—and in deep conviction!

II

Yet the other view trips both us and the Baron. His quotations from the opposite camp are too piercing to be ignored. Thus James Hinton, whose later wide latitude in sexual life does not utterly invalidate his earlier thinking, though it does give us pause: "If in the only worthy joy, . . . there is necessarily latent the element of pain. . . . If this is our Joy, then it is His also in Whose image we were made. . . . The life Christ shows us is the eternal life. He emptied Himself, and the pain became manifest. . . ." [30] C. S. Dinsmore strikes to an even deeper poignancy: "As the flash of the volcano discloses for a few hours the elemental fires at the earth's centre, so the light on Calvary was the bursting forth through historical conditions of the very nature of the Everlasting. There was a cross in the heart of God before there was one planted on the green hill outside of Jerusalem." [31] William Temple, a young man in the Baron's time, became a theologian of great stature in his middle and later years, and he is quoted as follows: "The life Divine is the Christ-life, . . . and . . . that means real suffering and sacrifice—until all love is returned." [32]

These quotations strike one haunting note: "God was in Christ reconciling the world to himself." [33] That word may not appeal to a modern skeptic, but even he if he is a thoughtful man cannot be utterly unmoved. Actually the Baron agrees with his critics, as least in measure, for he also bows his head before the dark light of Calvary. Yet with a sharp difference. They find God in Christ, while he finds "Two distinct and differing Natures of Christ." That is to say, he adheres strictly to the Creed formulated by the Council of Chalcedon.[34] He is categorical:

"There is no Suffering in God . . . Sympathy, yes, indeed, overflowing Sympathy . . . but no Suffering; and Suffering, indeed overflowing suffering, in Christ, but as Man, not as God." [35] There we have it. Or do we?

A systematic theology is not the concern, still less the competence, of this book. We are writing for the man-in-the-street and in the home who is not a theologian, except as every man necessarily plays that role. That man is surely dismayed by this split, to the point of schizophrenia, in the nature of Christ. Is there a cleavage right down the nature of Christ, a great gulf set, so that on one side he is man, and on the other side God? Our heresies are right in their resolve to bridge the gulf, though not necessarily right in the bridge they propose. Unitarianism bridges it by saying that Christ is altogether man, nobler than other men perhaps, but yet only one more man making one more guess; Unitarianism then puts its trust in (an outmoded) doctrine of evolution and the dubious scientific method. Fundamentalism bridges the gulf by proposing that Christ is altogether God: he "knew all along that he was God," and presumably heaven was emptied when he arrived on earth. So Fundamentalism says with Neotus and Cleomenes, against whom Bishop Hippolytus made his protest: He who was "wounded with a spear . . . is the God and Father of the Universe." [36] The rest of us find in Christ a paradox, but not a gulf. His life is whole, and the total Event has piercing unity. He is above us, yet with us. Besides, we must come to him not through philosophic debates about his "nature," as though he were static fact in a static world, but through the vitalities of history, through the actualities of the street on which we live. Of which more hereinafter. . . .

We cannot believe in a heartless God. We cannot understand how there can be Sympathy without Suffering. The very word "sympathy" means to "feel with." This inability to understand may be an "infirmity of noble minds" [37] or of minds not-so-noble. Even so we cannot imagine what we cannot imagine. The word "Father" is in the Lord's Prayer. Of course it is "in heaven" above our poor parenthood, but the word "Father" still has its meaning. The Baron says that our sympathy comes *after* suffering, while God's suffering comes *before*. Thus he ships the angularities of time into the Godhead! Can any reader imagine a sympathy before suffering? We say of a child, "He little knows what awaits him." But that sympathy, while it is *before* the *child's* suffering, is *after our* suffering. The real trouble with the Baron's plea is that he wrote it for the London Society for the Study of Religion! [38] Pain is never objective and never an academic study. So the academic answer is sure to be in some measure false!

III

Then what are we to believe? Which of two faiths shall we hold: that God is above all pain, or that God suffers with us? If we are wise we shall *accept both avowals!* Is some reader saying, "What a shabby 'out'!"? No, we propose no easy refuge, no cowardly refusal to choose between contradictory terms. When life and thought show us that two "opposite" faiths both have claim on us, we accept them both even though we cannot see how they fuse. This book has tried to avoid philosophic abstraction. Therefore, it is the more worth remarking that philosophy itself is obliged to confess antinomies. An antinomy, according to the dictionary, is "a contradiction between two principles each taken to be true." [39] God as Otherness unstained by our guilty transience, God as our "Great Companion": how shall we make those two convictions jibe? We cannot. Yet both have been revealed to men in the long human pilgrimage. The Bible, which is a book of history, a history which to some of us is the vital core of all history, again and again makes both avowals. In early days the Straits of Gibralter were known as the Pillars of Hercules. They were supposed to mark the limits of the world. *"Ne Plus Ultra"* was the motto inscribed on the Pillars: "No Further"! Ships going beyond the Pillars would fall off the world's edge! On one side there was what we have called "The Dark Continent," on the other the supposedly enlightened continent of Europe. But there was no final "strait" or gulf: the bases of the Pillars were joined beneath the sea. So with an antinomy: its two beckoning faiths are the visible points of twin mysteries which are one in the abyss of the Mystery.

Of course, we are now confessing our mortal ignorance. Our best thinking penetrates only so far into the vast hinterland of mystery, and then—"No further!" In our probing into the enigma of natural evil, we asked, "If evil is evil, and God is good, and God is God, how could evil ever have found entrance into our world?" In effect we have written,

91

"We accept the premises of that question, and we shall continue in the hopeful conviction, but we do not know the answer." [40] Karl Barth in his mighty ponderings tells us that evil is the reality which God sets behind his back, to which he speaks the eternal "No!" [41] That is worth the telling: it echoes our own knowledge that "evil is evil," and that when we see a friend dying of cancer or a village swept away by a tidal wave we cannot play around with so tragic an issue by proposing that "good and evil are only in the mind." Barth stresses also our "invincible surmise" [42] that God is good and that God is God.[43] But he has not solved the problem of the origin of evil. How did evil get in front of God so that he could set it behind his back? The same inevitable nonfulfillment attends Paul Tillich's doctrine of nonbeing.[44] How does that *non* become "demonic"? If the answer is that *we* make it demonic, whence *that* power? For myself, I cannot conceive even the subordinate reality of *non:* what is not is not.

We are further confessing that life in its revealings comes as paradox. That word also involves apparent contradictions. It means that which goes against our glib and commonly accepted answers—*para,* contrary to; *doxa,* opinion. How can we be genuinely free, and yet under the sovereignty of God? But we know that both faiths are true. We "go our own way," and it is *our* way, only to find that it leads in a direction opposite our choice. To cite another instance, the word *psychosomatic* is a paradox, written as one word without the hyphen.[45] So with the "two natures" in Christ. The Creed of Chalcedon might itself have saved the Baron, for it said of Christ's nature that he was "without confusion, without change, without division, without separation." [46] The modern approach to Jesus Christ is not by a static proposal of two static "natures," for our life is not static, but through history: an Event set in the ongoing unfolding of events in the biblical story. But the paradox remains: Jesus Christ is both judgment and mercy. Wise men accept the fact of paradox. Heresies arise because some men, cherishing the neatness of their minds more than the mystery of life, choose one term of the paradox against the other, only to find that no man can split a paradox. In Baron von Hügel's essay he decries "the sorry rationalist alternative," [47] and then chooses one alternative in the inviolable life of a paradox! We should add in gratitude that the very mystery of life, its refusal to honor the little tidiness of our minds, gives our days an infinite zest. A paradox is a nettle in a world of nettles:

> The world is a nettle; disturb it, it stings.
> Grasp it firmly, it stings not.[48]

IV

When we grasp the nettle of paradox, we do not fear to walk through nettles. When we consent to live in a house called Antinomy, we look out on a magnificent view. Sir Thomas Browne when he met mystery would exclaim, "Oh, the far heights!" [49] Moreover, guest-moments visit us, through which (or through whom!) we know that seemingly contradictory verities are yet unity. Nature is an instance: it is both law-abiding and free. We see *in* nature or we print *on* nature what we call "natural laws," but nature refuses always to wear that dress. A day or two ago as these words are written, a friend came down a nearby trout stream (named the River Jordan!) in a flatboat. He marked the variety of trees, their unprophesied waving, the wanton wind, the river's artless winding, its ever-changing eddies and ripples and rapids, the play of colors, the unpredictable light and shade; and then he suddenly remarked, "Nature is so untidy!" He had seen the freedom of nature, its wild abandon, its incredible beauty and destructiveness. Our neat "laws" and patterns do not go very deep. Nature is always overwhelming our conceited scientific minds. How long shall we cling to artificial formulas in the poor proud claim that we have spoken some final word? You and I have discussed that item! C. S. Lewis once remarked that if we had planned the solar system we would have arranged the planets at equidistance or in mathematical precision! [50] Thus in nature there is a paradox of order and freedom. Likewise in nature there is a paradox of otherness and sympathy! For we can say with Francis Thompson, "Heaven and I wept together," yet in the same breath confess with him,

> In vain my tears were wet on Heaven's grey cheek.
> For ah! we know not what each other says.[51]

But we do not doubt that nature is one life!

We find the same paradox in every neighbor. He has a certain otherness. There is in him a sanctum which we cannot invade, a privacy which we should honor. Francis Thompson sees that truth even in a bride pledging life-loyalty to her man on the eve of their wedding ("I bind thee to my inmost heart, my true"), for Thompson makes his proper comment:

> Ah, fool! but there is one heart you
> shall never take him to! . . .
> Its keys are at the cincture hung of God.[52]

Jean-Paul Sartre, aware of this otherness, calls it hell: "Hell is—other people." [53] But why should it be "hell"? Why not heaven, the place of the Main Contact? For our neighbor is also our neighbor, the man who is nigh to us. Why should Sartre discount that other term of the paradox? He does not say "people are hell" while his followers listen to him with eagerness verging on idolatry, in that tavern on Montmartre. Still less does he so speak of Simone de Beauvoir. Perhaps only a broken time could find guidance in Sartre's brokenness: he is one moment rationalist, almost in the succession of Kant and Hegel, and the next moment existentialist, but without power to follow through that bold gambit. His statements are frequently blind "faith," that is, lacking the beckonings which other faiths can claim. But be that as it may, our neighbor is a paradox of otherness and nighness. This is true even of husband and wife. Thus every neighbor grants us both the zest of the unknown and the joy of love. Our neighbor is paradox, but he is not cleft. He is one life.

V

Sometimes there is a lightning flash which lights a whole hidden world, which almost grants us to see the deeps of ocean where the bases of twin peaks become one Ground. They say that a drowning man remembers all his life in an instant: his moment-by-moment life is suddenly simultaneous life. His time becomes the eternal Now. We all share that miracle in some measure. For an hour in which we wait to hear news of surgery on someone dear to us is many hours, and an hour of ecstasy makes the clock a liar: "It could not have been an hour": it was hardly more than a moment. Someone asked Mozart if he "heard" his music as he composed it. He said he did, and then added startlingly, "Nor do I hear in imagination the parts successively but I hear them, as it were, all at once!" [54] The sequence of notes was sometimes for him one chord. So you and I, with no claim to be musicians, do yet understand how the dissonant penultimate chords enrich the final rest-chord. In such moments joy and pain are one. Does suffering thus live in God? We cannot guess, let alone know. But seeming contradictions are not what they seem, and strange unisons (and orisons!) live just below the surface of our broken lives.

The instances multiply. The lightning flash reveals the hidden world of a neighbor. Then his very otherness enlists our love. It is the gift of great drama to grant us such revealings. Sociology and economics are needed vocations. The "laws" they trace have a certain function, especially in an age when technology is almost compelling us to an urban fashion of life. But these "laws" cover the mystery of human life even less that the "laws of nature" cover the "untidiness" (the liberty, terror and beauty) of the natural world. Then we need drama—and the better drama of worship. In *The Death of a Salesman* [55] we see Willie Loman coveting esteem yet having no gifts to merit esteem, trying to "get by" on "a smile and a shoestring." We know his cardboard world must either crumple or be blown away. We can almost hear the footsteps of oncoming doom. There is a terrible "otherness" in the judgment that condemns his posturing, a Fate as inexorable as Fate. Yet the play for us is *catharsis,* a purging of the self. How can the purging of personal life, this clean constraint, be other than personal? Meanwhile we are sorry for Willie, but we do not pity him: he is too much like ourselves. Almost we love him, and we would gather him into peace and power if we could. That is to say, the seeming opposites in our human life are now reconciled. So when death takes someone dear to us: his evil and weakness, though we would not deny them, fall away from him as not really belonging to him; or, at any rate, our harsh judgments are stilled. Thus death itself becomes a messenger of grace.

We are saying that there are times of insight when apparent contradictories harmonize or are made one life. H. Wheeler Robinson rightly reminds us [56] that any creative task, carving a block of marble, writing a poem, painting a portrait, is at once pain and joy. He continues: neighborly concern shows this same paradox. An instance could be that of a doctor performing an operation. The doctor knows the pain of responsibility, the pain of cutting into the flesh of a fellow human at risk, yet the venture is still held in both zest and quietness. Then what of the martyr? We do not know, for few of us risk martyrdom. But when we do, we know both the pain of men's blind scorn and at the same time an awareness that we are now one with Life. Thus the English martyr, climbing his scaffold, cried, "Thanked be God, I am even at home!" [57] Can we guess from our own deepest life that suffering and above-all-suffering are one truth in God? We can only guess. Maybe "the Lamb slain from the foundation of the world" [58] is the burning Ecstasy. Meanwhile you and I must live in the labor pains of a paradox. "We know that the whole creation has been groaning in travail together until now; and not only the creation, but we ourselves, who have the first fruits of the Spirit, groan inwardly as we wait for adoption as sons, the redemption of our bodies. For in this hope we are saved." [59]

VI

Has this chapter been too hard a journey? If it has, the hardship comes not from my better brain, for it is not better (how can any man claim a better mind?), but perhaps because my job gives me more chance to ponder life—a chance denied in the same measure to a farmer or a mechanic, whose special skill brands me a tyro. The chapter began with the proposal that we who are creatures cannot mend our lives, because we depend on the Creator, and that therefore we are always homing, at least in our deepest hopes. We wrote in that opening paragraph that the "problem of pain" cannot find any answer unless God enters our suffering, his entrance thus becoming our door of deliverance. Then the question came: "But how can God suffer?" Therefore this chapter, with its confession that "now I know in part." [60] We confront a paradox: If God suffers, he is limited and infected with death, and so is not God; but if he does not suffer, he is both heartless and denied the insights which suffering alone sometimes brings to us, and once again is not God. Yet a paradox is not an untruth or a deception, for both its terms are verified in daily life: we are free, yet under Sovereignty; we are individual, yet social; we are body, yet psyche. If the conviction of a suffering God flatly affronts the mind which God himself has given, we had better forget the whole business. The purpose of this chapter has been to show that there is no such affront, though Mystery always "stops us."

Each chapter thus far has had a postscript about Jesus Christ. These successive *addenda* have been a deliberate strategy. So we now underline the fact that *both* Baron von Hügel and his critics, he believing that God cannot suffer, they sure that he must suffer, turn their eyes to Christ. He believes that Christ suffers, though only in his human nature; they believe that "God was in Christ reconciling the world to himself" [61] and that Christ is not divided; but both camps believe that in Christ is the true and living Word. The Baron as we have seen trusts in the "Sympathy" of God and in the "Sufferings" of Christ,[62] while his critics take the further step: "Now that the cross of wood has been taken down, the one in the heart of God abides, and it will remain so long as there is one sinful soul for whom to suffer." [63]

Thus the prodigious faith that Jesus Christ is the "breakthrough," God's invasion of our history! The very temper of our time makes such a faith a "thing incredible." [64] A college student recently retorted to me bluntly: "Jesus means nothing to me." Another student, on the way from the meeting, defended him from any charge of flippancy. I had made no such charge, for I was won by the honesty. The defender said, "He means that we all go the same way to the same morgue." Breakthrough or morgue? That is the next question, with no sidestepping either the dawn or the midnight.

7. Breakthrough

I. The Event

It is hard for our generation to confront the claims of Jesus or even to think about him. College students ask, "Why Jesus?" One good answer would be, "Why not?" But the temper of our time makes such an answer seem unreal. There is perhaps some twisted comfort in remembering that "he came to his own home, and his own people received him not." [1] The comfort is twisted because we should not find solace in that original blindness, but it is comfort because he simply outlived that first rebuff. He outlives our indifference because he keeps coming back, if not to the center of our thoughts, at least to the edges of them. Our dramatists and poets sometimes mention him. But we are ill at ease with him. He does not belong in our culture. But has he ever really belonged in our world?

One main reason why we consign him to the ragged edges of our life is that we do not see that truth is an Event. We are scientific, though science is only analysis exercised on sense data. Our mind has deeper levels than analytical mind. But the test for us is science, and Jesus cannot be scientifically "proved." Therefore we dismiss him and ask,

"What's the use of Christian faith?" Perhaps one use is to save us from the utilitarian blasphemy. When we are not scientists we are philosophers. Thus students are invited by almost every college bulletin to "come and seek the truth," as if truth were buried treasure on the campus, or secreted on the persons of professors, or hidden in the print of textbooks. Whatever truth may be, it was presumably here before we arrived and will be here after we are dead. Perhaps soon some college may invite students to an honesty by which truth may find them. That will be the day! But truth for our time is a scientific formula or a philosophic theory. So we overlook the sharp event in favor of universals such as "humanity" or "the absolute." Intellectual pride dotes on universals.

But suppose truth finds us through events. That notion is repulsive, for the world (we think) is our world: our clever minds will soon construe all mysteries and our clever hands soon build a stainless-steel paradise, and we shy away from events because they are always in some measure beyond our control. Suppose there is one Event which gathers all other events into a strange sovereignty. Oh no, that would play havoc with our universals and equations. Therefore we relegate Jesus to "one more religion," and then we consign all religion to "emotion" and "subjectivity": two more universals. Then we propose that "tolerance" in these matters is the prime virtue. The fact is, of course, that Jesus cuts clean across "religion." So tolerance becomes sheer evasion of an existential choice. Then it becomes a new form of self-righteousness: "I am a tolerant man, very different from you bigots." Then it becomes a condescension, for Jesus does not let us "tolerate" people: he requires of us a certain kind of stern love. Meanwhile atomic death is suspended over us, and planes bent on destruction roar across our world because of our imprisoned science and our dilettante philosophy, and because the truth we propose to "seek" (as if truth were our onion) has tripped our conceit. Yet we still ask, "Why choose Jesus?" The answer is blunt: We did not choose him. We do our best day by day to get rid of him. He chose us, and still lays hands on us. So we look once again on him.

I

Historically, as history is usually written, he is not worth even a casual mention. The historians of his time passed him by, and our historians find in him a very small concern. He came from "up in the hills" of a conquered land in the Middle East long before our time. So our modernity asks of him what his "superiors" asked in his time: "Can anything good come out of Nazareth?" [2] Too bad God didn't choose to work through our "great" land, in one of our "great" cities, by means of our "great scientific progress"! Somewhere there is a cartoon showing a neighbor of the Hanks family talking to the owner of a crossroads store in the back country of Kentucky. The storekeeper asked, "Anything new?" No, said the other man from his horse and buggy, "Nancy Hanks got a young 'un, but nothing ever happens up our creek." Well, Mary of Nazareth "got a young 'un."

The whole affair was lowly to the point of ridicule. If God wishes to make a Breakthrough he should not arrive in "Galilee of the Gentiles," that is, in a region which could not boast even the staunch Hebraism of Judea. He should not choose a town of little note and a craftsman's home. Nor should the Man of the Word lack all learning except for the training given by the local scribe in the synagogue school. They say he worked as carpenter or builder until he was thirty, and legend has it that he was the mainstay of a widowed mother and his younger brothers and sisters. Of course he may thus have done far more for workers than communism or capitalism could ever boast, because he was personal-Event and personally involved (with how deep an involvement!), while we with proud and abstract minds speak in "isms." We exalt our ideologies and forget our neighbors. Above all, the Breakthrough should not have been in a conquered land. Doesn't God know that the safeguard of freedom is a "strong defense," and that freedom from outward aggression is the only real freedom? Or was he just sorry for the vanquished? Or was the strange history of Israel waiting for the Word so that then he might be the vital core of all history?

The incredible littleness of the Breakthrough continued. The little child from a little home in a little town in a little land, when he was about thirty years of age, was baptized by John the Baptizer in the River Jordan.[3] That day there was a stirring and shaking of spirit, as if a Voice had summoned Jesus and sealed him to a task which he had long pondered, and of which now he was no longer in doubt. He chose twelve followers "to be with him," [4] and told them what he believed about God and man. The rabbis gathered their disciples after the same fashion. But Jesus was no rabbi, even though his church has remembered only reluctantly that he was not a "professional." His teaching was not that, not stated instruction, but often only stories so artless, so true to life that even now as we read them we are taken by surprise. For suddenly they steal up on our blind side. Only fragments of what he said have survived the corrosion of time. If God *was* intent on the Breakthrough, why didn't he safeguard every syllable? Surely he would have been wiser to wait for *our* time, for we have tape recorders, electric multigraphing and copying machines, radio and television. On second thought, we might not have allowed Christ to speak on the radio or appear on television, for fear he might alienate the "potential market." In any event God missed a chance to perpetuate Christ's words unless (these troublesome second thoughts) he has a better way of keeping them alive. But the whole affair was ordinary to the point of the commonplace unless (that pesky "unless" again!) his glory is lowliness, and by the same tremendous paradox his power is love.

Unfortunately the words of Jesus seemed and seem somewhat left-wing. Neither the John Birch Society nor the Communists of that time found in them anything to praise. He was not a peddlar of either economics or politics, but what he said found its instant relatedness in those two realms. His stories steal up not alone on our blind side, but on the blind side of each successive culture. None of the then-dominant loyalties took comfort in them. As for the Essenes, men who, despairing of the world, sought the monastic life in some Qumran comradeship, what could they make of his dubious friendships in the godless city? As for the Zealots, men who believed against all political realities that they could drive out the Roman legions by a few spears and swords, they were angered when he said: "Put your sword back into its place; for all who take the sword will perish by the sword." [5] As for the Sadducees, the rich landed gentry who controlled the emoluments of the Temple, the original "large" contributors to the original reactionary groups, they were sure he was subversive. As for the Pharisees, why should he cross their path? They and the scribes had liberalized the too-rigorous interpretation of the Torah. They were the Puritans of that time. They were fine patriots too, the kind who said Israel had a treasure of faith to share that was far more important than a role in world politics. But Jesus told a story about a tax-gatherer (for Rome against his own people) confessing his sins and winning the instant pardon of God, and of a Pharisee telling God of his rectitude, only to find that God was not listening.[6] What could Jesus mean? That spiritual pride is the worst kind? But what sort of story is that? Aren't we supposed to be good?

What Jesus said about God was the focus and circumference of his teaching, though no man has yet probed the center or gone far enough into Obedience to find the circumference. We say, "God is dead," or talk in universals about "the Ground of Being," but to Jesus God was more real than the main artery of a man's neck. He spoke of God in pictures because God can never be defined. God defines us. God is our Shepherd, our Master in the world-house, and our Father. The main line of our life is toward God. If that vertical is not set, no house can stand. But the vertical is to no purpose if the horizontal is not nailed to it: our love for our neighbor. "Thou shalt love the Lord thy God . . . and thy neighbor." [7] The words "as thyself" *may* mean "as thine own," that is, as if he were our kith and kin! The Otherness of God is traced in Christ's words and prayers, but there is assurance of an astonishing Intimacy: God is waiting for us in the next room, nay, in the next thought. God is God: earth is his footstool,[8] and he has power to cast soul and body into hell;[9] yet we may say as we pray: "Our Father who art above the heavens." [10] Jesus spoke constantly about the kingdom of God: a new start in history through his own coming, so that the old age was dying, and a new age was breaking on our weary world. Strange view of time and history! Not like our philosophic time or our objective history! So his words were a crisis of decision, *the* crisis and *the* decision. Those who turned from him would end in the "darkness of the old age": [11] those who followed would know "there's going to be a great day," for they would already live in it.

Of course he was killed. But why should God's Breakthrough end in death? That surely was God's worst blunder! Jesus had offended the rich: he said their wealth distracted them from both the love of God and the love of their neighbors. He offended the poor: he congratulated them in that their poverty reminded them that life is short, that they are pensioners of God's world, that God's grace and not their own wit sustains them: "Blessed are you poor" [12]; but he refused to follow them in any mob movement. He offended the Zealots: he would not let them use him as a national flag for a bloody insurrection. He offended the Pharisees with whom he had much in common ("religious people" come off badly in his parables); he warned them against "religious" pride and any notion that they were "better men" than the ungodly. He offended both the Roman governor and the highest Jewish council. Both the governor and the council feared that Jesus might become a flame of political revolt, the governor lest he should lose his job, and the council lest bloodshed should sweep away their privilege. So he died. It was a nasty death. Romans were not crucified: it was too degrading a death for a Roman. When a Jew was crucified, his body was taken down before sunset lest the field should turn sour and yield no harvest. The end of a little career, in a little land long ago and far away, was a messy little gallows. The small pilgrimage ended in a smelly little curse. That's all, brother!

II

But that was not all, though why—who knows? Why is Jesus remembered? Why should he trouble us? That petty affair in Galilee, that tempest in a teapot with rather acid tea, is no concern of modern man. Even to propose it is to sell out to a ridiculous disproportion. Let's keep things in balance. But the world does not balance, at least not by our scales. Jesus *is* remembered: there's a church down the street, a rather shabby affair, yet it's there. We trounce it, partly in truth, but partly because whipping a whipping post helps us forget Jesus whom people such as ourselves nailed to something worse than a whipping post. Yet he keeps coming back, as in Bach's *Mass in B Minor*. We try to remember only the music, for we are cultured people. The trouble is that we can hardly take the music without thinking of the faith that composed it.

Then why is Jesus remembered? Maybe the remembrance is not remembrance: he himself said that by his very Presence he would convict and redeem our world.[13] But for the moment we use the word "remembrance." Why the remembrance? Not primarily because of his "teaching." It was not a system of thought in any event, but sparks struck off from our flinty earth by a race-horse spirit. That is, the thing he said was addressed to the occasion, as when he exclaimed, "Look, over there, a sower going out to sow!"[14] Of course the "teaching" is treasure. It

103

shows the Man. But God in the Breakthrough (if so small an affair could be called a breakthrough) was apparently not too concerned to keep every word or even the very word. For consider: Jesus spoke in Aramaic which few scholars now understand or read. Someone has said that if Jesus had been only a teacher, instructing his disciples as long as he lived and dying at last in his bed, there might have been a short paragraph about him in the *Encyclopaedia Britannica* to the effect that he left no deep imprint. Perhaps our agonized search for his very words is another way of avoiding him. *Life Magazine* [15] recently gave large space to a proposed Temple of Religions, to honor six great "teachers," all of whom allegedly taught the Golden Rule. Jesus was bracketed with the other five as a peddlar of the Golden Rule. But of course the Golden Rule can mean anything, lust for lust, for instance, if it is not interpreted by his Spirit. If such a temple were built it would hardly be worth a trip across the road. When did "teaching" alone save anybody?

Then why is Jesus remembered? The next answer is astonishing. Not *in the first instance* by his cross. In the second instance, yes, but not in the first instance. Had the Cross been the whole story, it would have been worse than tragedy: it would have been tragedy locked forever in a tomb—after a murder. Many martyrs have died, but no New Testament has been written about any one of them. Tragedy is just that—tragedy: the blood-red sunset without any succeeding dawn. The Roman governor and the council got rid of Jesus. They bumped him off, and dead men tell no tales. The disciples wept. The "teaching" had been fine, such of it as they understood, but now the "teaching" made no sense. They were sadder but wiser men: "I am going fishing." [16] A good thing to do if all that life can give is an aspirin tablet to dull the pain! Ah, the pain, which is still our theme! Why does the New Testament bring pain into a new light and a new power? Why is the judgment in pain now cancelled? Why is pain now cleansing and daybreak and even a vocation? Not in the first instance because of the Cross, for, had that been all, the problem of pain would have been compounded by his pain, without any chance of a glad answer.

Jesus is "remembered," or he quietly comes, *because he rose from the dead*. The accounts of his resurrection are hard to reconcile. People who deny that plain fact and who therefore propose arbitrary "reconciliations" are no help, for they lack honesty; and people who demand "scientific evidence" are even less help, for science, though it is a worthy and needed discipline, has only a one-dimension mind scrutinizing a merely sense-dimension cosmos and so can give us only brittle and broken fragments of the truth. The Resurrection accounts are rapture rather than cold "objectivity." They leave us not knowing if he rose first in Galilee or in Jerusalem or in both places, if he came in the same body or in a new body, if an empty tomb is the focal fact or the sheer joy of his followers. Perhaps in Galilee, according to his behest [17]; perhaps in a new body by which he entered "the doors being shut," [18] perhaps in the sheer surprise. Yet we must not dogmatize. The Breakthrough has strange facets and stranger omissions. Maybe God will not let us get imprisoned in an affidavit. If we had it, we could still say, "Perhaps it's a forgery"; and it would still be in Aramaic. Perhaps God is not interested in a tape-recording. If we had it, the same doubt could intrude. The fact that the "teaching" and the death could not of themselves account for the con-tinuing Presence is itself much stauncher assurance!

Yet the accounts are a treasure. They underscore surprise. A man dying under a curse and then returning from the dead would be no blessing, at least not if he were one more man making one more guess. We are not sure even how much people believed then in the life after death. The Pharisees did; the Sadducees did not, and that conflict deepened the cleavage between them and Jesus, for he rebuked them: "Is not this why you are wrong, that you know neither the scriptures nor the power of God?" [19] What the general public believed we do not know: they probably drifted then as now between vague faith and vague doubt. But there is no question that the resurrection of Jesus took his followers by surprise. The Bultmann proposal [20] that they "came to believe" does not do any justice to the Gospel record. They were "surprised by joy." [21] Nay, more: they were overwhelmed by the power of the Most High God, for their word for it was not "risen" only, but "raised": "Whom God hath raised." [22] That mighty word repeats a dozen times in the New Testament. *The resurrection of Jesus was the Breakthrough.*

There is other evidence, but not the kind demanded by a law court. Call it *witness* in the sense of unquestionable testimony. Indeed, one of the names for the early followers was "witnesses of the resurrection": [23] "the Author of life, whom God raised from the dead. To this we are witnesses." [24] The testimony was in themselves. One day they were hope-

105

less, the next brimming with hope; one day cowardly so that they ran away from his cross in fear, the next day braving his foes and laughing at death; one day dull of understanding, the next with piercing insight into what he had said and done; one day shut up within themselves despite his love, the next with strong faith in God and accompanying love for all their neighbors. They were not liars concocting a "story": they confessed rather that if they falsified what happened, "if Christ has not been raised . . . we are even found to be misrepresenting God," [25] and therefore liable to the second death. They were not victims of illusion or a martyr complex: they would ask, "If the dead are not raised at all . . . why am I in peril every hour?" [26] They knew that only a fool dies for a fiction. Our attempts to minimize and explain away this strange daybreak (they said, "Our sun is risen in the west!" [27]) are toy pistols leveled against the Springtime.

There is also the witness of the New Testament, which we try to reduce to "one more religion." The fact is that the New Testament is always on guard against "the religious man," for he is always trying, by ethical discipline, or by cultivating the mystic vision, or by obeying the law, or by keeping a ritual, to make his own way to heaven, as if he were god. The New Testament is of its own kind. There is nothing like it. For while it is continuous in one sense with the Old Testament, it is sharply discontinuous: it is the Book of the *New* Covenant which God has made with men through Jesus Christ. It is the good news of the Breakthrough, that is, of the Resurrection and of the present Spirit of Jesus. Today I tried to count in a concordance the number of references to Jesus in the New Testament. Eyes grew weary in a joyous pain. There are perhaps a thousand, and not one of them speaks of him as dead. Not one: this is the book of the living Lord. And of the church, which is his living church because he lives. Yes, the church is checkered, and there have been many Pharisees and parasites among its members. The more wonder that it survives! The more wonder that it has some secret both of self-examination and renewal! We do not know what the years may bring for the church, but we do know that it has already met and outlived every antagonism and every convergence of hostility and indifference. So the New Testament and the church add their testimony of praise. Jesus is remembered, or comes, because he rose from the dead. That is the Breakthrough!

106

III

Then (in the second instance) the light of the Resurrection is thrown back on the Cross. If God raised him from the dead, then God was in his dying! God through his chosen One was in the midst of our transgressions! There he suffered for our sins, and there he conquered both sin and death. Just as the birth of Christ gathered all the ranks of men— shepherds, wise men, priests such as Simeon, the carpenter Joseph, the inn-keeper, the evil King Herod, with Mary as host to the Mystery— so with his cross. But at the cross there were few to uphold him. The watching women, through whom the gospel may have come to us, with Mary and John: they were all. The others fled, with one of them denying that he ever knew Jesus, and another selling him to his foes. But all *our* favorite sins converged on the Cross: the ruthless might of empire, precursor to our modern empires and our modern wars; the greed of the traders whose tables he had overturned, and *our* greed which has turned both radio and television into a cheap, reiterated huckstering; the ecclesiastical pride of the temple, and *our* churches with the incredible pomp of the Vatican and rich Protestant churches of the suburbs trying to forget the city ghettos; the treachery of friends, and all *our* local failures in friendship; the alternate bloodlust and cowardice of the mob, and the violence of our streets; and the quiet homes where most men lived too quietly, as *we* live taking great care "not to get involved." There all our favorite sins converged. But Another was there *incognito.* That is why we have doctrines of the Atonement. The doctrines are children of the Resurrection-light. How else could they have come?

So God in Christ is in the pain of our transgressions, which may have been the ancestor of all pain, which certainly is the bitterness both of natural evil and the dark legacy of history. The Old Testament has glimpses of vicarious suffering, foregleams of the Cross, as in the "Suffering Servant" passages in Second Isaiah: [28] "He was despised and rejected by men; a man of sorrows, and acquainted with grief." [29] The prophets foresaw a time when the mercy of God would redeem our age-long disobedience. Even so the Old Testament never escapes the house-arrest called law-disobedience-penalty. That liberation came only when God came in Person, and when that Man was raised from the dead. Then, because God was in our pain, suffering for our sins, pain was *purged of judgment* and *stripped of any final power*. A second Adam (that is the New Testament name!) [30] broke into the dreary defection and the dark legacy of the first Adam and his progeny, and turned the tide of battle, not as an afterthought or as a patch on a blunder, but in fulfillment of a purpose from "the foundation of the world." [31] "The first man Adam became a living being; the last Adam became a life-giving spirit." [32] Thus what we call "the problem of pain," though it remains after Christ, was no dreary "problem" to his followers. They never dreamed of calling it by that title. In the New Testament it is set in a new climate: it is framed in light.

Our philosophical and scientific time demands "proof" of the Deity of Jesus: "How do you know he is Divine?" I myself, in a poor endeavor to meet the modern mind on its own terms and in its own restricted angle, have tried to systematize an answer. Always it has been a foolish attempt. For how can we define and domesticate the ways of God? To define means to trace limits. The task can be partly fulfilled in science which deals with objects and sense measurements; that is, we can partly define what is finite. But we cannot corral the Infinite: God defines us, for we are his creation in our finite creatureliness. If the first followers of Christ had been asked to "prove" him, they would have said, "How can I 'prove' my father or brother or mother?" The question would have seemed a gay absurdity. Indeed that word "mother" was sometimes their very word: Christ had opened a new world to them, there was now a "new and living way" [33] between *our* world and that world (soon to be ours in fullness); so, though their Jerusalem was still in pain of travail, "the Jerusalem above is free, and she is our mother." [34] The only "proof" of Christ is in the history-testimony which we have described, and in the manifestation of his Presence, and in our brave faith.

All doctrines of the Atonement are rooted in metaphor. Why should that surprise us? In this gladness there can be no poor literalism. Still less can there be any test-tube demonstration. How can a man "prove" rapture? He can only exclaim and weep with joy and laugh. That is how the Breakthrough is described in the New Testament, and the description is its own evidence. So the power of God through the Cross is *victory*. Is there not a story of a peasant in an ancient crucial battle turning the tide of the desperate struggle with the sweep of his ploughshare and then refusing to give his name? [35] So another Peasant entered the ancient warfare with the devil and conquered not with a ploughshare, but with a gallows.[36] The power of God through the Cross is *pardon*. We cannot pardon either ourselves or one another, for we do not create our life and world, and our defection is against the whole order, against the Creator: only he can pardon, and this he has done: his was the prayer, "Father, forgive them," [37] and his the incredible answer in grace. The power of God through the Cross is *ransom*. Slaves in the early church knew the meaning of that metaphor! Sometimes a slave would be given his freedom, and sometimes because his master had been liberal he could purchase freedom. So God in Christ purchased our liberation, not by a price paid to the devil (Christ did not bargain with the devil, but overcame him), but at cost of love.[38] The power of God in the Cross is lowly *service,* for Christ humbled himself to become a slave.[39] That metaphor is in a modern play which tells how a distant almost unknown brother of a bishop and of a ne'er-do-well (the black sheep) arrived for a visit; and how the two did not know he had arrived, because he was *The Servant in the House!* [40] He cleaned the shoes and scrubbed the floor. He came down the backstairs at Bethlehem. The power of God in the Cross is *justification*,[41] a metaphor drawn from the Roman law courts: we have a Friend in court with rulership of all courts, and through him we have unmerited acquittal. The power of God in the Cross is *sacrifice:* "Behold the Lamb of God, who takes away the sin of the world." [42]

There are other metaphors: expiation, reconciliation, atonement. None can more than hint the wonder. All of them together fall short. The trouble with a scientific age and of a philosophy which itself has sold out to merely scientific and logical tests is that we have neither rapture nor metaphors for rapture, but we also must try. A former colleague wrote a fine little book entitled, *The Crucifixion in Our Street*.[43] The dust cover had a picture of an Eastside tenement street in New York City, with clotheslines strung across the street, and the clothes props cutting the lines in the sign of the Cross. Sometimes we try to describe the rapture as health, the root meaning of salvation, through transfusion of blood. Mankind is sick, and pain is the onset of death. Only pure blood, where ours is impure, can "save" us, yet only our "number" of blood. So "The Word became flesh." [44] This blood simile is actually another New Testament metaphor, finding new form in our time. But a materialistic age, thinking it has explained the world, when it has only manipulated it with gadgets, does not easily find new metaphors. Thus the pain of preaching in this generation. Maybe our very brokenness, when we are honest enough to confess it, will give us some new-old picture: "This is my body which is broken for you." [45] The light of the Resurrection means that God is in the Cross. He is with us in all our pains in both love and power. Surely our time, though perhaps only when a worse brokenness has come upon us, will leave the shallows, and find once more the depth of the New Testament joy.

IV

There is much else to be written about the Breakthrough, especially as concerns our faith. The Beckoning is null and void for us except as we respond to him. The Great Day is not forced on us. God in lowly love respects the freedom which he has given. That is why he came through a Craftsman in a conquered land long ago, who died on a cross. We can draw the shades on the Daybreak, close our eyes, and sleep through even "The Great Day." That crux engages us in the next chapter, with some further tracing of the meaning of Easter and Calvary for our study of pain. Obviously this chapter should have come first in this book. But in that position it might have seemed a dogmatism and even an affront. It seemed timely to show first that our skills cannot remove our pain, "the Blank misgivings of a Creature," [46] and that our easy answers do not answer. Therefore, the present order of the table of contents.

Perhaps the sea of faith which has been ebbing for four centuries (we are not clever authors of modern skepticism, but its victims) is now at the tremulous turn. Modern writers now speak of a new "Age of Longing." [47] Soon we may begin to doubt our doubts and to believe our beliefs, which are the vital movement of the creature toward the Creator. Then there may be a new age of faith in which we shall relegate know-how and the endless patterning of life and sense-measurements to their proper, valuable, but subordinate place. Existentialism, if brought into due proportion, may help us. Many interesting books on philosophy have been published in recent years, such as that of my own teacher: *Space, Time and Deity*.[48] But the only *exciting* book for me in this field since

Bergson's *Creative Evolution* [49] has been the existential *Irrational Man*.[50] The new philosophy at least sees the nonsense in the Cartesian catastrophe: "I think, therefore I am." [51] The nonsense is multiplied, as follows: first, the "I" is "snuck in" at the beginning of the sentence, and inevitably comes out at the other end, turning the whole sentence into assumption pretending to be argument. Second, we cannot just think; we have to think about something or someone. Therefore, he should have said, "I think about my world: I am and my world is": we and the world share is-ness. Third, thinking philosophically implies the use of only one dimension in our many-dimensioned mind: e.g., we are aware of ourselves thinking: we live in self-transcendent mind which is the real land of mind. Fourth, the whole sentence puts the cart before the horse, for he should have said, "I am, therefore I think."

The above is written with a grateful bow towards the existentialists in the hope that we are moving to a new age of faith. They are at least aware of the impact of the event. They know that a sailor's knowledge of the weather is a deeper kind of "knowing" than that of the meteorologist, and that truth is found through history rather than through the mind's rationalisms. In all this they are one with the "drive" of the Bible. Indeed, some moderns come halfway back to the Scriptures. William Golding in his *Lord of the Flies* writes about original sin, without yet understanding that there is a Breakthrough; and Albert Camus tells of "The Fall" of man, of "Paradise Lost," though he died before his chance to write "Paradise Regained." There is a certain stark honesty in existentialist thinking—and some blind assumptions. Perhaps that realism is a necessary prelude to a new age of faith. At least it knows that scientific formulas only tickle life, and that philosophic abstractions may easily avoid life instead of confronting it. Therefore the insistence of our earlier chapters on the reality of pain, the fact that natural evil and historical evil *are* evil, and on our human inability either to explain pain or to master it. But the people of the Breakthrough overcame pain, by faith in answer to a Beckoning. So we may conclude this chapter by pointing (we can do no more within our limits) to some harvests of their witness.

The Sabbath became Sunday, even though the first followers were Jews and though the Sabbath was bastioned in both the Decalogue and in the covenant-centuries. Why the change? Because Christ was raised

111

on the "first day"! Thus the impact of his resurrection! The change means little to us, for we lack imagination: we have spent too much time probing into matter and tinkering with it. Yet even we should be startled by the fact that when skeptic writes to skeptic, or gangster to gangster, or politician to politician with only political power in mind, they date their letters from the birth of the lowly Christ. Did he not say that his coming inaugurated a new age in history? By the same mighty token the black day on which he died became *Good* Friday or *Holy* Friday. *That* day good or holy, when his enemies jeered at his dying, and the crowd gaped, and his friends fled? Yes, when it is seen in the light of the Resurrection. For then the Cross is no longer a crucifix: it is empty, and the focus of all praise.

That light fell on men's minds, giving them a new kind of wisdom. Dietrich Bonhoeffer has written [52] that if we try to judge an action by the agent's motives we have to go back to the dawn of time, that is, through the man's conscious and subconscious mind, and thus through all his parentage; and that if we judge an action by its results, by our American pragmatism, asking if "it works," we shall have to wait for the other end of time, for only then will all the votes and aftermaths be counted; and that we cannot make either journey. Bonhoeffer lived and died by faith in Christ. One day perhaps his *Ethics* will be studied in colleges alongside "systems of ethics" which can never be systematized and which are always vulnerable to Bonhoeffer's fine comment. The early church asked just one question in the crux of decision: "What is the mind of the Spirit?" They consulted the Risen Christ. They could not ransack the past, much less read the future. They deeply wished to know what Christ asked of them then and there, and left past and future in his sovereign hands. No, they did not receive specifics in every instance or even in many instances, but they were given a clear direction, and light step by step as they traveled. Several years ago, a council of churches after much prayer and searching of the Word, asked the one question, and then proposed certain moves in the strike-bound coal industry. The council was trounced and traduced for "interfering with business," though they had no such desire and indeed came to their task with misgiving and reluctance. The outcome? No immediate outcome. But during the next few years every recommendation of the council was followed under the impact of events. While I write there has appeared in *The New York Times* a full-page statement on the Vietnam crisis by a group of church leaders who have recently visited that tormented land.[53] Prophecies are dangerous: it is not given to men to read the future. But, to court that danger: their proposal will be seen in history as making far more sense than is given to business or military or political leadership. A certain new kind of decision-making came from the Resurrection.

And a springtime of creativeness! Our unbelieving generation is drawn despite its doubts to the great cathedrals of Europe. We sometimes forget that some of them were built by the whole community in voluntary labor, and that a man and his sons would work a lifetime on a carved screen. The marching pillars, the high vaulted ceiling, the ground plan of a cross, the aisles leading to an altar, the reverberating diapasons of the organ—is this all false? Only truth could have built it. And what of art quickened by the faith, such as the Raphael "Madonna" or an El Greco canvas of the Crucifixion? "Time would fail" any man "to tell." And what of music? Is it not amazing that in a planet of pain one group of people should week by week sing praise, with the "Hallelujah Chorus" as type and climax? There is a village in Pakistan where the village leader "requested" the tiny outcast church to accept a plot of ground on the edge of town in exchange for a central location near the leader's home—because he was afraid his (Muslim) wives might hear Christian singing! [54] Yes, the art changes, and should, for all things change. Thus the new architecture of the Swiss churches, and the new music of the Roman Catholic Mass. For creativity goes to deep, deep ground: this Jesus whom God raised, being God's Word, is the Eternal Word: "All things were made through him, and without him was not anything made that was made"! [55] The light of Resurrection was thrown back, all the way back, on the first creation!

A new kind of sainthood emerged. Not the sainthood we have eulogized in some calendar of the saints, for such saints are in some cases only pietistic imitations of true saints. Many of the so-called "saints" would be awkward company at a picnic. Their pious "thou shalt not" would be worse than a sudden rainstorm. There is no "holy tone" in the New Testament word for saint. Indeed, the word is always plural: there are no singular saints, and the saints have no "merit," at least not in any angular theological claim. The saints are simply the good folk

113

in Christ. They are forgiven sinners. They know, far more clearly than other men, that they have no merit. In the pain of our mortal life, the heaviest burden of it due to human pride, how could any man *"merit"* the gift of God in Christ and his being "raised"? Does any man *deserve* such pardon and such hope? So the true saints ask little of this world's goods: just enough to ward off carking care, not the too-much which would distract from the praise of God and the glad doing of his will. They are neighborly, not because they are better than their neighbors, or because they believe that human skill can get rid of all the world's ills, still less because they wish to parade a compassion. No, but it is because there is a catalyst in pain, and a Mercy which holds all our sufferings to redeem them, and because they must bear their glad witness to his love and power. Behind the sometimes-repellant facade of churches intent on prestige, that new kind of sainthood lives on in lowly folk. St. Francis refused the church being built in his honor. Indeed, he climbed the roof and threw down the tiles in anger.[56] Of course! Then he would go to the nearby village with his group to preach, and would dance in the village green, and when he was asked, "But weren't we planning to preach?" he would answer, "We did." That kind of sainthood is not elsewhere found.

Add to all these gifts a new kind of hope! That simple word raises great issues which we must later discuss. Let it be said here and now, in little more than a few sentences, that life is a thrust into the future. If the road is blocked, if life is a dead-end street, life ceases to be life: it becomes death. So the author of "The Revelation of John" told a church which had "soiled its garments" that "you have the name of being alive, and you are dead." [57] What else? If a man or a church becomes "set on itself," it is "set"—fixed, locked in, unable to move, and its end is the mortal end. That is why skepticism moves towards despair, and why G. K. Chesterton remarked that the face of an utterly hopeless man, even though seen only for a moment in a passing crowd, might strike us a blow.[58] People complain about the clumsy word "eschatological"— about both the word and the doctrine. *Eschaton* in the Greek means end, and eschatology is the study of the hope in Christ. Let it be written here, in prelude to what we shall say later, that if life is not hope, it is not life. If the hope is realized, there must be a new further hope, or the realized hope becomes a dead-end street. Thus the seemingly simple

114

words of a tremendous little letter, perhaps as tremendous as any ever written: "For in this hope we were saved. Now hope that is seen is not hope. For who hopes for what he sees? But if we hope for what we do not see, we wait for it with patience." [59] Incidentally that word "patience" has ingredients of suffering as well as of steadfast waiting. For those who first knew Christ the dead-end street had a secret door and a light streaming through it in which pain and sin and death were overwhelmed. That hope will not perish from our earth.

But the events of biblical history culminating in one great Event are not enough: they fail unless a man grasps them in faith as they have first grasped him in mercy. Suppose that on the Monday after the first Sunday the disciples had said, "We were probably fooled." Suppose they had not said, "This, this I trust!" The Breakthrough is God's initiative, but it is no Breakthrough for us without our response. So to our next stretch of the glad road: Breakthrough as Faith.

8. Breakthrough

II. The Faith

Truth is another name for God. So truth for us is first by his coming, and then by our responding trust. His coming is not by some aroused emotion or by blackboard demonstration, but by "his mighty acts." Truth is through events and the Event which beckon our glad obedience at cost and risk. It is strange indeed that we could ever have believed that truth is some cogitation or some algebraic formula. For philosophy itself depends on the event, namely, on the created world; and if suddenly time were reversed, like a movie made to run backward, the philosophy of time would have to change: it could no longer be what my professor called "the time-space continuum." Likewise science itself depends on the event, on revelation, on what is disclosed and given, for the scientist can "discover" only what is *there* to be discovered: the atom has been waiting to be split since the foundation of the world, and science proceeds by the beckoning of single events, such as an apple falling from a tree to hint the "law" of gravitation. All our studies, though they talk sententiously about "truth," are children of the event. Drama has a "plot," a sequence of *happenings,* and tells how people respond to what *happens.* Economics in our complex society goes back to a man watching a round stone roll down a hill, and then inventing a wheel for transportation; or to another man asking why steam issues from a boiling kettle, and contriving a steam engine. Our "technological society" results from a sequence of events. Yet how much depends on what events we try to ignore or choose to honor, on our response!

I

Some events we cannot ignore, for they rule us. Our birth, of a certain family, a certain land, a certain era in history, with certain gifts of hand and heart, is not our choice, but it is a determining event, of which Paul writes with piercing contemplation: "But when he who had set me apart before I was born." [1] The event of death likewise we cannot sidestep or govern. We may hasten it by eating lobster Newberg at every meal and getting drunk every day, or we may postpone it by sober living, but we cannot remove it or evade it. The twin mysteries of birth and death proclaim the Sovereignty. Isn't it strange (and incredibly shallow) that we spend little thought on the great events of birth and death, but invest a fortune in both money and years on ways of selling a bottle of deodorant, with television pictures of people grinning at the bottle as if it held the secret of perpetual youth? All events have an element of sovereignty, but some we cannot change at all: we can only respond in this way or that way.

Other events *we* can initiate, though only from materials given to our hand, only under the sovereignty of the created world. Thus we can use nuclear fission to make a bomb to destroy a city, and then hope that other men will respond to the event in fear and surrender. It is a vain hope, for there is that in human life which stands above time with its fears, or we would not be able to say, "Time is swift." Our event at Hiroshima, far from ending war (its announced purpose), only carried war into the nuclear age. Therefore, we must confess even of events which we "rig" that they have a life of their own beyond our control. The red and green traffic signal is *our* event, by our invention, and by the prescribing of our laws, yet even that small and obviously "contrived" event goes "beyond us." For red is by nature warning, the color of fire and the color of blood, while green is by nature safety, the color of the green earth by which we are fed. Besides, we have no guarantee that our neighbor as he drives his car, absorbed in "trouble at home," will observe the red light. He may smash into our car. Then there is a new event to which at least two families must respond. We talk airily about universals and formulas, for that manner of speech flatters our intellectual pride, but we are ruled by the event. Even our "own" events have harvests or shatterings which we cannot foresee. Dimly we know that the event is beckoning, for we keep asking, "What's *happened?*" and we turn eagerly to the television newscast and to the newspaper. The phrase, "it came to pass," hides all the mysteries.

So consider the anatomy of an event. Did not Kierkegaard infer that if he asked Hegel for directions to a street address in Copenhagen, Hegel might give him "a map of Europe where Denmark would be no larger than a steel pen point"? [2] The map is the proper symbol of our equations and universals. Existentialism does not yet know the why of its outright acts of faith or unfaith, but it has this merit: it pins us to *act*ualities —the acts of the Sovereignty and our acts. The anatomy is as follows, at least in main thrust. First, *an event comes from the totality:* it can never be fully predicted and its results can never be fully tabulated, because it springs from the whole history of mankind and the whole creation of the world. Take as instance Hitler's invasion of France. We write knowingly (or not so knowingly) about it after it happens, but all history is in it and all geography, and that is why when it happened we exclaimed, "But we thought that kind of ruthless warfare did not belong to our time!" Next, *an event has its own invasiveness,* its singularity, almost its arbitrary inruption. We say of it, happily of a marriage which we approve or sadly of a funeral that grieves us, "Why did *you* walk into my life?" Yes, an event walks in without invitation and without manners enough to knock on the door. "It came to pass": it *came,* often without warning and always in some measure beyond our control. It "takes place": it *takes* it, and the place is *our* place! To subsume an event under some law kills it and robs us of its rightful challenge. For, third, *an event is a gauntlet thrown down in our path.* Every event obliges us to stand outside ourselves (isn't that power a strange gift?),

118

and ask, "You, myself, what will you now do?" The necessary answer to an event is an act, even though it may be an act of default. Any event summons us. Charles Williams tells of a retired army officer secretly coveting a knighthood, and learning that his rival had won the honor. He can now congratulate his rival or withhold his hand. He withheld, determining to hate the fact, and that response was one more step in *Descent into Hell*.[3] This is the simple anatomy: mystery (or totality or God), invasion, gauntlet. And we have not scratched the surface! The world waits for a book entitled simply, "Event."

II

But, someone may ask, surely we can choose to which events we shall respond? Yes, but not for long, and not with impunity. The scientist can choose for a time to attend only to events which he can partly control in his laboratory. He can say, "I am determined to honor only empirical tests: there is no other 'truth.'" But then greedy men or power-drunk men lay hands on his "discoveries." There is an atomic explosion outside the laboratory door. The scientist cannot then wash his hands of the whole affair. He must now respond or default as a citizen and father and person. Meanwhile nuclear fission may blow his laboratory into limbo. Or, to take another instance, we may choose to respond only to the invention of machines that will eliminate human labor and bring more money to "my" business, but the choice is only for a time. For the Negro ghetto, filled with unskilled laborers who have been eliminated, may erupt in violence, and the violence may be directed toward the rich man who has had no concern for his poor neighbor; and meanwhile the machine with its inevitable systematizing of all life may mechanize us, so that we hardly know why we are so ill-content with our acquired cash and comfort. Yes, we can choose both event and response. That is our freedom. But only for a time, for our freedom is under Sovereignty.

Then the same someone asks if in our blindness we may misread events, and even take the small for the great and the great for the small. Yes, we may and we do. That is part of "the problem of pain." But once more the misreading is not for long, for events keep happening to our gain or loss. Within the last few days our newspapers have told of two men—one of whom won a fortune at the race track and exclaimed, "Money is divine!" (he was only being more honest in idolatry than a million neighbors); the other, having won such a fortune some years ago, told how the money had robbed him of desire to work, broken his home by divorce and alienated his children and friends, so that he exclaimed that the day of his "good fortune" had actually been the most unhappy day of his life. Which man spoke "truth"? The first man spoke in the first flush of the event, the second in its unpredictable aftermath. Or was it unpredictable? A good deal of water has gone under the bridge since the first man on earth lived for cash. Meanwhile events keep happening.

Then which is the focal Event of human story? Which Event gathers all others to give them light and power. The Dialogues of Plato? But they are "of the mind" and of their age, and remote from "the man in the street." The invention of printing? But even a marvelous modern offset machine can print the flood of pornography that darkens our time, or it can print the Bible. The first thrust of science? But science has brought the bomb without giving us any power to use it to our good. Then is it the first school, precursor of an education which billboards proclaim as "America's Greatest Blessing"? But the quiz shows with their story of deception practiced on a whole nation, for the sake of advertising, for the sake of money-gain, featured educated men: only so could the shows be conducted; and it is therefore clear that education also can be perverted. Meanwhile only one Event has split the calendar into before and after, the Event of the birth of a certain Man who never tried to split the calendar. The Roman emperors of his day tried, and all failed though they had the swords and the powers and the cash, while he risked oblivion by accepting death under a curse. Does that Man speak to us of the Totality, the Mystery, from beyond our calendar of births and deaths? Does he resolve the enigma of pain, not by an explanation, but by an event called Calvary? Does he change the curse of the Cross by conquering death and showing himself to his friends beyond death? Does he convict us at the very moment that he welcomes us despite our shabbiness, and by his very welcome convict us? Does his refusal of any timebound "god," his unswerving devotion to the one God, provide a talisman by which we can judge our crisscross of loyalties? Each of us

120

must answer for himself, and we cannot answer unless we turn from our engaging distractions and confront him in some final honesty. He flings the gauntlet in love at the feet of our world. Our concern now is with the gauntlet and our response. The *totality* of the Event: "It came to pass in those days, that . . ." [4] "the Word was made flesh." [5] The *invasiveness* of the Event: "Behold, I stand at the door and knock." The *gauntlet* of the Event: "If any one hears my voice and opens the door." [6]

III

So we write about the response of Christ's first disciples to the total Event of his life-death-resurrection. The history of their land and people should have prepared them for the coming of God's Anointed, because that hope, vague or clear, keeps breaking through their literature like a recurrent yet fading springtime. They were the chosen folk with whom God had established his covenant, and their strange persistence to this day is no disproof: it is its own validation. But some of them misread events. Their political hankerings had been again and again denied, for their land, surrounded by great empires, had repeatedly been a middle-ground battlefield. They themselves had been carried into captivity. Yet, such is our human pride, they still dreamed of national power greater than that of their foes. A few perceptive spirits clung to a better hope, even to believing that Israel might become a vicarious sacrifice: "He was wounded for our transgressions, he was bruised for our iniquities." [7] It would seem that Mary and Joseph, together with Elizabeth and Zacharias and Simeon, belonged to this group, for they were "looking for the consolation of Israel," [8] that is, for the coming of the gentle Messiah. But most men in Israel hoped for a Messiah with the sword and "garments rolled in blood." [9] Two unknown disciles to whom Jesus revealed himself after death seemed to have entertained that same fierce hope: "We had hoped that he was the one to redeem Israel" [10] —as a slave nation is redeemed from a master nation. So they were both prepared and unprepared for the Great Event.

The "proof" of the Event is that it overwhelmed the curse of the Cross, for, even if his first friends had imagined him as a "Suffering Servant," they would have been horrified by the proposal that he would die as a common criminal under a curse. Their amazement at this reversal of all

121

standards can be seen in their language even after his triumph: "This Jesus . . . killed by the hands of lawless men. But God raised him up, having loosed the pangs of death." [11] So his first followers had for their joy this mighty demonstration of God's power and will. It was as staggering as if our television should some night have bold headlines on its newscast: "Criminal knocks at the prison gate after death in the electric chair." Faith therefore was easier for them than for us. Yet it was harder, for they had to meet the enemies of Christ at risk of a like martyrdom. By signing a *libellus,* a slip of parchment testifying that they had offered a sacrifice on the altar of Roman gods or the emperor, they could escape death. How easy to say and to believe that their Lord's appearing was what our skeptical time is prone to argue: a wraith, a dream, an illusion! By their glad and brave response to the Event truth lived in them—and for us.

Then what of our response without which the Event becomes void, at least until we return to him and he to us in the thunders and pleadings of our unregenerate time? It is an easier response in that we are not persecuted. Our devotion has been so tepid that nobody thinks us worth the trouble of fire or stake. But the response is harder in that Jesus does not startle us after a criminal death by his resurrection presence. The moving story of Thomas' doubt about the Resurrection, with the comment of Christ, "Have you believed because you have seen me? Blessed are those who have not seen and yet believe," [12] seems to mark a turn in God's providence: the time of Christ's appearances is ended. You and I must travel by other signs which are better than signs: by the Holy Spirit.

Yet we are perhaps better equipped for response than the first disciples, for we have *their* pioneering (at what cost!), and the New Testament (without any *in memoriam* word!), and the church (its persistence the more marvelous because it has been so pockmarked with worldliness and cowardice, though with a continuing secret life), and the evidences of the Holy Spirit in art and architecture and music and lowly folk, and a calendar split down the middle. If we are denied the vivid conviction that came with his new coming, we have "proofs" denied to Peter and John. Perhaps we have a better chance for courage: "Blessed are those who have not seen and yet believe." That last Beatitude awaits faith in our time. Admittedly the faith seems a very tenuous thread, as tenuous as the optic nerve by which we become aware of our incredible earth and sky, but by that so-slender bond we are open to the Holy Spirit and his mighty works.

IV

We should not bridle at the word "faith," for our whole life is an adventure in trust. The proposal, fashionable in our time, that science travels by strict investigation while "religion" (vague word!) spoofs itself by "faith," would hardly do credit to a grade school. For science is shot through with faith both in its beginnings and in its continuance. It believes matter is worth studying—against the major drive of Greek philosophy, and it *is* worth studying, though not unless other deeper themes are studied. It believes that mind can comprehend matter, though the two realms seem severed: How can a man "know" about a stone or tree? It believes that the universe *is* a uni-verse, one song, though no man can guess what the next astronomical explosion of hydrogen may bring, or trace the bounds of a boundless sky. It believes that time is nonreversible, that the next experiment will "go on" and not return on itself. Yet how can that or the other tenets be proved? For all we know, time may take off like a corkscrew or a boomerang next Thursday. Or *do* we "know" better? Yes, but not by scientific "investigation." All our life is by faith, for we travel with the line of light at our toes, and we do not know what a day may bring. Crossing a road is by faith. Investing money is by faith. Going to work is by faith, for we may suffer a heart attack. Marriage is by faith, not as a lottery, but as a mated adventure, as a life commitment: not with the back door of divorce always open (though divorce is sometimes the better of two second-best choices), but with more thought of children to be born than of ourselves. Why should anyone bridle at the word "faith"? Anyone and everyone lives by faith.

As to faith response to the Event of Christ, we cannot ultimately escape it, for all other events constrain us to their Master-Event. God is God, and man is man the creature, and at long last our only choice is to agree with God's choice of us or go on living in rebellion. But, by paradox, our freedom to choose our transient life instead of Christ is honored. That is, there is no coercion in this present world. We *need not* respond to the Christ-Event. As of old Christ is given into the hands of ungodly men. We may crucify him again or, more cruelly, ignore him. Most people nowadays ignore him, the indifference being worse than the railing, for the railing at least acknowledges both his presence and his strange power. When the Word becomes flesh, God accepts all our weakness even to death itself—and then again the Resurrection. So there is in one real sense no coercion, or (should we say?) constraints are very gentle: our freedom is honored. God knocks at the door, but he does not pick the lock or smash the barrier.

But the choice is a life choice. It is not like the choice of an avocation or even of a vocation, and certainly not like the choice of a "religion"! That last-named nonsense is typical of our shallow time: "I have chosen the Buddhist religion," or, "I want to marry this man, and so I shall choose his 'religion.'" The choice of Christ is not ours in the original instance: he chooses us, and we must then decide if we accept his choice. He splits the calendar, even though we do not wish to reckon time by his birthday. He returns from the dead, though we are sure we have got rid of him on a gallows. We can be worthily a scientist or a dramatist without a whole-life commitment, for to be a scientist or dramatist does not necessarily determine how our life shall be lived. But our response to Christ is "all or nothing." It is "for keeps." It is addressed to the will, not merely to emotion or to our intellectual interest. To believe means to live-by-your-leave. The Event, in far deeper sense than other events, obliges us to stand outside our life and ask, "What now shall I *do?*" We cannot "take it or leave it" as if we were choosing a necktie or a house. But we can "take it *and* leave it" in some final defection. We can "take it" and never leave it, because the Christ who first chooses us, and whom we then choose, chooses us again in our choice, and holds us by his Spirit, so that we also can say: "I know whom I have believed and I am sure that he is able to guard until that Day what has been entrusted to me." [13] That "whom" is the item: we do not believe a creed; we trust a Person who has first given us his trust.

V

What comes of our response to the Event of Christ as regards pain and evil? The New Testament is a watershed in this issue. On one side

124

is the Old Testament emphasis on judgment, enigma, and penalty; on the other side the morning of a new day, so that Paul could say: "For the sake of Christ, then, I am content with weaknesses, insults, hardships, persecutions, and calamities; for when I am weak, then am I strong." [14] That list covers almost all forms of suffering, the words "for Christ's sake" are determinative, and "content" could just as well be translated "I am happy with"; for Paul knew that his very weakness provided opening for the divine grace. Books on suffering have in many instances failed to mark this almost complete change of climate in regard to human pain. To the New Testament pain is not morbidity or hopelessness or retribution. It is still devil's work, but the devil has been overcome and the penalty has been cancelled. So pain is now cleansing, illumination, and vocation: not in itself, for in itself pain is incipient death, but because the Event of Christ has changed the bitter waters into a pool of healing. These three words, "cleansing," "illumination," "vocation," shall soon engage us. Meanwhile we mark the miraculous change.

(a)

As for *"natural evil,"* the man who trusts the great Event knows that it is conquered. For Christ met natural evil, and "was raised" from the consequent death. He came in the flesh, and so knew and endured

> The heart-ache and the thousand natural shocks
> That flesh is heir to . . .
> the whips and scorns of time.[15]

This suffering comes to dark climax on the Cross. There the sun struck like swords, and flies buzzed round a helpless head. There the blood ebbed, and darkness came at noon. The story tells us that an earthquake shook that hilltop, token of the strange hostilities and terrors of the natural world, but also of nature's protest against the foul deed of Calvary. The hill was called Golgotha, "the place of a skull," [16] because it was either shaped like a skull or littered with skulls, symbol of the death which awaits every man, the death which seems to be the final mockery of life. All of which means that Jesus died not only by the hand of his enemies, but of "natural causes." Natural evil converged on the Cross.

But he was raised from the dead, and thereby triumphed over both pain and death! The enigma of natural evil is not solved, at least not in any ink-and-paper demonstration, but it is overwhelmed in light. We are not given any explanation, but we are given a victory. Therefore the explanation can wait, for it no longer deeply matters. Nay, more: The victory carries back through time and illuminates the whole creation. For Christ is the eternal Logos (that is the Greek for "the Word"),[17] the out-thrust of God's creative act, the One through whom God said, " 'Let there be light'; and there was light." [18] Therefore Christ's first followers, under the tremendous impact of the Resurrection and the Cross sang and shouted their tremendous credo: "He was in the beginning with God; all things were made through him, and without him was not anything made that was made." [19] Our whole cosmos from its very origin in mystery has been in the hands of Christ! Why the world is flawed and why our human life should be seduced by "the snake" we do not know, for it is not given to man to eat "of the tree of the knowledge of good and evil." [20] But evil has been under control from the first, and its days are numbered. Easter and Calvary, which are one Event, are God's seal on evil's doom.

(b)

For the man who trusts the great Event *"historical evil"* also is conquered! For all the powers of historical evil converged on the Cross, and they were not enough. Christ is *in* history. He "was made flesh." [21] He is not a theory, but our actual life; not "universal man," but the specific man, Christ Jesus. The Bible is not a book of science or philosophy, but a book of history and of man's response in belief or unbelief. So Christ is not to be confronted as if he were isolated fact or static fact whose "nature" we can then debate, and as if we were spectators armed with microscope or textbook. He is not static, and we can never be spectators. *He is not isolated* but belongs to a specific stream in history, that of Israel with whom God made a covenant, not for their private prestige, but that through them his "mighty acts" [22] should be made known.

The very name "Jesus Christ" (more accurately "Jesus the Christ") proclaims his involvement with history-past and history-yet-to-come. For Jesus was a well-used name in Israel, almost as common as William or John in our birth certificates. It meant "Jehovah saves," but Jesus shared it with many now-forgotten brethren. He fulfilled it while they could only hope. So the history of Israel came to focus in Christ: Israel's long breaking of the covenant finally broke him, and Israel's still-unbroken longing and hope found in him its glad completion. As for the name "Christ," that is the Greek word for Messiah, and Messiah means God's Anointed (King). That name in its Greek form was prophetic of the thrust of Jesus into the history of the ancient world. For *koine* Greek, the Greek spoken in the streets, is the language of our New Testament, because it was the language used across the ancient world, binding man with man and land with land. Thus when "certain Greeks" [23] came seeking Jesus, they were for him the harbinger of spring, the promise and portent of the new age, though only through his death and beyond death. So he said: "The hour has come for the Son of man to be glorified. Truly, truly, I say to you, unless a grain of wheat falls into the earth and dies, it remains alone; but if it dies, it bears much fruit." [24]

The dying was Calvary, and the "earth" was black "historical evil." The very place of death was legacy of the baleful past, for (it is his word) "it cannot be that a prophet should perish away from Jerusalem"! [25] The dark entail of Israel's itch for political power was at Calvary, for there violent men on the left who trusted to violence, and reactionary men on the right who were resolved at any cost to Christ to keep their status and cash, joined hands to kill him; and a rampant empire, token of all the empires which in the past had ravaged Israel, executed the sentence. At the Transfiguration, [26] that other hilltop where Jesus foresaw Calvary and consented to God's strange will, he spoke with Moses and Elijah—Moses who forbore in pain his nation's lapse into Baalism and was denied entrance into the Promised Land; and Elijah who led another struggle against defection and Baalism, and was regarded in Israel as forerunner of a new age, and for whom a chariot of fire "swung low" and carried him to heaven.[27] All Israel's history, dark and bright, converged on Calvary; and our history also, our shifty politics personified in the shifty politics of Pilate, our hardened churches symbolized in the hardened temple, our mob finding voice in the mob which shouted "Crucify him!" [28]

Yet he conquered historical evil, for God raised him from the dead. The dark entail of human sin could not destroy him. The Cross is empty now and set before worshiping eyes. His word stands: "In the world you have tribulation; but be of good cheer, I have overcome the world." [29] We are still not told why we suffer from dead men's sins: only that that kind of world is now overcome. "Tribulation" is from a Latin root meaning a threshing-sledge! The Resurrection and the Cross gave assurance that historical evil is now robbed of power, and that it never had any final power; and the telling is not by word alone, but by the Word whom God raised from the dead. If we ask, "Then what of those who lived and died before his coming?" or, "What of those living now who have never heard of him?" these questions also have their answer: History is not yet complete. He has already split history into B.C. and A.D., and "the year of our Lord" has only begun. In its culmination all men shall understand and praise, and those who lived in dim longing shall "receive double" not only for their sins, but also for their waiting: "The kingdom of the world *has* become the kingdom of our Lord and of his Christ, and he shall reign for ever and ever." [30]

(c)

As to our personal evil and the pain that comes from present sin, it was sin precisely like our sin that killed Christ, for sin is always the anxious pride of the creature by which we try to be our own god. In the ongoing of the years the form of temptation changes: there are no carbon copies of history. Each man, each nation, each era must make its own choice under new options, yet the options in essence do not change, for always the alternatives are man's futile will or God's overruling will. As for natural evil, that does not change, for the natural world is cyclic: its strange "freedom" is within limits, but plague and fire and earthquake bedevil every generation. If the form changes, it is because of man's greater freedom: we can partly predict and anesthetize pain (if we know soon enough), and by modern transportation rush help to areas of disaster; or we can multiply pain by our wars or by the frantic tempo of our greedy culture. As for the mystery of pain—why the snake appears in our natural world and as seducer in our world of human decision—the mystery remains: We do not know, though we do know that we cannot shelve responsibility for our choice.

The pain that comes of sin is the focal item in the whole "problem," and in the midst of it stand a Cross and a Resurrection. Our name is Peter who denied, and Thomas who doubted, and Andrew who fled, and Judas who betrayed. Of us, you and me, the prayer is spoken, "Father, forgive them; for they know not what they do." [31] They did not know, as we do not know, because they didn't care, or because the world distracted them, or because their human wisdom miscarried, or because the customs of the time blinded them. Do we not drive from comfortable homes to successful businesses through Negro slums? We also are the prisoners of the accepted patterns of the world. A gentler age may wonder how we could be so callous and blind. Yes, the prayer is spoken of us. Yet because God raised him from the dead the prayer is *already answered* for us. *We are forgiven!* Satan has already "fallen like lightning"! [32] When the prodigal returns home, or our prodigal world, there is no fumigation, no isolation ward, no required probation, no hard labor in any prison, no exacted requital. There is only, "This my son . . . let us . . . make merry." [33]

As for the *mystery* of pain, the mystery of all evil including our evil, that remains. But we know now that it is gathered into Light. It is constitutional. In this life we cannot escape it. It darkens in the word of Jesus when he was betrayed, for he was speaking both to Judas and beyond Judas when he said: "But this is your hour, and the power of darkness." [34] Yet betrayal has only an hour, and the power of darkness is broken because God both shares our pain and overcomes it. "The Word was made flesh" [35] . . . and "was raised" from the dead. Have we not said that pain wrings from us a double cry—"I am mortal. Where is my salvation?" We need no longer ask "where": "Believe in the Lord Jesus, and you will be saved." [36] The Twenty-third Psalm finds new meaning in the Good Shepherd, for now we do not fear "the valley

129

of the shadow of death," for he is with us and spreads a table for us "in the presence of" our "enemies." One of my sons tells of sitting between two hospital beds, where one man was moaning in his misery, and the other was stoically or rebelliously silent. Thus he sat for a long time, until the moaning man stopped moaning and challenged him: "Did Jesus hurt?" The answer was glad and instant: "He surely did!" The moaning stopped, and both sufferers were confronted by the focal truth. Jesus not only "hurt" in and for our hurt: God raised him from the dead. Thus the astounding change of climate in the New Testament. Judgment is now love, darkness is now light, and pain takes on a new life—in cleansing, illumination, and vocation. Not of itself, for pain in itself is "hurt" and incipient death. Not of itself: "it is the gift of God" in Christ.[37]

VI

This faith is not popular in our time. Perhaps it has never been widely popular. Perhaps it is intended to be always the seed of the new age. As to that, we do not know. But the parables of Jesus—that about the necessity of letting weeds and wheat grow together until the judgment-harvest,[38] for instance—do not encourage an easy optimism. Indeed there are voices in the church telling us that many former functions of the church have now been assumed by the world—"charity" and learning, for instance—a claim obviously true; and that man has outgrown belief in God and is getting along quite well without him—a claim by no means true. These voices offer our passing culture as the incredible test of Truth! The prime issue is not the church, but the focus of faith. If the focus of faith is Christ, the church comes of itself, or, rather, from him, for it is his "Body." How can anyone intelligently say that modern man has outgrown the need for God? Or ever proclaim that we are "getting along very well" without God? Our industry lives with a gaping lesion: the strife between labor and capital. Our politics breeds wars that may destroy the whole world. Our culture is a hideous contrast between slums and suburbs, and between race and race. Violence makes our streets unsafe, and nervous ills multiply. "Getting along" is precisely what we are not doing: we are falling apart—for lack of a creative faith.

There is a line in Shaw's *Saint Joan:* "Must then a Christ perish in torment in every age to save those that have no imagination?" [39] The question is disfigured, for there is not "*a* Christ," but only *the* Christ; and the main trouble is not lack of imagination, but blind self-will. So we *believe* that supply-and-demand is self-regulating, though it is plain to see that our economy can produce (e.g., automobiles) far more than it can consume. We *believe* that "enlightened self-interest" (a contradiction in terms) will of itself bring public good, though it is clear that selfishness atomises our common life. We *believe* that science is salvation: science fiction to many a high-school lad is not fiction, but a guaranteed promise; and we keep on believing, though the erstwhile categories of science are steadily corroded, though science is limited to mensurable matter, and though its findings are now used to add to the horrors of war. We *believe* that "education is America's greatest blessing" without asking the nature of true education, and therefore our schooling has become a poor cult of facts:

> That frost of fact by which our wisdom gives
> Correctly stated death to all that lives.[40]

The facts are now so multitudinous that we almost drown in facts. Our universities are split into alienated "departments" with almost no traffic across the various gulfs, because we do not face this issue: we can learn only a trace of all the facts and must now ask what facts are best worth studying. But we have neither norm nor courage to confront that issue. So education is a vast cafeteria in which everything is served (Plato or platypus or the study of pornography), and the student survives only by a stomach-pump. The conduct of our national elections hardly proves us "an educated nation." Meanwhile we deplore what is called the "sentimentalism" of faith in Christ, which actually is the only realism, and we send heralds through the streets announcing that we have outgrown God.

These strictures could be multiplied: philosophy now accepts only empirical or logical tests, though empiricism is a fractional mind intent on a fractional world, and logic itself rests back on mysterious "axioms." Politics, to cite another instance, knows that communism is a false faith, without knowing why, and therefore confines itself to a poor counter-punching, blind to the fact that poverty and desolation always *invite* communism (though they do not necessarily *cause* it), and that our wars bring more desolation. But enough of strictures. There is no joy in filing them. Indeed their only major use is made clear by a dream of Shelley: a hooded figure stood at his bedside, then drew back the hood to reveal a vaguely familiar face, and said: "I am your memory. Are you satisfied?"[41] Soon we may confront our bright and brittle world, far more brittle than bright, for the brightness is the shine of tinsel, and admit that actually, despite all our protestations of "having a good time," we are not satisfied. Then perhaps there may be the first gleam of a new age of Faith.

Meanwhile Christ still stands at the door and knocks. It is a gentle knocking. We do not hear it because he stands at the back door while we are in the rumpus room busy with our gadgets. He does not pick the lock, much less break down the door. He stands there until ancient hostilities gang up on him, and hurry him to a Hill outside the city gate. Then again he is "raised," and comes again to our door offering surcease for our suicidal selfishness. Perhaps our "angry young men" have their role: they are telling us that *they* are not satisfied. Perhaps existentialist "despair" is far better than luncheon-club optimism. These revolts may make a breach in the wall, openings for a new and better faith. Thus there is a strange little interlude in Samuel Beckett's *Waiting for Godot*.[42] The play seems to say that it is the fate of men to wait for God—who never comes. Messengers promise his coming, but he never comes. Meanwhile there is between and beneath the lines of the play a protest against our callousness and a plea for some kind of sympathy. The two main characters still wait as the moon rises in the darkening sky, for men must always wait. One man footsore has taken off his shoes. Then this unexplained interlude with little to prophesy it and less as sequel:

> Vladimir: "But you can't go barefoot!"
> Estragon: "Christ did."
> Vladimir: "Christ! What has Christ got to do with it? You're not going to compare yourself to Christ!"
> Estragon: "All my life I've compared myself to him."

Vladimir: "But where he lived it was warm, it was dry!"
Estragon: "Yes, and they crucified quick."

Perhaps they did not need to wait! Perhaps the Christ had once more arrived in the Event—the Cross made always contemporary by his Presence. For that is how we are found again of the one true and only God.

9. The Way of Suffering

I. Dead End—as if
There Were No Breakthrough

When a pathetic bunch of flowers appears on the doorknob of your next door neighbor, you decide and act, whatever your theory of pain, evil, and death. Even though the mystery of pain darkens and deepens for you, you must still act in friendship or default. You must choose some beckoning, and answer in some faith. Likewise when the doctor tells you, "There must be surgery if you wish to live," you can whine, or rebel, or just "take it," or think first of your family, or pray in realistic courage. That is why this chapter is titled "The Way of Suffering." We walk the path, whatever our chosen path, for we cannot wait for explanations. Pain is not a theory but a daily onset. It is not academic but *act*ual. It is answered not by a philosophy, for every answer lives in mystery, but in a beckoning and in an answering resolve. Therefore this book has printed the word "problem" in quotation marks. The "problem of pain" is more than a problem for debate in a classroom or

134

argument in endless conversation: it is an invader, and we must grapple with it or try to run away.

So books on pain and evil, including this book, savor of impertinence. The books are on paper; the pain strikes at the nerve centers. "You have suffered much," said the visitor to the woman long crippled by arthritis. "So they tell me," came the brave, wry answer. Books do the telling; everyone of us does the bearing, with stoicism, for example, or in some secret light. Even when the books are written by men who have had their share of pain, as I have had my share, they are still only books: they are not the surgical ward or the sudden news of grief. Yet the books can reflect life even if they cannot transcribe it. They can hint at solving faith, and at the unfaith that only adds poison to the turbulent waters. So now we try to draw pictures of this-world-only answers, found on any secular street, some of them both brave and compassionate, on which the sign-board is "No Exit." Even so they may be better answers than those offered by merely "pious" or sentimental or unrealistic "churchianity."

We have kept saying that pain and evil trace the line, as with dagger point, between the dimensions of our two-dimensional life. We are *in* life, walking down Main Street and entering the drugstore; yet we are *above* life, for we can speak of ourselves almost as if we were another person: "There he goes down Main Street to buy Band-Aids in the drugstore." The other day I heard of a woman who said as she looked at her own portrait, speaking of the artist, "I am glad he understood that woman's hardships." Thus Nicholas Berdyaev has written:

Anguish points to the world above and is associated with the experience of the insignificance, precariousness and transitoriness of this world. Anguish bears witness to the transcendent and, at the same time, to the distance, the yawning gulf that exists between man and the transcendent. . . . Anguish can awake my awareness of God, but it can also signify my God-forsakenness.[1]

Brave, true testimony! Our language in this book has been simpler and more drab: pain wrings from us a double cry: "I am mortal! Where is my salvation?" The last two chapters have testified that God himself has crossed "the yawning gulf" in Jesus Christ. But what of those who in our skeptical time cannot yet accept the testimony? What of all of us in our times of "God-forsakenness"? "All of us" is the rightful phrase, for we should not divide our world into believers and doubters: we should be honest enough to confess the faith-doubt tension that troubles every man, so that every man must pray, if he prays, "Lord, I believe; help thou mine unbelief." [2] Then what of our grappling with the invader in our time of doubt, as if there were no Breakthrough? There can be no faith without beckoning. But the beckoning we choose, in denial of the fact that we are chosen, makes the difference. Sun hardens clay and melts wax: the difference in that instance is in the recipient, not in the sun.

I

Some people try to sidestep pain, and they find many an ally in our checkered world. As to physical pain, they can misuse the blessing of anesthesia. As to that bunch of flowers on the neighboring front door-knob, they can refuse to "get involved." As to the current war (there is always some kind of current war), they can say: "I'm over draft age, so why should I care?" As to the typhoon that has just leveled the neighboring village, they can say, "Let the government take care of it." As to their mistakes, they can pretend they are somebody else's blame or that they have made no mistake. I have just found the following in my Bible concordance, of all books!

Erratum
One page following page 71 has been omitted from the text at this point. It is printed on the reverse of this sheet with the pagination of 71a.

Notice: there is no confession that "we" made a blunder, but there is no ignoring of the fault, though the printer could have ignored it and left the reader wondering if he had misread his Bible. Many people try to sidestep pain and evil.

The pessimist tries. He takes his beckoning from the insensate cruelty of the world, ignoring life's joys. Even Albert Camus with his splendid realism leaves us troubled with his disproportion, for, though he seriously wondered in print if suicide is not the best option in an "absurd" world, [3] there are pictures of him in his Paris garden obviously happy with his lovely wife and children. But the pessimist says, "It's a rotten world! It's a cutthroat world!" He can find plenty of evidence. Then he says, "I'm going to get my share of happiness, if there is any, and to hell with the rest!" Some of our modern violence is more evasion than worthy rebellion. When the head of a large corporate venture was rather clearly guilty of misappropriation of funds, an employee remarked, "The other big boys get theirs, so why shouldn't he get his if he can?" The man might have added with truth, "You can bet I'll get mine if *I* can!" There was no acknowledgment of right and wrong, no standard of guilt or goodness, no pity for the victims of the embezzlement though he himself was among them, and no compassion for anybody. Why? Because it is not that kind of world. In his pessimism he was even ready to inflict pain on his neighbor; or, rather, he simply refused the sight of pain in the world, just as he refused entrance to any pains of sympathy in his own life. Camus also was a rebel, but of another kind, for his rebellion sprang from compassion. It was evasion of the joy, not a sidestepping of pain. We shall discuss it.

By sharp contrast there is another unimpressive kind of sidestepping, that of the false optimist. He says of pain and evil, "It is all in the mind!" That is what one woman said of birth pains, and refused anesthesia when her baby came. If only she had said, "I wish to bear the pain for my child's sake"! But she said, "It's all in the mind!" Suppose somebody had killed her baby with the excuse, "It's all in the mind"! Buddhism raises our questions in this regard, even while we should be quick to confess our indebtedness to that fine faith. Indeed, Buddhism is not consistent on this issue, for many a modern Buddhist insists that the Buddha postponed his entrance into Nirvana that he might the longer share the sorrows of our earth. I myself cannot find that emphasis in the Buddha's teachings, for he disclaimed any knowledge of the gods or of heaven, and offered a physical and ethical regimen for ridding the mind of "the stain of the world." I am grateful for the modern emphasis, but the impressive face of a Buddha image does not speak to me of life. It seems to me almost like a mask, impassive, tired, complacent, even slightly cynical—an evasion of the sharp impact of life's joys and griefs, with a slow dissication of death behind the mask.

Another unimpressive form of sidestepping is seen in our modern cult of "peace of mind." It would have us believe that there is no evil that we ourselves cannot overcome by a prayer-formula and "confidence."

"Positive thinking" can guarantee both an attractive personality and business success. This world is a world in which we can always "win friends and influence people"[4] if only we keep telling ourselves that "every day in every way we are getting better and better." When we set Jesus alongside this cheap evasion it dwindles into selfishness. For my part I cannot find in him any peace of mind: people like me caused him too much trouble. I do find in him the peace of God, but that is another item. Maybe we need a book entitled "Turmoil of Mind" to offset the spate of aspirin books which promise a brief, manipulated pleasure. Can a worthy man just forget his culpable blunders, the child he killed when he drove while drunk? Can he worthily forget the desolation in Vietnam? If not, then pain, kicked out of the front door, has returned through the kitchen. Perhaps the sufficient judgment on this wretched cult of popularity and success is the word to Crillon: "Hang yourself, brave Crillon! we fought at Arques, and you were not there."[5] Incidentally Crillon *was* brave: the adjective was not a sarcasm. It was his great misfortune to have missed the battle.

Still another form of sidestepping is that of the aesthete who in tribute to beauty avoids the sight of ugliness. Thus a certain seminarian who was taking lectures in the nearby university could choose from two routes for the journey, a shorter route through slums and a longer route through suburbs; always he chose the "happier" journey, saying, "God does not wish us to occupy our minds with ugliness." Unless, of course, God outrightly chose the ugliness of a hill called Golgotha "which means the place of a skull."[6] Kierkegaard in his *Either-Or*[7] has argued that the ethical choice cuts deeper and carries a greater burden of constraint than the aesthetic choice. That is certainly true if ethic rests back, as always it does, on some faith, and if the faith be faith in Christ. It is true in any event, for the human has more claim on us than color and form. It is worth noting that modern art is not concerned with prettiness. It attempts in inevitable ugliness to portray three dimensions on a two-dimensional canvas: thus the initial repulsion from the later work of Picasso. Sculpture now is sometimes in twisted rusty iron. In brokenness it portrays our broken world. Yet some men, under the plea of beauty, disclaim human misery. A commuter from Montclair pulls down the shade in his window on the train as soon as he approaches the hovels and

138

pigsties on the New Jersey meadows. He looks for the silver lining, pretending that there are no devastating storms.

We should notice that sidestepping pain never fully succeeds, for even if it pays off in the eyes, it fails at life's center. We may lock the door against misery, but we know the misery is outside the door, and that one day, any day, it may enter despite every lock. Meanwhile the repression spreads beneath the skin, for there is neither use nor wisdom in plastering down a boil; and soon there are ills of another kind, alienation from our neighbors, inability to concentrate, a neurasthenic fear of ill health, and all the pains of withdrawal. Every device by which we try to deny our creaturehood finally fails. Indeed, it becomes a canker. William James had a theory, which is partly true, that we do not run away because we are afraid: we are afraid because we run away.[8] The partial truth means that we exchange sympathy for fear, and realism for pretense, whenever we try to avoid the world's evil. It is a poor exchange. The renegade lives in an unreal world. So his fears become a fantasy; or in worse fate, his human life is finally lost in brutishness.

II

Other people, worthier than the runaways, *endure suffering with stoicism*. There are stoics in every sizeable street. They even use the word "stoicism," never dreaming that they belong in the school of Zeno of Cyprus. The first stoics were so named because they met in "The Painted Porch" (the *Stoa Poecile*) near the Agora (the public square where the city assembly was held) in Athens about 400 B.C. The popularity of early stoic doctrine is perhaps reflected in the fact that Paul in his sermon on Mars Hill in Athens possibly quoted Cleanthes who was Zeno's immediate successor: "Yet he"—God—"is not far from each one of us, for

> 'In him we live and move and have our being';
> as even some of your poets have said,
> 'For we are indeed his offspring.' "[9]

That first quoted line is possibly from Cleanthes, the second is definitely from Aratus' "Phaenomena." But we should be on guard lest such quotations mislead us. Paul was not fully endorsing them; he was seeking some bond between the thinking of his hearers and his own thinking. The "him" or God of the stoics was not personal, let alone concerned for our well-being. "He" was only a force or fire in all things and all men, and the circle of creation was just that, a circle, for after an age or two the whole world would return to limbo, and then begin some new circle which yet was the same old tracing:

> The heavens at last will end, as all things must—
> to let new heavens ripple out of dust.[10]

But to the stoics there was no heaven, least of all a new heaven: there was only animated dust cyclically returning to its dust. This idea, that our world is but blind Force or Fire, is not alien from the widespread stoicism of our time.

That ancient stoicism, which we know best through its Roman disciples, such as Seneca, Marcus Aurelius, and Epictetus, has bonds also with modern science, for it taught that all we know is through the senses. Thus Zeno today might say that love is only a titillation of the glands and anger only a rush of blood. Therefore, he might add, a wise man lives without passion or pity. He harbors no unjust thought but is content to fulfill duty and justice with steely endurance and self-sufficiency, for there is a god (a force) within the flesh. How notions such as justice and duty entered the picture is not explained. But the way of life is cool reason and a certain objectivity. The favorite Greek word to indicate this prime virtue of the stoics gives us our word "apathy." The stoicism which we find today on any Main Street does not go to these extremes, but it betrays its far-off ancestry, as witness its typical language: "That's the way things are," or "That's how the cookie crumbles" (and there's no escaping crumbs in our lap), or "We must just grin and bear it" (with a forced grin, not a secret laughter), or "Can't you take it?" (for you should not look for pity to your neighbor), or "What can't be cured must be endured" (for as a matter of fact this world can never be cured).

The reader can well supply other expressions from literature:

> For men must work, and women must weep,
> And the sooner it's over, the sooner to sleep;
> And good-bye to the bar and its moaning.[11]

We can read of one very poignant instance in *King Lear* as following:

> I do remember now; henceforth I'll bear
> Affliction till it do cry out itself,
> "Enough, enough," and die.[12]

It was a vain hope, for the trouble is that trouble does not die, at least not "of itself." It brands both body and mind as with a hot iron. In Gloucester's case the iron was actual and held in the hands of hatred, and it gouged out his eyes! Gloucester's best hope was that he might soon die, and that death is death. But such a hope is the death of hope.

Then what are we to say about stoicism ancient or modern? We should admire, for there is no whining or self-pity in this doctrine. There is instead a certain Spartan courage. It puts to outright shame our wretched cult of "peace of mind." Have you not marveled at the power of ordinary folk to endure? They lose their kith and kin in a colliery explosion, and after a few tears, say: "I guess we must just keep going." Perhaps they have some hidden hope of what lies beyond our mortal pilgrimage, for they still use such words as "heaven" and "hell." But they do not trust the hope, for they cannot see it. They also, like Zeno, live by the senses. But there is a measure of realism about them. They do not bemuse themselves by singing, "Look for the silver lining," in the pretense that there are no storms!

> God pity all the lonely Folk
> With Griefs they do not tell
> Women waking in the night
> And men dissembling well.[13]

Yet the word "pity" is out of place, for there is no pity in stoicism; or, if there is, it is no longer stoicism.

Stoicism is not normal. Its alleged realism does not "see life steadily," much less "see it whole." Why should we refuse entrance to joy or grief? They come, joy with its laughter, and grief perchance hiding a better treasure. The renunciation of self-pity we can endorse, for sin is the false pride of the creature, and self-pity is the core of pride. But what of pity? Seneca says, "The solace that comes of having company with misery smacks of ill-will." [14] *Ill* will or good will? Epictetus was at first a slave in

141

Nero's bodyguard, though afterward he was freed and became a professor of philosophy. Did he feel no pity when Nero lit the followers of Christ as torches to make a Roman holiday? Did he not admire their fierce joy as being better than apathy? Did he feel no protest at Nero's sadism? Yet Epictetus wrote: "I will take lunch now, since the hour for lunch has come, and afterward I will die at the appointed time." [15] For myself, I would have liked the slave-philosopher better if, after he had seen Nero use a fellow human as a cheap candle, he had vomited his lunch and joined some revolt against Nero.

The complete stoic would be almost a monstrosity. Imagine him, his features fixed and impassive, on a camping trip! Imagine him, an unwrapped moving mummy in the living room! His posture is a forced posture. That is, it goes against the grain of life. We die, so why fear death? Such is his question. He says, oblivion is oblivion, and no man need fear oblivion, though obviously the stoic does not know that death is oblivion. The trouble is that we love as well as fear, and that a mother's love knows no fear. Can we meet our child's death with scientific objectivity? We might hate ourselves if we could. Karl Barth is surely nearer life as life finds us when he writes: "Some day a company of men will proceed out to a church yard and lower a coffin and everyone will go home; but one will not come back, and that will be me. The seal of death . . . will bury me as a thing that is superfluous and disturbing." [16] But he writes in brave protest and glad faith, which is far better than a Spartan apathy. Stoicism is outside the biblical witness, and it is four centuries before Christ. It so proclaims itself. In any event we cannot get rid of the "problem" of pain by quietly strangling all the questions.

III

There is another response still outside the Breakthrough, which is in some forms finer than stoicism as stoicism is finer than escapism, namely, *outright rebellion*. It can take low forms, as when a greedy man draws the natural anger of his neighbors and then exclaims, as if he were an innocent sufferer, "Why has this happened to *me?*" Life has little wholeness for a man locked in the "me," for he himself has become a broken-off fragment. The revolt takes pathetic forms, as when a man overtaken by the sorrow of his daughter's death defies God: "God took my daughter: I shall never again darken the door of a church!" The pathos lives not only in the proposal that God can be mortally wounded if a man stays away from church, or the sky stained if a man flings a tar brush at it, but in the fact that such a man is not likely to be much concerned when his neighbor across the street loses *his* daughter.

But the rebellion can take high forms, as in the case of Job. We speak of "the patience of Job," but he was not patient either with the mystery of God's ways or with the glib explanations of suffering offered by his friends. He demanded of God to know why misfortune had devastated his farm, tragedy had killed his children, and loathesome affliction had racked him from head to heel. The sentence translated in the King James Version as, "Though he slay me, yet will I trust him," is much more correctly given in the Revised Standard Version:

> Behold, he will slay me; I have no hope;
> yet I will defend my ways to his face.[17]

As for those who too easily equated the extent of his misfortunes with the horrendous measure of his sins (they themselves being by the same measure righteous men!), Job let them have it from both barrels:

> As for you, you whitewash with lies;
> worthless physicians are you all.[18]

With their lying explanations of pain they were actually blaspheming God:

> Will you speak falsely for God,
> and speak deceitfully for him? . . .
> Will it be well with you when he searches you out?
> Or can you deceive him, as one deceives a man?[19]

Strange argument! Job could not believe that God is love, at least not until suffering is reasonably explained, but he was still sure that God is truth! This rebellion is noble because Job was concerned for other people as well as for himself. His wife was of shallower mind. When her neat little patterns of belief were broken, when in her awareness of fine spirit in her husband she could not longer equate the measure of suffering with the measure of sin, she was ready to smash everything to get even with God. So she bade her husband, "Curse God, and die." [20] Job rebelled on the ground that a pain-stricken man has the right at least to some explanation. Incidentally there is in the story an amazing foregleam of the Breakthrough in Christ, for Job says to his friends about God.

> For he is not a man, as I am, that I might answer him,
>> that we should come to trial together.
> There is no umpire between us,
>> who might lay his hand upon us both. [21]

Faith in Christ can answer: "But there is, and better than an umpire: the Word made flesh!" But history had not yet brought that revealing.

The modern protest in its finer voices is even more definitely compassionate. Albert Camus has a story of a French schoolteacher in a remote Algerian school. [22] French army police leave an Algerian murderer in the teacher's care, they themselves being more than busy in a time of revolt. The teacher has no relish for the job. So the next morning he takes the murderer to a fork in the desert road, saying in effect "That is the way to freedom, and this is the way to the French garrison to which I am charged to take you. Choose for yourself." Reaching his school, the teacher sees the man trudging toward the garrison. Why? He can hardly guess. Because he knew his guilt? Because he despaired of life and almost wished it might be ended? Because he would show them that an Algerian could die defying them? He could not guess the reason and had little time to guess. For as he entered his classroom he saw scribbled on the blackboard a message from the Algerian rebels telling him that they would soon kill him, because he had betrayed an Algerian to the enemy. The story almost sobs with compassion for men half-blind in an absurdly ambiguous and insensately cruel world. Camus does not deny God: he hates him. Even of Christ he wonders how Christ could bear to remember that his birth at Bethlehem had occasioned the slaughter of innocent children. [23]

In "my book" (this book) such a protest is nobler than the dispassion of Epictetus as the sky is higher than the earth. Camus was not content to take his lunch and to die, each at the appointed time. Camus could hardly eat his lunch for thinking of the pathos of Algerian rebels, French gendarmes, a schoolteacher, and of the cruel web of life in which all of them are caught. There is a further provisional comment: the Old Testament spoke the Camus protest centuries before Camus, and in more voices than the voice of Job:

> How long, O Lord, wilt thou look on?[24]
> How long will you judge unjustly
>   and show partiality to the wicked?
> Give justice to the weak and the fatherless.[25]
> How long, O Lord? Wilt thou hide thyself forever?
>   How long will thy wrath burn like fire?
> Remember, O Lord, what the measure of life is,
>   for what vanity thou has created all the sons of men![26]

The Bible does it better than Camus! There is a further comment: rebellion does not resolve the pain: it only adds bitterness to the burden. Thus it is existentially "disproved," or is at least shown to be a poor way to meet the onset of suffering. There is a still further comment in the form of a question: Has Camus or any other man the right to debit God with all the cruelty and credit man with all the compassion? Yet this rebellion has noble marks. It is a sign of hope in our time that more and more men cannot stand the sight of a Negro ghetto. If the church can stand it, and the rebels then turn against the church, God in Christ lives with the rebels even though they do not see or confess him. But that brings us back to the Breakthrough, and for the moment we are discussing other ways of meeting pain.

IV

We continue in regard to rebellion—on deeper ground. We have said that there is in every man a tension of faith and doubt. Indeed, the doubt testifies to the inarticulate faith, or there would be nothing to doubt. Is there not also in every man a tension between hate-of-God and love-of-God? That soldier, dying in Korea just after the armistice had sounded,

145

said, "Isn't this just like God?" [27] He hated God for the cruelly untimely death, but—God had sent the armistice. Even Job was not unaware of God's tender care, for there is some evidence that he deliberately parodied a cherished psalm. The psalm had said,

> What is man that thou art mindful of him,
> and the son of man that thou dost care for him? [28]

Job in bitter parody says, "What is man . . . that thou should inspect him critically every morning, and cruelly test him every moment?" [29] The point is that Job could not so have spoken if he had been unaware of God's care. It is worth remembering that, since all things come from the creative Will, and since we are bound to say in mystery that God allows pain, our compassion also comes from him. There is always tension in us between the hate-of-God and the love-of-God.

We hate God because he lays on us too high a demand. Why should we be required to tell the truth when no man in this ambiguous world can be sure of truth? What *was* truth in that Algerian impasse? Or why should we be asked to show pity when if we really exposed ourselves to the world's pain our heart might break? We could be comfortable in this green and pleasant valley called Earth if God had not set snakes in the grass and swept the valley with storms and challenged us with snow-clad mountains and made us curious to know what lies beyond the mountains. There is a certain sloth in us, and we prefer to live without pangs of compassion or conscience. Then why has God vexed us with sense of past and future? Why can we not live in the present, with no memory of past failure and joy, and no concern for what tomorrow may bring? Surely Job had the right idea:

> I would not live for ever.
> Let me alone, for my days are a breath. [30]

Sometimes in this hatred of God we pretend that if there were no sense of sin there would be no problems. Thus Whitman thought he could "live with animals" because "they do not lie awake in the dark and weep for their sins"; [31] and Lenin seriously believed, or tried to make himself believe, that if economics could once for all be brought into the

Marxist pattern, we could dismiss the police force and live as peaceably as in a happy meadow.

We hate God again for what we deem his endlessly repeated breach of justice, or of what we think is justice. We look at a trainwreck caused by the heart attack of the engineer, or at a polio epidemic, and we cry: "Isn't this just like God?" [32] We argue that good men in this world ought to prosper materially (e.g., in long years and a large bank account) in the strict measure of their goodness, and that bad men should proportionately suffer material loss. But when we look at life we can find no such fairness or impartiality. Then we denounce God, and declare that we will have nothing more to do with him. As if we and our world could be anywhere except in the encompassing Mystery! Occasionally we have fits of doubt about our definition of justice. As for long life, Jesus did not live very long, and many a criminal is an octogenarian; and, as we watch the two die, we are not so sure about number of years being the measure of reward. As for material recompense, it is fleeting at best, and often proves anything but the best. If prosperity corrupts, and the instances are legion, is it blessing? If adversity chastens, and again there is no lack of evidence, is it punishment? Very occasionally we ask if any man is "good," and what would happen to *us* if we received just what we deserve. But we dismiss these doubts. We pour oil on our angers to see how fiercely they can burn. *We* know what justice is (though we don't!), and God is *not* just! So we hate God and fulminate against his ramshackle world. This hate made Calvary and tells us why armed soldiers could curse and strike a helpless Christ.

Yet we love God even when we try to hate him. Have not men spoken age on age about the Good, the Beautiful, and the True? Have they not spelled the words with capital letters? Do we not constantly inquire, "Is there any word from the Lord?" [33] The current skepticism which says too quickly, "No, there is not!" does not disprove either the longing or the hope. *Waiting for Godot* [34] tells us that God never arrives, yet men have spoken for ages of his coming. He finds us through the joys of the natural world, for storms, though their evil and violence remain, only punctuate the loveliness and the mercy. Harvest fields bring forth bread, the moon rises golden red over the lake, and our physical life is a very zest. Then we love God who is in, through, and beyond nature. We love him for the working of his spirit in our fellow men, so that we gaze and gaze at "The Winged Victory" in the Louvre, and listen and listen to the slow movement in Beethoven's *Seventh Symphony*. We love him for his daily providence in a world in which our whole life had changed if even one atom had changed. We love him, as we look at the photographs in our home, for the affections which compass our mortal life. We love him because, at the very moment when we are tempted by the devil, he tempts us to some compassionate cause at risk or to some white vigil; and because every man is at times tempted to be St. Francis.

Why does the "despair" of our time forget the joys of life? Samuel Beckett has said, when asked for the meaning of his play, *Waiting for Godot,* "If I knew, I would have said so in the play." [35] But that answer makes even the literary effort a species of nonsense. A child's picture of a boat may be such that everyone on board would be pitched into the sea, but the child at least knows what the picture means. Meanwhile Beckett takes joy in the theater, or he could not write with such appeal, and presumably he is ready to go on living on the royalties. Thus Sartre's "despair" likewise seems to be histrionic figure skating round and round a black hole in the ice: he is enjoying his protested "misery." As for Camus, my own admiration has devoured his every book, but I still cannot understand why he should shroud life under the term "absurd." [36] If by "absurd" he means that life cannot be corralled under our bloodless scientific formulas or our finespun webs of philosophy, he is right, and he thus brings us back to the glad or poignant thrust of the event. But if he means that life is merely comic or cruel, then we cannot agree. Both the doctor and the priest in *The Plague* [37]—the city called Earth is plague-stricken with all lines of communication cut—still knew they must minister to the victims of the plague, in however vain a hope. Therefore they knew not only that there is something authentic in human nature, but that they and every man are under constraint of *Love.* They knew that the lines are not cut. Camus' novels in their chronological sequence show a certain movement. Had he lived he might have explored the "something authentic" and the Constraint. Surely in the desolution of our times that is our present task.

Meanwhile we shall go on loving God even while we hate him. That ambivalence is written in an anonymous poem in regard to Christ.[88] There is first the hatred:

148

> Go, bitter Christ, grim Christ! haul if Thou wilt
> Thy bloody cross to Thine own bleak Calvary!
> When did I bid Thee suffer for my Guilt?

But the writer loved Christ even while he hated him, and longed for Christ even while trying to evict him:

> O King, O Captain, wasted, wan with scourging,
> Strong beyond speech, and wonderful with woe,
> Whither, relentless wilt Thou still be urging
> Thy maimed and halt that have not strength to go? . . .
> Peace, peace, I follow. Why must we love Thee so?

We cannot truly appraise the modern hatred of God until we see it as one term in an ambivalence. The man who cries out on God, "Must thy harvest fields be dung'd with rotten death?" [39] is not a blasphemer (he was in fact a most devout worshiper): he is in conflict. He may be much nearer God than a conventional churchgoer. Why? Because joy and pain, neither of which should be denied (as these words were being written word came that a plane has just gone down in Lake Michigan with twenty-seven people on board), leave us in conflict until we find, or are found by, some interpreting and transforming Word.

The rebel helps other men confront the reality of pain and evil. He pursues knowledge but is still aware that knowledge without reverence is doomed, and he cannot find room for reverence. Yet he finds room for compassion, and the Old Testament says of the compassions of King Josiah, "Is not this to know Me?" [40] and the New Testament quotes Christ concerning those who yearn over their jailed or hungry neighbors, "Truly, I say to you, as you did it to one of the least of these my brethren, you did it to me." [41] Meanwhile God comes and keeps coming in the twin mysteries of joy and pain—in an atomic science which suddenly knows that science itself is doomed unless men can learn to love, and in a Medgar Evers [42] shot to death in his own driveway because he believed that all men are brothers beneath the skin. All this brings us back to the Word without whom both joy and pain leave us under judgment without mercy (Camus' *The Fall*) or in the ambivalence of hate and love.

V

As for Christ, it is unthinkable that he could ever sell out to escapism. One wonders if our all-too-easy cult of "personality" and success, though it is preached in some churches, ever remembers that the Jesus (whom it is supposed to preach) was nailed up by the hands and died as a common criminal. There was no martyr complex in him. He loved life, healed folk, saw in all things the parable of God, spoke deeply of joy, and prayed for continued years—until it became clear that this was not his destined mission. Then he walked with open eyes straight into pain, and refused any opiate. His deepest pain was that inflicted by human pride: he was cast out by his home, by the rulers of his nation, by the crowds of the city over which he wept, and at last by his own close friends. He thus told us that the secret of pain is not on this side of pain, least of all for the man who tries to sidestep it, but clean through pain—on the other side.

Likewise he was no stoic. He accepted life both in its joys and its sorrows. He liked dinner parties and good conversation. He rejoiced in friendship. He saw in field and sky a deeper handwriting. He was glad at weddings, and wept at funerals. But he lived and breathed another friendship. Stoicism is not the best bravery: it comes closer to a deliberate dulling of life. It has certain courage, but yet is pitiable, not least because it forbids pity. It tries to turn our heart of flesh into a heart of stone, but never succeeds. It becomes withdrawn and thus isolated both from its own true life and from the joys and pains of other men. Jesus "set his face" [43] like a flint (that is almost the idiom in the Greek text), but only the resolve was flint: the adventure to which he set his face was the vital poignancy of joy and sorrow, the journey to the Cross.

Likewise Jesus was no rebel against God. He rebelled against the devil's work in our world, and his anger flamed against cruel men who trample or deceive the weak. But as for God, God was in him accepting pain—to triumph over it, by walking straight into ignominious death to conquer death. Why should Camus assume that cruelty comes from God while compassion is our virtue? Why did not Beckett remember that long ago there was One who lived and died for a man led by a chain or rope? As for the church, it is shabby enough but yet knows its own shabbiness. If the rebel-skeptic who pours ridicule on the church should ever wish to see a thorough job of dissection, he should go to a preachers' conference. Meanwhile the church stands, despite its own perfidies and despite the skeptic's scorn. It stands better than government or business or art. The attacks may be other than justified attacks. Perhaps (this is written by one who knows the failures of the church and his own share in them)—perhaps inner conflict, not to mention self-hate, always seeks a whipping post and finds some poor transitory comfort in applying the whip. Truth is still through the event, and only then through the church. Which Event? So we turn from ways of suffering that are aside from the Breakthrough to ways which walk in the New Age.

10. The Way of Suffering

II. Via the Breakthrough

Somewhere there is a story, which prompts an instant and painful, "Oh, no!" of a man imprisoned for years in a cell with an unlocked door, because he had never tried the door. The story is the more painful because it goes on to say that outside the door there was welcome and an open road to home. New Testament faith does not pretend that the door of pain-and-evil is always unlocked, but it does claim that Christ has given us the key, and that genuine life awaits us beyond the door. We now ask about the way of suffering in that faith. Escapism, stoicism, and rebellion are still locked in, for these roads all prove to be dead-end streets. What of faith in the Breakthrough?

Life is a journey, not a debate. The modern demand, "Prove it to me!" is a poor affair. For it is actually saying: "My rational mind is my god, and my god sits at home ringing up pros and cons. Don't ask my god to take any journeys, still less any chances." Such a mind is not even alive, for all that lives must venture. Every man must take his chance—on pilgrimage through joy and sorrow. Suffering with its ground of gladness is an encounter to be met in some faith vague or clear, not a "problem" to be solved by argument and "proven theory." We begin the journey as soon as we are born. Children cannot be spared it, despite foolish parents who say in a time of grief, "Why do we tell *them* anything about it—yet?" For children have their own pain which in their smaller powers is as hard to bear as the adult burden. Parents can partly shield their children from the storm, but they cannot dismiss the storm. One pilgrim can help another, "This is how I have met pain." But we are all on the journey, and we cannot wait for answers. As to pain and evil the academic answer is never found or given. But the New Testament folk say not only that they have found the way, but that they have been found of a healing and redeeming Presence.

The New Testament points to Christ, living, dying on a Cross, and raised from the dead, and then says, "He is the Way." [1] The New Testament does not claim that he is the neat rational explanation. Such a claim would take away chance of courage. It would reduce life to an exercise in geometry, with the answers at the back of the book and all the necessary "steps" supplied. In the New Testament the mystery of pain and evil is not "solved." It knows that evil is evil, and that pain is incipient death, but refuses to say that God "sends" evil, for God is good. Yet it is driven to confess that God "allows" evil. The New English Bible has that confession from the lips of Christ in regard to Peter's testing which would come with the death of his Master and the threat of Peter's own death: "Simon, Simon, take heed: Satan has been given leave to sift. . . you like wheat; but for you I have prayed that your faith may not fail." [2] The translation is not strictly justified, for the Greek reads more like, "Satan has demanded to have you for the sifting as wheat," but the New English Bible rendering is certainly implied, for "demanded" means of One who can grant or deny the presumptuous claim. Even so, we are not told *why* God thus had dealings with Satan, much less how there can be suffering, with its accompanying evil and its encroachment of death— in the Godhead.

But we *are* told that God raised Jesus Christ from the dead. That is to say, there has been a Breakthrough, a Daybreak, the beginning of a New Age. Nothing less can account for New Testament joy. The light is flung back on the Cross, for since the Word of God is in Christ's triumph over death, that same Word is in his cross: God is in the midst

153

of sin to cancel sin's ruinous power, and in the midst of pain to transform
it in such grace that a gallows becomes the focus of our adoration. The
light is flung back on all creation, for God made the worlds by that
same Word: "All things were made through him, and without him was
not anything made that was made." [3] So evil and pain, by whatever
mystery they entered the natural world and the historical order, have been
under control from "the foundation of the world." [4] Pain and evil, though
real enough in our broken world, are inferior, servile, and transient.
Nay, more: they are already overcome, they and their main garrison in
man's transgressions, for God has raised Christ from the dead. This
faith can be trusted or refused. But it cannot be whittled down by proposing that "we are getting rid of evil" when manifestly we are not, or
that Jesus is one more man making one somewhat nobler guess. New
Testament faith has split history into before and after. It is just such a
shattering faith, though in gentleness. It is the Springtime of human
story, or it is nothing. We simply falsify the New Testament unless we
say of the men who wrote it:

> They spoke, I think, of perils past.
> They spoke, I think, of peace at last.
> One thing I remember:
> Spring came on forever,
> Spring came on forever.[5]

The tremendous Event does not rest on our "thinking" or "remembering": it is written in the life and joy of New Testament life, and in the
witness of the Christian years. There is a "great divide" between the
Old Testament and the New. On one side the rivers run into the Dead
Sea, though men living there keep saying, "There may be joy beyond
that mountain range." On the other side the rivers run into "a sea of
glass mingled with fire," [6] into a new Red Sea through which God has
carried his own to a new Promised Land. Most books, even books within
the faith of Christ, seem to hear with only dim ears this note of redemption and joy. But if the Jewish funeral service is set down side by side
with the New Testament funeral service the difference fairly shouts, even
though most "Christian" burials still mute the glad triumph. Faith in
Christ sets the whole issue of pain and evil in the Daybreak. Thus a

154

disciple whose sufferings sear the mind even in our mere reading yet says in throbbing joy: "For this slight momentary affliction is preparing us for an eternal weight of glory.[7] We cannot laugh off such testimony. He continues: "He who has prepared us for this very thing is God, who has given us the Spirit"—of the raised Christ—"as a guarantee." [8] There is a Breakthrough—*the* Breakthrough. Pain and evil are viewed in the light of a new and staggering Event, and they are met in a new purpose and power. We now trace this new Way of Suffering.

I

These pilgrims accept pain. Acceptance is perhaps the key word, acceptance of what we cannot change, acceptance of both joy and pain. Yet it is a poor word, because all words pale before that Light. The acceptance is not morbid, still less a masochism. It is not cringing submission which says resignedly, "It is the will of God," as if the will of God were a dark tyranny. Jesus said that "my food is to do the will of him who sent me"[9]: God's will is like meat to a starving man. God's will is welcome to the prodigal, and healing to those who suffer. So what word shall we use? Acceptance is still, perhaps, the best we can find, provided we remember that sometimes in New Testament faith it means a challenge met concerning what we *can* change, sometimes appropriation, and sometimes outright welcome; but never a martyr-complex, never a pretense that evil is not evil, and never a dull stoicism.

We know what the word "acceptance" means in modern psychiatry. The psychiatrist accepts his patient without any initial praise or blame but only with intent to uncover the mental ill and to cure it. Thus the fine faith of this new branch of healing says of the patient: "This man is a candidate for health." If the man is so unruly or ugly that the doctor cannot establish empathy, he refers the man to another doctor. He is slow to accept an intimate friend as patient, for in such a case the necessary realism is harder to establish. There is a stage in the healing when the hidden hostilities of the patient fasten on the doctor who then "accepts" the hostility, knowing it to be a stage toward his patient's health. Then he leads the man to "accept" himself and to accept his world. The man must not be perfectionist on the one hand, demanding more of himself than human nature can bear, or too self-indulgent on the other hand so that he curses his circumstances to evade self-knowledge.

Psychiatric "acceptance" on the part of doctor or patient is beset by thronging questions even while it wins our gratitude. We are told that if the patient confronts reality and can gather confidence, the lesions in the psyche begin to heal. But what is "reality"? Not a mirror, for a man might cut himself on a mirror; and not anything merely "objective," for it heals. As for "confidence," in whom should the patient be "confident"? Not in the psychiatrist, for that would make the patient "dependent"; and not in himself, for he has come for healing because he lacks confidence. Then in whom or Whom? We should not ask the psychiatrist to desert his fine ministry to answer these questions, any more than we should ask a surgeon to substitute the reading of the New Testament for his surgery. Life has its complementary areas and functions. But each of us as men confronts the questions, for they underlie all other questions. Meanwhile we can be grateful for the modern word "acceptance." Paul Tillich uses it to tell us that our decision is this: Do I will to accept God's acceptance of me?[10]

So acceptance means to accept God's acceptance of us. In Christ God has overcome the sin that slew Christ, for God raised him from the dead. So sin is canceled in love, and sin's stronghold of pain is broken, for the worst pain comes from man's transgressions. Perhaps *all* evil thus comes, as issue from Adam's presumptuous pride, Adam being prototype of our humanity. In any event, "other" pain, the "plus" of natural and historical evil, could be borne but for the misery-penalty of human pride with its inevitable envy and strife. But this central bastion of pain-and-evil is now breached and broken. New Testament faith accepts this deliverance, not of our deserving, but in spite of our undeserving. Then, because God has thus accepted us, we can accept ourselves. "Reality" and "confidence" are now grounded in God. That is why psychiatry is blessing. Then joy can be accepted with double joy, because the happiness which all men know in measure, and which our modern "despair" seems resolved to ignore, is itself now not a poor transient gleam but is "rooted and grounded in love." [11] The Masefield creed which of itself is only "optimism," is now anchored in eternity:

> Best trust the happy moments. What they gave
> Makes man less fearful of the certain grave,

And gives his work compassion and new eyes:
The days that make us happy make us wise.[12]

All days now "make us happy"! Incidentally John Masefield wrote these lines in the title page of my copy of his poems. But the book was stolen from our living room, presumably by some autograph-hunter or book-collector. So now I must accept both the joy and the pain, for both are held in God's love-conquering grace.

Acceptance gladly takes a further step, as we continue to write about joy which we may refuse and pain which we cannot evade. That further step is welcome. H. Wheeler Robinson[13] has called attention to the hidden meaning in the line, a meaning justified in the Hebrew:

Weeping may tarry for the night,
but joy comes with the morning.[14]

The words "tarry for a night" mean "come as an overnight guest." In the evening-light the guest looks like a thug. He may carry daggers. Even so we must welcome him, according to the Arab and now deeper Christian law of hospitality. God knows all about him, for God has had the mystery of pain and death in his control from the beginning. It is useless when such a guest arrives to be afraid or stoical or rebellious: he has come "in the order of Providence." So the guest must be welcomed, the guest-room made fair with flowers, and the best meal prepared. Then we find in the morning light (the morning of this world or the Morning beyond death) that the thug is actually sent to befriend us; or the ugly guest disappears, to be followed by glad shouting: "Joy comes with the morning." [15]

Yet acceptance always spells renunciation of our will, at least in regard to constitutional pain. Earthquakes shake our world. History in its dark entail collects its fee. Our guilty blunders bring wretchedness, with double wretchedness when we see the pain they inflict on other men. Compassion invites many a pang. Length of years is host to growing weakness, and death waits every man round any corner. What to do? Not to accept in stoicism, for that itself is a dull death in the midst of life; not to rebel, for rebellion adds bitterness to the burden; not to escape, for there is no escape, and cowardice also compounds the pain. New

Testament faith *accepts,* in the sunrise of Christ's resurrection and in the mercy of Christ's cross. It kisses the spear, and finds that the spear carries not poison, but life.

II

But acceptance is sometimes the acceptance of a challenge—to change what can and should be changed. But, such is life, this acceptance brings a further nobler pain, as any man knows who enlists in a dangerous and compassionate cause. New Testament faith never asks us to say of a nasty swamp or a Negro ghetto, "It is there, and it is God's will." It is not God's will, for the very word "God" is bound up with the word "good." Swamps and ghettoes are not good. I know a man who at one time refused to shovel the snow from his driveway to his store because "God sent the snow." But maybe God sent it as challenge. Without challenge life would be misery. Thus acceptance means acceptance of a challenge and the fulfillment of a task—in love of men. The snow should be removed lest our neighbors flounder or lose their footing on ice. The swamp can and should be drained lest people suffer from malaria. The ghetto should give place to decent homes where men live together without any petty and ridiculous pride in the pigmentation of their skin. There are valleys in the Painted Desert which now blossom as the rose because men by God's grace have brought in water. Surely the new garden is God's will, not the former desert.

Yet this acceptance, while it eliminates pain for some men, invites pain for those who undertake the task. It has been written that dishonest mortar was responsible in part for the San Francisco earthquake. All right: we must take issue with men who use dishonest mortar, as Jesus took issue with traders who traded with undue profits on the ignorance of the poor, and thrust their booths into the temple court of the gentiles as they would never have thrust them into the inner court of the Jews.[16] So Christ in anger overturned their booths. Yet not with impunity! He died because of economic and racial "radicalism," and because of "passivity" in his country's nationalistic pride, as well as for what his foes deemed theological heresy. So now the answer to pain for New Testament faith is invitation to another kind of pain! As these words were written, the newspaper came with account of a speech given before a luncheon club. The speaker was well-heeled. The speech took account of the present violence of our streets and said in word and in effect that "unless there is more respect for property rights" the country is going to the dogs. If property rights are always to come before human rights, things before men, perhaps we deserve that fate. G. K. Chesterton spoke of "the easy speeches that comfort cruel men"![17] So the acceptance of a challenge is no sinecure: it invites pain, as witness three bodies in Mississippi clay.

But there are warning signals in regard to the New Testament acceptance of a challenge. The acceptance is in the name of a faith (Christ crucified and raised), not in the name of a human pride. The proper word is, "This I do as witness to God's grace in Christ," or "This I do to testify that human life is precious" (the implicit humanist creed), *not,* "This I do because human skill can get rid of pain, and because I have found the final ideology." Between those two attitudes there is a great gulf set. Human skill cannot get rid of all evil and pain. The attempt, as in our wars to end wars, has multiplied pain. As for any ideology, it is the final conceit, the incredible pride that claims to have found the ultimate pattern of man's life for all coming time. We accept a challenge as witnesses, not as conceited architects of civilization. That dear lad, the hero of J. D. Salinger's *Catcher in the Rye,* rubbed out a dirty word on the wall, and then thought of all the dirty words on all the walls! [18] We do what we can and all we can—as witnesses to the Breakthrough. We bear the new pain. Then we remember what Jesus said, that we should get rid of weeds as far as we can, and after that "let both grow together until the harvest." [19] Someday we may be ready to confront his realism. Yet the Daybreak-faith makes us sure that the whole field is in the control of "the Lord of the harvest." [20] So we tackle removable pain, whether in slums or in a hospital, as witnesses to the Event, not as if we were Atlas.

The other warning is as sharp: We shall not know what love of neighbor means except in that love which suffered on the Cross and raised Christ from the dead. No word has suffered more abuse than the word "love." Homes are broken, shame is spread, and children are left forlorn because this woman's husband and that man's wife established a "love-nest." Or a child is born out of marriage, to carry a lifelong stigma, because "we loved one another." Or parents indulge their children because "we love them, and we remember how little we had when we were their age." How are we to know what love is? All wisdom is *given,* not devised by our minds, for we are creatures, and we shall know love only as genuine love is given—in the Word made flesh, dying, and raised from the grave:

> Thrice blest whose lives are faithful prayers,
>   Whose loves in higher love endure;
>   What souls possess themselves so pure,
> Or is there blessedness like theirs?[21]

Faith in answer to the Breakthrough accepts the challenge to change what should and can be changed, and does so in love, the Breakthrough itself giving the manner and the power.

III

We propose now three words to describe the Breakthrough faith in regard to pain and evil. These we shall explore in subsequent chapters. In this chapter they are only summarized. The first is this: *we travel learning.* There is little to be learned from suffering *in itself,* for the entail of suffering in itself is death. But where there is a catalyst in the bitter waters, the catalyst being the Event of Christ, the waters are changed so that they grant us knowledge and wisdom. This fact holds also our joys, which *of themselves* tempt us to a silly "self-reliance" (as if death were not already stalking us) or a sillier false optimism. The Old Testament has a story of a tree being flung into a brackish pool to sweeten it so that Israel could then drink what beforehand would have poisoned them.[22] No, the tree was not the Cross, despite some preachers (except by some profound doctrine of the preexistent Word), but it is a foreshadowing and parable of Christ in the deadly stream of our pain. This learning from pain and evil is not perfect in this world: there are no human angels, and

> Life, like a dome of many-coloured glass,
> Stains the white radiance of Eternity.[23]

Faith is often checkered by doubt, for our minds are finite and our will wavers. But faith returns, not least by the venture of prayer, and we travel learning from both joy and sorrow.

Thus Bill Smith who lives on Main Street in any town says with better wisdom than any philosophy could give him, "Experience is a great teacher." He means dark experience as well as the bright stretches of the road. Irvin Cobb has a book filled with laughter entitled *Speaking of Operations*.[24] In retrospect he can see the comic side of life in a hospital. He did not tell, though he would have told had it happened to him, of one hospital victim, who, having been punctured with this syringe-needle and that syringe-needle, and having been poked by this doctor and that interne, saw to his horror a man arriving with a large bucket and mop. "What's your racket?" asked the shrinking victim. Said the man, "I've come to wash your transom." Why do we all like to speak of operations? Because to that measure we "have proved ourselves," or, rather, since that phrase savors of our incorrigible pride, because we have known ourselves undergirded and strengthened. This knowledge is of a deeper kind if we accept the challenge of what ought to be changed, with the accompanying vicarious pain. Thus a missionary doctor in China, stoned in the Boxer uprising, exclaimed with blood running down his face: "Now I am a follower of Christ." In a wisdom beyond words he could speak of "the power of his resurrection" because he had shared "the fellowship of his sufferings." [25]

It is no back-tracking, but only an underscoring, to remark that pain teaches how much human kindness (as well as how much indifference) comes with pain. No back-tracking, for Jesus made the same remark: "For I was hungry and you gave me food, I was thirsty and you gave me drink, I was a stranger and you welcomed me, I was naked and you clothed me, I was sick and you visited me, I was in prison and you came to me." [26] Through suffering we know this human kindness— and can then share it. Perhaps suffering is not too great a price to pay for such a boon. If we rail at pain instead of accepting pain, we shall not fully know this sympathy or share it. Sartre hardly mentions it. Our modern cult of "nothingness" and "despair" ignores it. Sometimes skepticism contrasts the kindly humanist with the pharisaic "Christian," though the contrast is in gross disproportion, for a genuine faith in Christ has girdled the globe with hospitals and hospitable homes which humanism did not build. Jesus never discounted this friendship by describing it as "humanism": he called it the bond between God and man because it is of God. Therefore of those who befriend their neighbors his astonishing word: "Come, O blessed of my Father, inherit the kingdom prepared for you from the foundation of the world"! [27] So we may not brag about any kindness we may show, though that was Abou Ben Adhem's wretched pride in a wretched poem. Abou asked a visiting angel what he was writing, and when the angel answered that he was keeping tabulation of "those who love the Lord," Abou asked again if his name was registered. The answer being, "Nay, not so," Abou answered "cheerily":

> I pray thee, then,
> Write me as one that loves his fellow-men.[28]

The prig! If Abou *really* loved his neighbor, the angel goofed, for he had forgotten what Jesus said, and Abou's name should have been entered! Again, if Abou really loved his fellow men he could not have bragged about it. Those of whom Jesus spoke were astonished to find they had done anything of merit! When shall we understand that what is *in* life comes *from* the Creative Source? When shall we learn to live in gratitude rather than in self-assertion? Acceptance of pain teaches us just such thankfulness.

And a deeper wisdom! My mother, when her children were sick-abed would say, "Flat on your back? It's a good position from which to look up!" But only if the "position" is accepted, not if we become stoics or rebels. When pain and evil strike, they trace the line between the two dimensions of our mortal life. We cry, "I am mortal!" Then, knowing we are mortal, standing therefore above mortality, we cry, "Where is my salvation?" Then, aware of what Berdyaev calls our "God-forsakenness," [29] we cry again, "O God!"—and the door is opened to his coming. For those who have marveled at the Breakthrough he is already present. How else could we know? Not from pain in itself: only from pain under the catalyst of the recognized or unrecognized Christ. In the approach of death our poor earthly props are broken. Then we can rail: "Must Thy harvest fields be dung'd with rotten death?" [30] or we can pose as stoics, "Well, that's the way things are!" or we can pray, and, if we trust the Great Event, we can know him present with us. It's a safe guess that most men will go on praying. The modern "God is dead" proposal means that God is not and never was, for a God who can die is not God; and it means that the mind which pretends to trace

God's living and dying is its own idol-god; and it means that all our words (our "earth" which hints heaven and our "time" which acknowledges eternity) are nonsense. By pain of disciplined mind plus the uprush of the mysterious subconscious, scientists and poets alike come to their discoveries, which are God's gift before they are man's finding. By pain of poverty and rejection Debussy's gift was refined as by a "refiner's fire," [31] until he gave a new turn to music in such subtlety that he distilled poignancy into peace. These instances are road signs from a distance pointing to the truth that has become incarnate in the Cross and the Resurrection. By pain, under the catalyst of the gospel, we learn of God.

III

The next word in "acceptance" is this: *we travel loving*. The "manner of love" is made clear in Christ. He "accepted" even a cross still telling us that we are God's children, and praying "Father, forgive them." [32] So we accept man's contumely or nature's evil, not pretending that we are ever free from the transgression that deserves the pain, but knowing from Christ that if this "weight" is "accepted" it can become wings. Such acceptance on our part is hard to come by, as the priest found in Camus' *The Plague*. He was prone at first to say in judgment that the city deserved the plague, thus forgetting his own guilt. When the compassionate and unbelieving doctor took issue (since pain is still a mystery), the priest changed his moralistic tune: he admitted that "the love of God is a hard love." [33] So it is, an impossible love indeed without another Spirit. Yet it is measurably possible, though still streaked and fitful, to those who trust the Breakthrough.

Thus we try to love our neighbor in our pain. We know that the wheel-chair patient who is acid and cantankerous is a pest. We know for ourselves that we ought not to daub our misery on our neighbors, and they know (whatever their measure of sympathy) that we ought not to darken their day. The Seventy-third Psalm has a man roundly cursing the scheme of things for its manifest "injustice" but suddenly stopping in the middle of the diatribe:

If I had said, "I will speak thus,"
I would have been untrue to the generation of thy children.

> But when I thought how to understand this,
> it seemed to me a wearisome task,
> until I went into the sanctuary of God.[34]

When he thought on God, even though he came before the time of Christ, he knew his fulminations were a perverse enjoyment of his cursing, with no issue except bitterness and emptiness. So our "tragedy" accepted becomes cleansing both for us and our neighbors. We should and can think of them. They are watching. For love's sake we should act in a decent courage. This love goes far to overcome pain. A loving mother hardly knows weariness as she tends her sick child, though she is weary. The martyr literally finds that his agony of fire is caught up in apocalypse. In any event *we travel loving* our neighbor.

Likewise we travel trying to love God. The priest was right: it is "a hard love" when we look at plague and tidal wave, but not when we look on Christ whom God raised from the dead. Unless we love God, even in a vague and uncertain faith, we cannot long love our neighbor, for any worthy love of our neighbor sees in him a "value" (wretched word!) too precious to be the plaything of cancer or drought. That is, the best humanism honors in every man that which binds him to eternity, that in short for which Christ died and was raised. Our political speeches are filled with windy talk about "brotherhood." As for me I find it very hard to love my brother man in a subway rush or when he holds me up on a dark street on a dark night, unless I keep looking on Christ. Then I can measurably love him—in the natural and historical evil which we share, in the pain which he may inflict on me, and even in the pain which I inflict on him. Is any realistic love possible unless all men are held in love? Artificial respiration is not artificial: it is the special use of the air first given to all men. "We love," by means of transformed pain, "because he first loved us." [35] Indeed, the love of God, acknowledged or unacknowledged, articulate or inarticulate, always precedes the love of men. The vertical of the Cross, the line between God and men, is first set; then the crossbeam, the line between man and man, else it falls.

IV

The third word is this: By night or day we *travel worshiping*. Worship is the inevitable movement of the creature toward the Creator. In-

THE WAY OF SUFFERING: BREAKTHROUGH

evitable because, if it is thwarted, it does not die but takes false forms. If we do not worship God, we shall not cease to worship: we shall worship the state (as in Hitlerism) or an economic system (as in Marxism, which is so all-compelling a worship that people in the "cult of personality" do not count); or we "adore" success or comfort. Public worship, even at its poorest, even though it may be only half-aware of God, is yet the salvation of the state, for it saves the state from self-idolatry. But how to worship God in the midst of pain? By the disclosure of God in the Breakthrough! At Calvary God's own Man worshiped in very agony and death: "Father, into thy hands I commit my spirit." [36] We are not Christ, but we can live in his Spirit, for he is raised from the dead.

Any man understands that to worship God only in fine weather is a shabby affair. It savors of the blasphemy which would pat God on the back with, "Keep it up! You're doing fine!" Who are we to know what is "fine"? Besides, in the Breakthrough God has shared our pain, even at the cost of Calvary. What right have we to "ditch" God or charge him with less wisdom than we can boast whenever things go wrong? The hymn, "Now Thank We All Our God," [37] so they say, was written in the midst of plague. That fact, if it be fact, does not downgrade the hymn. Our Thanksgiving Proclamations have too often thanked God for our prosperity (which is right to do), while other lands go hungry (which charges God with favoritism or credits us with special virtue). The church is castigated in our time, and sometimes deserves the whipping. Yet many times my telephone has rung in the night, and a voice has said: "Father has just died. Please come and say with us the Twenty-third Psalm." At such a time and place the words come alive:

> Even though I walk through the valley of the shadow of death,
>   I fear no evil;
> for thou art with me;
>
> . . . .
> Thou preparest a table before me
>   in the presence of my enemies;[38]

even in the face of the enemy called death! Such a faith is its own proof. There is no argument against such worship: it has its own "Hallelujah Chorus" in the midst of grief:

Surely goodness and mercy shall follow me
all the days of my life;
and I shall dwell in the house of the Lord
for ever.[39]

We cannot explain the pain, but this can be said: Pain gives us the chance to offer God an unbribed worship, a love untraduced by "prosperity."

When a child dies, to offer him to God is not easy. When an operation confronts us, to offer that as strange gift to the Giver of all life is no sinecure. But we may lose the child in shadows and doubts unless we thus worship, and the operation may become a dull stoicism or even the bitterness of rebellion. "Great peace have those who love thy law" [40] of love made known and made present in Christ! Would we rather that Christ had died quietly and safely in his bed? Would we rather he had died cursing God instead of praying? No. Then why don't we confirm his own strange choice? If we keep asking that question we shall not find an academic answer to "the problem of pain," but we may find a way that leads to light. Paul was a true disciple. That word means "learner." He said, though probably through the lips of one who was devoted to him, "I am now ready to be offered." [41] Paul thus speaks of his approaching martyrdom. The word "offered" means "poured out as a libation on an altar." Thus the new translation: "I am already on the point of being sacrificed." There is no rebellion in Paul, but on the contrary all joy, for he is one in joy with "all who have loved" Christ's "appearing." [42] Would we rather Paul had escaped from prison to die in hiding? No, that "offered" is a grand affair. It is instinct with worship. It opens our clay-shuttered eyes. Surely Paul at that moment was not unvisited.

V

These are high matters. No man can explore such a lonely-bright-quivering land without clumsiness. Yet we shall try. For the present we have proposed that only by faith in the Breakthrough can pain-and-evil be stopped on their way to death, and turned into dark angels. If we ask petulantly or angrily, "Why has this happened to me?" there is no answer, for the question is locked in "me," and is therefore locked. When a parishioner whose son had just been killed in battle demanded of his minister, "Where was God when my son was killed?" the minister answered, "Just where he was when his own Son was killed." If we say stoically, "That's the way things are," we are in a little better light, but we are still pulling down the shades. If we rebel, we are acknowledging God but denying the strange Event of Christ. If we say, looking at the Cross and the Resurrection, "This I believe, and in this trust I try to live," our weak hands are caught and held in other Hands, though we still can find no words in which to capsule that vitality. It was a man like ourselves, a man with blood on his guilty hands, a man who had to tear out life by the roots to get rid of his pride of rank and pride of mind, who said, "For the sake of Christ, then, I am content with weaknesses, insults, hardships, persecutions, and calamities; for when I am weak, then I am strong." [43] Psychiatrists think him a bigot, even though he wrote in his Letter to the Galatian Church a charter of freedom. Humanists think him a dogmatist, even though he wrote a poem on love which has brought glad tears to countless eyes. Theologians reckoned him "old stuff" for a time, but now, after two world wars, return to him in "the theological revival." His word is rooted—in Christ.

To learn from pain, to love in the midst of it, to offer pain as worship is not easy. Do we wish such ease? Perhaps our present "despair" *is* easy, for what is easier than to curse our fate? It was easy enough for Ulysses to thrash with chains the flooded river that barred the path of his armies, easy—and futile. Half-success in "acceptance" is better than "no bread," for the God who has visited us in Christ and raised him from the dead takes our poor intention for our deed. My students are fond of telling how the Sea of Galilee has clear water because the River Jordan flows through it, whereas the Dead Sea is dead because it has no exit. The parable flatters our activisms. But the Dead Sea does have exit—upward. It surrenders to the burning sky. Therefore, the scientists tell us, there are deposits of potash around its shores, enough to fertilize all earth's fields for five centuries. That also is a parable. There was no exit at Calvary, except upward. There under a burning sky that seemed to have no eyes a Man offered himself and his pain to God. It would be sacrilege to try to point the moral! So: no moral. Only Life.

11. Pain as Cleansing

The Breakthrough, the Event by which we know
that pain and death have been dealt the fatal blow, does not remove
suffering, for suffering is constitutional in this world. Indeed it increases
suffering for those who trust the Breakthrough, for they now take on
themselves the sufferings of their neighbors in obedience to the behest of
Christ: "A new commandment I give to you, that you love one another;
even as I have loved you, that you also love one another!" [1] He loved
us by way of an accepted Cross. So we, though only as his empowered
servants, try to love our neighbors.

Honesty requires a further acknowledgment: The Breakthrough does
not dispel the mystery of pain. We still do not know from what lair
the snake came on Adam and Eve. We still cannot answer the oft-
repeated question: "Why does God allow evil?" Since writing the last
chapter I have read two more books on the vast theme of God and pain,
each of which attempts an intellectual answer to the enigma.[2] Both leave
me not only unconvinced, but rebellious, for not even a toothache can be
intellectualized; neither book comes within hailing distance of the man
who watched his six children killed in a railroad-crossing accident and
whose wife died a little time later in childbirth. The Breakthrough does

not tell us why the devil has so much power in our world. Yes, we shall continue to say "devil," though without any dogmatism, because that name best interprets our experience, as when we exclaim under the threat of senseless or malicious cruelty "What the devil!" To children of the Breakthrough God will still at times seem outrightly cruel, and because they have compassion the pain of the world will itself bring an agony of pain.

But the Breakthrough means that pain and evil are parasitic, however real; and transitory even though dark in dismay. This is our deep surmise even without the Breakthrough. The Event of Christ validates the surmise: joy is the ground of our life. Nay, more: the Breakthrough assures us that God is in control, that pain is always within his bounds, and that the devil is his servant. So pain is in a new climate. We need not now spend endless hours probing for the *origin* of pain in our world, for the question has changed to, "What is the *purpose* of pain?"

I

We shall be wise to pause on that last sentence. Perhaps the cult of origins has been for years a will-o'-the-wisp. We ask, "What is the origin of human life?" and end in the fear or the sarcasm that we are "descended from monkeys." Or we ask, "What is the origin of religion?" and conclude that all religion is a mass or a mess of superstition. By the test of origins science itself is made a mockery, for science began in the original curiosity, the first monkey searching for the first flea. It is now clear in any realm of study that every new event has a veritable newness and cannot be predicted or predicated from its antecedents. Events do not *come from* evolution: they *arise in* evolution. The very word "evolution" is therefore superficial, for what we confront is continuing emergence. Perhaps the better word is "creation." In a jolly book called *The Cruise of the Kawa*,[3] a take-off on travelogues, the crew finds a bird which always flies backwards. The reason? It doesn't give a red cent where it is headed but must know where it started! Can any man living in time hope to discover time's origin?

While we are discussing our futile cult of origins, we may as well pay our respects and disrespects to the modern emphasis on the word "problem." This cult is the bad fruit, amid many good harvests, of our over-

169

stress on science. We propose that marriage is a problem. Then we look for a formula as clear as an equation in geometry, or as instant as the bestowals of a vending machine; and if we do not find it we escape from the "problem" by the back door of divorce. Yes, I know: divorce is sometimes an honorable front door, the smaller of two evils. But that fact does not turn marriage into a "problem." It is a mated venture. Ditto in regard to foreign policy: "the problem of Vietnam." But life is not that kind or any kind of problem to be solved: it is a life to be lived. It is a journey in love or hate. It is a tapestry to be woven with whatever threads, long or short, bright in color or dull, our birth has given us. It is a venture, not a problem. The Breakthrough delivers us from both the cult of origins and the cult of problems. We are now "in the clear," though the mystery is not resolved. We now ask for the purpose of pain.

II

The first answer is that pain, delivered from judgment and false remorse, *becomes cleansing.* Tragedy was always catharsis. This fact our race has long known. The very word "catharsis" comes from the Greek and was used early to describe the purgation of the emotions through the Greek tragedies. The *Antigone*[4] with its account of a woman breaking the law to give her traitor-brother's body a decent burial, and thus herself being condemned to die, cleanses us of both fear and pity, leaving an open door for worthier emotions. Of course, the Greek tragedies speak of Fate rather than of God. So the opened door closed again—on the same old emotions. But after the Breakthrough pain really cleanses, with a new hope! Therefore our neighbor may say, "Every once in awhile I go to the movies for a good cry." If the opened door closes again, the "good cry" becomes a self-indulgence. It may become worse, namely, fictitious sympathy wasted on fictitious pain, so that the heart is hardened against a neighbor's actual grief.

To the children of the Breakthrough the Cross is *not* tragedy. It is beyond tragedy. For tragedy has no open end. It is meaningless. But the Cross under the light of the Resurrection is the conquest of tragedy. So the catharsis that now comes from pain, as it cleanses us from fear and pity, invites through the opened door the new motive of love: "Beloved, if God so loved us, we also ought to love one another."[5] Who

170

of us would not choose Mozart's *Requiem* rather than some happier strain such as that of *The Magic Flute?* Or *Hamlet* in preference to *The Merry Wives of Windsor?* Merriment has its place, but on the surface, not at the deeps. Jesus laughed, but only a shallow mind would prefer a laughing Jesus to a crucified Christ. Why? Because suffering has cleansing power. The cleansing is proportionate to the worthiness of the suffering. The sight of a man broken in an automobile accident purges our emotions, to our loss if we do nothing, to our truer cleansing if we try to help; but Medgar Evers[6] dying for the cause of peace and racial concord brings a profounder catharsis. Then what of Christ sharing our agony of doubt ("My God, my God, why has thou forsaken me?"[7]) and dying rather than answer hate with any weapon except love or meet violence with any weapon except a prayer? What of Christ then raised from the dead? This is the ultimate and creative catharsis. Such cleansing goes far to reconcile us, if we walk the path which Christ has pioneered, to the enigma of pain.

III

We can now specify the cleansing: it is cleansing from sin and the desire to sin. We have said that there is a plus of pain beyond the suffering caused by our human irresponsibility:

> Streams will not curb their pride
> The just man not to entomb
> Nor lightnings go aside
> To leave his virtues room.[8]

But the bitter core of all pain comes from "man's inhumanity to man"[9] and from his denial or forgetfulness of God's commands. Biblical thought is consistent on this issue: we might ride the waves of other sorrows if the sorrow of iniquity were canceled. The Breakthrough assures us that it is canceled. If a man should presume on the pardon, if he should keep returning to his well-loved transgressions with a casual "God will forgive," his sin multiplies and deepens, and soon he loses the awareness of God. Meanwhile God does forgive, though the casual man may become unaware of pardon.

But the man who judges life by the Breakthrough, by the Cross in

171

the light of the Resurrection, is not casual about his sin. It is bad enough that what we gloss over as "social disease" should blind a child, and even worse that a drunken driver should kill a child, but the most piercing and convicting evidence of sin's cruelty is seen at Calvary. There the best in our human story was done to death heartlessly by the worst. "You don't know: you haven't seen": said the British chaplain after the death of Joan of Arc by martyr fire.[10] Until that moment he had justified the deed and had even believed that her death was required. But when he had seen it he was both broken in heart and cleansed. Any of us can evade the sight of the Cross. But if we dare to look at it, still more if we look into it, we soon know that Someone is looking at us from the other side. Then we know with pain that our name is Judas or Peter or Thomas. Thus we are cleansed.

We can never make amends for our assault on the life of men, still less for our grieving God. Our sin is always against the creation, not primarily against ourselves or primarily against our neighbor, for we are not the creators of human life or of the cosmos. The psalm is right: "Against thee, thee only, have I sinned." [11] So we cannot mend the world of the damage we have done. We can confess to those we injure, and in some instances we should. But in other instances we should not, for the confession might deepen the animosity. And how are we to confess when those we have injured are dead? The confession to an enemy or to an injured friend, when it is wise to offer it, is not amends: it is testimony to God's forgiving grace and to a resolve on newness of life. Have you not wondered what Paul said to the relatives of men and women whom he had martyred in the days when in a supposed righteousness he had lived "after the most straitest sect" of the Pharisees?[12] How he would have resisted our title bestowed on him of "saint"! He would have protested again, "I am chief of sinners"! [13] He could only accept the grace of the Breakthrough, and try to live in it.

All of which means that the marks of sin are not erased. The prodigal who went into the far country and the prodigal who stayed at home[14] both carried the branding of their folly to the end of their days. The one wasted his "substance" of life as well as cash; the other, who "served" his father for cash instead of loving him, grew hard in that wretched role. Moreover the memory of sin, by which the past works in the present, cannot be expunged. But this nemesis is not now nemesis: the bitterness

172

is cleansed away by God through him whom he has raised. The penalty is pain, but it is no longer penalty: it is a precious discipline. The sinner is purged of a false self-reliance and of all pride. He judges no man, for he himself is a forgiven sinner. He tries to live in love with all men, for he himself has been loved incredibly in the grace of God. Pain purges him.

IV

Now we can specify both the sin and the cleansing: *the children of the Breakthrough are cleansed by pain from a false worldliness.* Faith in Christ does not hate the world, and characteristically it does not forsake the world. The anchorite may have his place, but it is a small place, for if all men were anchorites our human life might cease. The faith finds joy in the world, as Christ found joy in birds and flowers, in sunrise and sunset, in daily work and in homes, for God made the world, and its ground is joy. That order of monks, called "The Gravediggers," who daily dug another spadeful of earth for their own graves, is a dark parody on the gospel. The world of nature and of men is God's handiwork. Again and again we can and should trace the autograph.

But the man of the faith does not love the world, for it has a fatal flaw. Pain forbids him to love it. A poem which was popular a few years ago makes little sense:

> A haze on the far horizon,
>   The infinite, tender sky,
> The ripe, rich tint of the cornfields,
>   And the wild geese sailing high,
> And all over the upland and lowland
>   The charm of the golden-rod,—
> Some of us call it Autumn,
>   And others call it God.[15]

It could better be called euphoria, a form of drunkenness. For the "tender sky" is sometimes a tornado, and cornfields are sometimes rotted by rain or made barren by drought, and there are vultures as well as wild geese, and there is poison ivy as well as golden rod. In short, nature is flawed, and every man suffers the pain of natural evil. This pain cleanses him of nature worship. But in the faith he is sure that nature also is in travail, waiting the final redemption. Meanwhile he refuses to blink at the fact of earthquakes, tidal waves, that avalanche which just the other day overwhelmed a Swiss hostel, and the volcano which only yesterday erupted in the Philippines.

Likewise the faith does not hate the world which man has made as subcreator. The children of the Breakthrough rejoice in Michaelangelo's mural of the Creation and in the Grieg "Liebestod." They are grateful for more mundane gifts by which our daily life is made civil—thatched cottages and soaring skyscrapers, country lakes and the thrust of expressways, books and kitchen aids and well-stocked stores. These are "amenities," a word which in its origin means "pleasant." A paved street leads us quickly to our friend's house, and "a garden is a lovesome thing, God wot!" [16] Men make burial caskets also; Admiral Nelson kept one in his ship's cabin always to remind him that soon he would die, but the Admiral was morbid rather than realistic: the faith rejoices in the world which God has enabled men to fashion.

But the faith does not love that world, much less worship it: pain forbids. For man's life also is flawed. The devil has more than a foothold in us. Skyscrapers can be the sign of man's uplifted pride, and then they fall like any Tower of Babel, as witness the bombing of London and Berlin. Expressways are roads of daily death because men would rather save a few moments for their unimpressive pursuits than save life. Paved streets are used by gangsters' cars, and gardens are infested with death-dealing bugs and weeds. And men *do* make caskets because we all die, and because then we must be put away decently lest our death should become a public nuisance. So the faith makes no idol of a computer. It is a thing of steel and may mechanize us. It can measure only things in a merely mensurable world, but, because we easily fall prey to our own proud work, it may make us prisoners in a world of weights and measures. Yes, it can almost instantly reckon the right track of a rocket, but the rocket can be used to destroy a city.

Here is the deep wisdom of the Bible concerning the world: "Do not love the world or the things in the world. If any one loves the world, love for the Father is not in him." [17] That is to say, the pain of natural evil rules out pantheism, and the pain of human evil rules out humanism. Pain points us beyond both nature and man to the mystery of God.

174

Humanism now confronts the fact that a bomb may wipe out both humanity and the planet. Never was a faith so beggarly. Humanism can survive only by closing its eyes, only by the pretense that evil is not evil, and that death is not death; only by the obdurate belief that evil is a passing defect which science, education, and "freedom" can overcome. Atheism in our time is a much more impressive creed, but the atheist must still speak of Truth when he refuses to speak of God. Meanwhile pain cleanses us under the Breakthrough from any love of the world. Could we have known God at all except for pain? Could anything else have pointed us beyond the world and human life? What a question! The answer is "No, only pain is the road to God." But we should not dogmatize because we are dealing with mysteries. Meanwhile the faith is purged by pain of any false clinging to the world.

V

Pain cleanses also from lovelessness. Pain *by itself* has no such power. Two world wars have darkened over our planet and killed off perhaps as many as a hundred million people, but the world is not cleansed of lovelessness. Indeed, disillusionment and sporadic wars are now the aftermath of the carnage. Pain *of itself* leads on to death. Without the catalyst to change pain all suffering is oncoming night. But we are writing now of pain in the light of the Breakthrough. Two small children[18] seeing in a strange church the cross in the chancel asked their parents: "Why do they have a plus sign in church?" The plus sign, so they assumed, belonged only to maths in the grade school. Pain with the plus sign cleanses us of lovelessness. God in Christ has shared our pain on Calvary and proved his power over pain in a conquered tomb. So in gratitude "we love, because he first loved us." [19]

We are obliged in truth to reiterate: Pain of itself is no guarantee of cleansing from unconcern for our neighbors. King Lear driven from the palace by his ungrateful daughters, finding no shelter except the hovel of a down-and-out beggar, began to think, perhaps for the first time seriously, about all the beggars in his realm:

> Poor naked wretches, wheresoe'er you are,
> That bide the pelting of this pitiless storm,
> How shall your houseless heads and unfed sides,

175

Your loop'd and window'd raggedness, defend you
From seasons such as these? [20]

The king adds that he had taken "too little care" of such misfortunes. Perhaps he *was* concerned in his remaining days, perhaps not: we soon forget our neighbor's troubles.

There is genuine compassion in many a humanist, perhaps because in his revolt against too many uncaring churches he is worshiping Christ on the hidden side of the altar, perhaps because God leaves himself nowhere without witness. By the same token there are many "followers" of Christ who have no care for their neighbors. Therefore he must ask again and again: "Why do you call me 'Lord, Lord,' and not do what I tell you?" [21] Dr. Samuel Johnson is said to have replied to Sir William Scott when the latter complained of a headache, "At your age, sir, I had no head-ach." [22] When Johnson *did* have a headache he was not necessarily more sympathetic: he may have become surly. The man who claims about the unemployed, *"I've* always been able to find work," does not necessarily learn social concern when *he* loses *his* job. In the depression of the 1930's he and his kind were known to commit suicide. What we are here intent to say is this: If a man dares to look on Christ (it is quite a dare!), and when he "thinks through" the Cross and the Resurrection, and when his prayers are steadily in sight of the Cross, he is joined with his neighbor in love and cleansed of unconcern. We are born with some measure of this sympathy, as witness the traveling salesman whom we know as the good Samaritan. [23] But in Christ that inborn grace, the image of God in us, is driven deep and becomes regnant. Christ told that story, and lived it—to the limit of Calvary. Nor has the church utterly failed. Once we flew from Bangkok to Chengmai. We looked down on crocodile swamps and frowning mountains and wondered how the early missionaries ever found a path. In Chengmai there were two fine schools, an excellent hospital, and a hostel where upward of two thousand lepers were being cured. Thai Buddhism did not initiate that work, and no ethical cult in our land could claim it.

Thus the church is or should be a company making common cause with the world's pain. This we shall discuss at length, for this is the focus of the church's present failure. But it is not complete failure, for the church, by the present spirit of Christ, has power of astringent self-

176

criticism. Its love is thus renewed and has never centrally failed. The church is "the body of Christ." [24] If one member suffers, all suffer. Such membership in love is not locked within the church, for love if it is genuine cannot be locked: Christ in his body of flesh "so loved the world that whoever"! [25] Charles Williams calls this love "the co-inherence," [26] and rightly declares that it has never been fully explored. He suggests that a man genuinely living in the Calvary-love and Resurrection-victory of Christ may be able to say to his neighbor in sorrow, "Let me carry it for you," just as he would speak of a suitcase. Have we ever really dared to live in Christ's present Spirit? Once after I had preached in the Church of the Crossroads in Hawaii a little Korean lady came and said, "I'm glad you like my Jesus." I'd bet that she is not unconcerned when her neighbors suffer.

VI

Once more, *pain in Christ cleanses us from the dominion of time.* Pain *in itself* accents time, for pain wrings from us a double cry: "I am mortal. Where is my salvation?" Thus pain *in itself* underscores the fleetingness of time and life. Is it Martin Heidegger who has written that we live between two negatives—the past which is *no* longer with us, and the future which has *not* yet come? [27] He is only partly justified, for the past *is* present with us in memory, and the future *is* present with us in hope. The catalyst of the Cross cleanses the memory and purifies the hope. But that word about the two nots has its thrust, for often our days seem no more than a moving point traveling through nothingness. No man can see the harbor from which his voyage began, or the port beyond the sea toward which he journeys.

Thus the hurriedness of our present culture. We keep manufacturing more and more labor-saving and time-saving machines, but more and more we are slaves of work and victims of time. Soon it may become clear that our machines are a compulsive affair like alcoholism, and that we make machines because we are intent on forgetting time, not in saving it. This issue reveals again the penury of humanism. It has no answer to the ever-recurring questions, "Whence my life?" and "Whither bound?" Even when it speaks sententiously about "living for the ages"

177

it blinks the fact that "the ages" also are transience. No loyalty within time is free from this blindness. The only worthy loyalty is above time.

But pain, even pain without "the plus sign," convicts us of transience: "I am mortal." It obliges us, from a hospital bed for example, to ponder our life. We think then of the expensive toys on which we spend our strength, and we exclaim, "What shadows we are, and what shadows we pursue!" [28] Could we ever have known eternity except for the pains of time, or God except for the piercing conviction of our transience? Now add "the plus sign." God has raised Christ from the dead. Therefore the word of Christ in the Cross is above mortality. Therefore his presence with us *is* presence and power, not mere memory—if, indeed, any memory is mere. Therefore pain under his catalyst calls us away from time, and cleanses us from time's tyranny. The children of the Breakthrough are not in a hurry and not in any sloth. They do what they can without haste and without laziness, and do not flagellate themselves for what they cannot do, because the pains of time (the painful longing for a lost rapture, and the painful waiting for a coming resolvement) have already been gathered into the healing eternities of God.

These are high matters. The reader must explore them—through his pain. Carlyle said nobly:

The illimitable, silent, never-resting thing called time, rolling, rushing on, swift, silent, like an all-embracing ocean tide, on which we and all the universe swim like exhalations, like apparitions which *are,* and then *are not:* this is forever very literally a miracle; a thing to strike us dumb.[29]

The Faith has an answer, the New Testament being the most daring of all books, namely this: Christ came in "the nick of time," and the nick is now as wide as the Breakthrough. Those who live in him are friends of time because they have a loyalty beyond time: "The world passes away, and the lust of it; but he who does the will of God abides for ever." [30] The nick of time is an outright breach in time—the year A.D. 1.

VII

The summing-up is this: Pain under the Breakthrough is *cleansing from self-centeredness.* Russia *decries* the "cult of personality." This means in Marxist doctrine that the man is nothing and the system (Marxist economics) is everything, and that the man is but a throw-up of the system. Basically it means that life comes only of primal matter. But of course the system is not everything, for every system has its day and goes its way. In America we *exalt* the "cult of personality." The real actress is one who has her name in electric letters on the theater marquee. The successful businessman is the head of the firm who has made a fortune. We write books on "how to be a real person." Even the anti-poverty program advertises "Be Somebody." The youth conference asks me to speak on "The Search for Self-Identity." But a person who soon must die can no more be the center of the world than the system, for he is a creature—created, dependent though given a strange independence, contingent, mortal. When some lady charged Carlyle with being eccentric, he replied: "Not so eccentric, madam, if you only knew my center." [31] How can the center of life be ourselves—or any system which our hands have fashioned?

Pain, even pain in itself, makes nonsense of any self-idolatry, for any pain is the forewarning of death. But the danger of pain *in itself* is that it invites us to believe that we are nobody. This pessimism is no better than the pride that strives to be somebody. The younger prodigal went into the "far country" determined to be somebody—and ended in a pigsty. Then in his misery he concluded that he was nobody: "Treat me as one of your hired servants." [32] Thus our world, made chaotic by atomized individuals determined to be somebody, has fallen on insensate strife: the planet is hollow with graves and red with blood. Now in our despair we fear we are nobody, as witness our oft-repeated cliché: "He has an inferiority complex." We are even ready to listen to the scientist who, from categories which belong only in the limited world of science, tells us that we are a midge breed infesting the skin of a minor planet which itself may vanish. All of which shows us that neither man nor the planet is the center of life. Only the Creative Spirit can be center, the Spirit focused in the Christ whom he has sent. The New Testament is quite explicit: "And he died for all, that those who live might live no longer for themselves but for him who for their sake died and was raised." [33]

Pain in the light of the Breakthrough cleanses us of all wish to be somebody because now Christ is "all in all." That is why St. Francis, one of the few saints in the calendar who would be fun on a picnic, climbed to the roof of that church being built in his honor, and threw down the tiles: a church belongs only to Christ. But the action of Francis did not condemn him to be nobody. He was already somebody because Christ had chosen him beyond all deserving, and in spite of all undeserving. We speak sententiously about "the dignity of man," but "dust to dust" has little dignity, and the white man's parody of justice in Alabama has none at all. Today's paper tells of the outright flouting of justice in the killing of a young seminarian civil-right's advocate. The only "dignity of man" is that each of us is confronted by the mystery of God (as when we know that life is mortal), and by his seeking us in the love of the Cross and the joy of the Resurrection. That gift in his pain and our strickenness-in-judgment-and-mercy overcomes our being nobody, and cleanses us of the itch to be somebody. Thus the paradox: "He who finds his life will lose it, and he who loses his life for my sake will find it." [34]

Likewise we are *cleansed of any trust in our own wisdom*. If we say, "I am resolved to act from high motive," we stand on uncertain ground, for every man's motives are mixed. Freud has shown us how easily we rationalize, even though he was trapped in his own net: it hardly occurred to him that he could rationalize. There is some gain perhaps in a scrutiny of our motives, but also some danger, for by that probing the mind soon preys on itself. We are on equally uncertain ground if we judge an action by its probable results, for again and again such attempts to read the future have been confounded. Colonialism was justified as "the white man's burden," though it was much more the white man's greed; and its initial fruit seemed to be good in that the life of "underdeveloped nations" was "enriched." But now the votes are coming in from the remoter precincts (of God's sovereignty), and we see the scorching of Java, the swamp-carnage in Vietnam, and apartheid-cleavage in South Africa. We have no wisdom to read either our own hearts or the far issues of history. Then by what test shall we judge an action? By the mind of Christ, set forth in the Bible, pondered by the beloved community called the Church, and honored at risk of pain by the confrontation of God in our personal solitude. You say the church has failed to ask that leading question? If so, that fact only proves the point. You say

that such an inquiry would give no specifics? It gives a true direction and
the next step. Since we must walk always with the line of light at our
toes, we should not ask for more than the next step, plus the flashes
which again and again show us the road.

Pain and the Breakthrough cleanse us also of a false mysticism. The
local congregation goes to church seeking a "spiritual experience." If
that quest means the presence of Christ's Spirit, well and good. But the
Spirit does not always comfort us, much less grant us regular Sunday
rapture, much less an emotional jag. The word "Comforter" means in
the Elizabethan English of the King James Version the "Strengthener"—
for the *doing* of the truth. But in our time the preacher is judged by his
power to incite a momentary fire which as quickly fails, leaving only
cold ash. For the man who wills to obey the Presence moments come
when the veil is drawn and he hears "things that cannot be told, which
man may not utter." [35] But Paul arrived at that experience by the fellowship of Christ's "sufferings." [36] There is a place for mysticism in the life
of the church, but not if it is clutched at and contrived. Perhaps it should
be occasional and no more: we are not asked to surrender the inde-
pendent selfhood which God himself gives. The end of life is not
"absorption in the Infinite," where easily we forget our neighbor's pain,
but the fulfillment of our limited freedom in the glad and painful doing
of his will. The church should now ask why the song, "We shall overcome" [37] has far more verve and power than, "O that will be glory for
me." [38]

We are cleansed even of longing for a lost innocence. Why does the
businessman speak longingly of "the old swimming hole"? Is he at-
tempting the journey back which no man can travel? Why do we all
sentimentalize about "the good old days"? They were not good: the
Victorian age broke in two world wars. Why do we get weepy and
starry-eyed about the joys of childhood? Children also have their burdens
and must carry them on smaller shoulders. Why do we dream of the
Garden of Eden when it was there that Adam and Eve (Mr. Man and
Mrs. Woman) took their tragic turn? Why does a political party resolve
to "hold to our traditional policy" in a world destined to continual change?
We find many paths by which to run away from the present demand
of the Eternal God! But the Event of Christ, always contemporary be-

181

cause his spirit searches our world, cleanses us from a false nostalgia and commits us to the joyous fulfillment of today's tasks.

One of the books mentioned earlier in this chapter has this looking back on a lost Eden.[39] The book is cast in the form of a dialogue in which the main speaker almost dogmatically justifies the pain of our world. Those who try to answer him, the artist, the agnostic, the scientist, the atheist, all conveniently understate their case. At one point the protagonist almost shouts: "I demand that hell be given back to the world."[40] As if our poor purblind race were not already stumbling through a shabby hell! The book is not long on compassion! The final voice is that of a priest who first endorses the main contention, and then offers faith in Christ if not as an afterthought, then as only the coping stone on a building raised by one man's mind. Faith in Christ is not an addendum to anything: it is all or nothing. Then the priest gets trapped in his longing for a lost Eden: "We learn that God's intention was originally that man should live in felicity, and that it was the fault of man himself which made his lot different."[41] Yes, man is at fault. But whence the power to default? Meanwhile did God goof in his anticipations? Are history and Christ himself a patch on a blunder? This is not the New Testament word. There the work of Christ is ordained from "the foundation of the world."[42] Yes, that conviction deepens the question: "But why by such a road?" To that there is no intellectual answer. Again and again we come on walls of mystery. But such an admission is better than charging God with entertaining naïve hopes, and then patching what he could not foresee. The Christ-Event in its present joy and power cleanses us from any mooning about a lost Paradise.

VIII

The litany for Holy Saturday in the Roman Catholic Church has a line which begins *"O felix culpa"* ("O happy guilt").[43] Why "happy"? Because without the guilt we might not have known the victory of forgiving grace. No longer need we agonize over the origin of evil, which origin we can never trace by mortal mind, or wonder why the devil should have any role in God's providence, for God through the Cross—a gallows become a shrine—has proved his power to use even evil and guilt to his own redeeming purpose. By that same token we need not propose that God was taken by surprise by Adam's sin, and therefore had to change the Divine plan, as if God had no more than human prescience.

Of course the "happy guilt" raises precisely the question which Paul raised: "What shall we say then? Are we to continue in sin that grace may abound?" [44] The only answer is Paul's own answer: "God forbid!" [45] He continues: "How can we who died to sin still live in it?" [46] You and I know redemption now and cannot transport that truth back into the past when we did not know and then say: "I'll make a thorough job of sinning that I may experience a fuller grace." That jugglery in time is not possible; and if it were, a man has no right or skill to play sleight of hand with God's costly goodness. That nasty perversion might bring the blindness which cannot tell good from evil. A man may not presume to act the part of God. In the "Mr. and Mrs. North" comedy he says to her, she having been guilty once more of trying to "rig" other people's lives though with every good intention, "You mustn't be Providence. You don't look like Providence." [47]

Yet the *felix culpa* is just that, for though the contradiction of the two words cannot be resolved in logic, it is already resolved in history and in life. Pain, when the light of the Resurrection and the Cross is thrown on it, is cleansing. It is much more, namely, vocation and insight. But that is for our later chapters. When we know this *purpose* of pain we can carry the burden of pain's mystery. Once I heard Maude Royden say: "The Faith does not give us the reasons for tragedy: it gives us power to meet it and to transform it. Then it gives us the reasons, or, rather, it would, if we any longer cared about them."

Imagine the incredible "man from Mars" (incredible because God's creation has no duplicates, and if there *is* life on that other planet it might not be "man") visiting our planet. Imagine him in church. He might say: "We also are aware of the Presence. Only so could we know our strange finiteness. But what is that on the altar? A gallows? Then why is it empty and in gold? We on our planet would never dream of worshiping the Mystery before the sign of a gallows!" Why *do we* so worship? "O happy guilt that won so holy and high a Redeemer!" [48] God knows the secrets of pain. We can only slowly learn. He has told us that the answer to the "problem" is not an answer to a problem, but a courage of faith in response to his strange, strange beckonings. The "answer" is not despite pain, or in the respite of pain, but straight through pain. "For the foolishness of God is wiser than men, and the weakness of God is stronger than men." [49] But think of God being most Godlike on a gallows!

12. Pain as Vocation

The word "vocation" means calling, a manner of life in response to the call of God. The word is out-of-fashion. We no longer ask the guiding questions: "What are my gifts, given by life or God? What is my unique sense of human need? How are these questions answered under the level though unseen eyes of Christ?" No, our word is "career," which comes from the French word *"carriere,"* which means a race course or a street for vehicles: we choose how and where we shall get into the rat race. But the true word will return, as witness college men and women *called* by the Peace Corps. In the book, *The Secular City,* Harvey Cox almost proposes that it is there in the secular city that we find our true vocation.[1] For him the word "secular" replaces the word "sacred." But secular comes from *saecularis* (once in an age) or *saeculum* (breed or generation), and there is no life in the merely transient. What he should have said is that the word "secular" is not found anywhere in biblical thought. There the only word is "sacred"— only the work of God in his creation. Then he could well have said, what I take him to mean, that in *our* false dichotomy of secular and sacred, what *we* call secular may be more sacred than the locked-in pietisms which *we* label sacred.

In the whole realm of vocation nothing is stranger than that pain itself should become vocation. This item is one of the sharpest and most startling differences between the Old Testament and the New. The Old certainly has a prophecy of the vocation of vicarious pain, as in Isaiah:

> Surely he has borne our griefs
>   and carried our sorrows; . . .
> But he was wounded for our transgressions,
>   he was bruised for our iniquities;
> upon him was the chastisement that made us whole,
>   and with his stripes we are healed.[2]

Most scholars tell us that this passage refers originally to a Godly "remnant" in Israel, though they agree as to the cogency by which we quote the words about Jesus. But the quotation is still pathos: there is no light of Resurrection on it.

It is sharply distinguished from New Testament in another particular: it is lonely rather than a Companionship. For in the New Testament the vocation of pain is a sharing with Christ not only in his vicarious sacrifice, but in the joy and power of his resurrection. Thus the words that repeat with many a variation: "For it has been granted to you that for the sake of Christ you should not only believe in him but also suffer for his sake."[3] Notice the repetition of "for the sake of." He has "tabernacled with us":[4] the word is a reference to the sacred ark of the covenant set in the midst of the huddled tents of Israel. For forty years Israel followed that ark, though at awestruck distance. When the enemy conquered or stole the ark, Israel was desolate. But then the enemy god, Dagon, standing near to the stolen ark, was found fallen, his head and arms struck from him.[5] Men grew strong just by passing in front of the ark: new life from the hidden Presence flowed into them. Christ is the bond of the New Covenant: "Jesus, the mediator of a new covenant."[6] The ark of his presence led men in a strange pilgrimage through Calvary and the tyranny of death, and he is still Presence. Men grow strong just by thinking about him. When they follow him in the vocation of his pains-in-love they become "heirs of God"! Thus: "When we cry, 'Abba! Father!' it is the Spirit himself bearing witness with our spirit that we are children of God, and if children, then heirs, heirs of

186

God and fellow heirs with Christ, provided we suffer with him in order that we may also be glorified with him." [7]

I

Pain as vocation in Christ is the pain of *cleaving to faith in him in the midst of an alien world,* and doing so without pigheadedness, proselyting, or a martyr complex. The paragraph just written seems naïve or benighted to the eyes of our culture. The college student who holds that Christ is the Truth is regarded as a pietist or a bigot even though he may be one of the most thoughtful men on campus. Our current trust is in science, though one hour's pondering is enough to show us that the merely analytical level of mind intent on a merely sense-data world can find truth only within its own narrow confines: it cannot find life-truth. Compare the formula for matter with the children playing on the grass in the neighboring park. Then you will know that the formula is a vanishing ghost waving at reality before it vanishes. You may also know that the formula in the hands of violent men may decimate our planet, and that we may all be killed by applied science. Yet our world still trusts to science, not alone for the limited truth it can bring, but for whole truth which is always outside its bounds. How hard to hold the faith in such a world!

The student in humanities hopes that he will come on the truth through philosophy. He *may* indeed thus come on the scope and depth of the *question,* but not on the answer. Someone has defined a materialist as a man to whom everything matters except everything. The philosopher, and indeed any student in the humanities, is splendidly aware of everything. To quote a popular song, he has "the world on a string." [8] But his particular string is the exercise of the universalizing dimension of mind expressed in abstractions. This is the point of Kierkegaard's complaint about Hegel, to the effect that if he should ask for directions to a street address in Copenhagen Hegel might give him in reply a map of Europe.[9] Philosophy now shows promise of taking another direction, namely that of recognizing that the cosmos is an event, and that we live in events. Faith in Christ goes further: we must look for *the* Event which has first looked for us and which gathers in and interprets all other events.

187

But that day is not yet: we live in a skeptical time, for which an obscurantist church or a church conformed to its culture is not without blame. Therefore the pain of cleaving to the faith. Of course events finally validate the faith, but the word is "finally," and meanwhile the faith is hard to hold. We know it should be so: a faith with no odds to meet would not be worthy of the name. To believe in God only in fair weather, and to ditch him as soon as rain falls, would be a childish affair: a man should at least ask if there is a purpose to the rain. To follow Christ as Truth-Event only when *our* will is done would be self-idolatry. Job was nobler than his wife. She bade him "curse God and die," [10] because her shallow pattern of faith was rudely broken, while he still believed, though with many an honest doubt, until the day came when he saw God in the depth and height of Mystery and forswore once for all any trust in his own poor protestations.

But the holding of such faith is hard. We cannot force it on our neighbors, or ever clutch at the poor comfort of the proselyter who is more intent to bolster his own insecurity than to save his neighbor. The faith requires us to honor our neighbor as a center of freedom for whom Christ died. We may enter into dialogue with an unbeliever, but only as we first listen to him and try to understand his life journey. Even then we may be required to keep silence lest speech deepen misunderstanding. We cannot deny the encroachment of our own doubts: that would be dishonest, and if there were no doubt faith would sink into flabbiness. We cannot ever pity ourselves: that is the core of an unworthy self-concern. Joyously we cleave to the faith. Pilgrimage for the follower of the faith is often through darkness, with occasional lightning flashes revealing the road. But always "we see Jesus": he kept faith against all unbelief, and bore the pain, and overcame the world. "Stand firm thus in the Lord" [11] is man's vocation in the faith. It is a vocation of secret pain, but the pain brings both cleansing and insight.

II

The vocation of pain in Christ *is a calling to bear witness for him* in a world which meanwhile "is in the power of the evil one." [12] The witness is made, for instance, in *the midst of inexplicable pain and natural evil.* A friend whose tongue was removed because of cancer, and who had to write what he wished to say, gave me this message on his ever-present scribbling pad: "It is strange to live without the sense of taste." Notice: "It is strange," not, "It is rotten and unjust." His courage is better than the rebellious raving of some "angry young man." Thus a blind organist, who knew all the hymns by heart and who would open the hymnbook on his organ rack lest people should pity him for blindness, would say: "I have keener ears to compensate for the loss of sight." We cannot trace the origins of pain or ever find the neat "answer" to the "problem." Meanwhile pain nobly borne is witness and even apocalypse to those who watch. To that vocation we are called because of the redemptive pain of Christ.

This vocation of witness (to cite another instance) is *fulfilled by the way a man acts in unanswered prayer*. A man prays for worthy cash, but his unpaid bills are doubled. He prays for his child's life, but the child dies. What to say and do? If the man has pondered life he is aware that God's "no" is as clear an evidence of God as God's "yes." For how could we ever know God if his will did not cut across our will? If our every wish were granted, we would be our own God, quite sure that by the waving of our wand we rule the world. We would then be as conceited and comic as Rostand's rooster who was convinced that his crowing brought the day and that the sun rose at his call.[13] But such ponderings are poor comfort when what seems a rightful prayer is rudely crushed. Some help comes from remembering past joys, and that the ground of life is joy. Friends standing with us in the crux of experience are a better help. The best help is the knowledge of Christ whose prayer, "Let this cup pass," [14] was not answered, and who by obedience became the Savior of men. But the pain of the witness remains: "This I believe against the gathering night!" Such a testimony is a light in the darkness, and to that vocation we are called.

But the main arena of the witness is in the social concerns of our world. Only an appalling misrepresentation of the claim of Christ could make him a peddler of private platitudes with no word for our common life. Indeed, only an appalling blindness to our human nature could be guilty of such gross distortion. Our life is body-psyche, and therefore, if faith in Christ is to have any validity, it must speak about the work of a man's hands and the housing-area in which he lives, as well as about his "spiritual experience." Moreover our nature is individual-social, not the

one or the other, but both; and therefore Christ is a truncated Christ
who speaks only to our private concerns and not to our public life. There
are pains private and public that cannot be changed and must be borne.
But there are pains private and public that come of human greed, and
must be both judged and redeemed. Christ died not solely because he
was charged with theological heresy, but because he opposed the kind of
trade that invaded the temple and the kind of temple that cared only
for prestige and profit. To propose that Christ is a celestial Dale Carnegie
teaching us "how to win friends and influence people" [15] is blasphemy at
the very foot of the Cross.

Christ told his followers flatly that the faith, far from shielding them
from pain, would invite pain, which they could sidestep if they coveted an
easy path. They must take up a cross, and follow, if they would be his
disciples.[16] They would have to endure tribulation in the world.[17] Mark
clearly: "In the world," not merely in the struggle with private doubts.
They would be hailed before courts and rulers and beaten and killed.[18]
There is small fear that many a tepid "follower" in our day will suffer
any such fate! But Christ himself was brought before courts and rulers
and was crucified, and that end came not because he peddled the
"positive thinking" that gives us "success" and a "pleasing personality."
Until the church knows again this vocation of the pain of public witness
it will be bereft of both joy and power. Million-dollar downtown
cathedrals or suburban structures with educational wings rivalling the
ramps of an airport, do not atone for failure to visit the prisoner, to tend
the sick (who in Christ's time were regarded as demon-possessed), and
to make a home for all homeless folk.[19] The church has veered away
from the Path. It has become "conformed to this world." [20] It has aped
business to seek success through multiplied bricks and multiplied "members." It has sought to impress the world. But God is not impressed, and
a true member is not a name on a church roll: he is an arm of the Body
of Christ. The church has forgotten the vocation of witness in the world,
the witness which spells accepted pain.

The long list of references under the word "suffer" in a concordance
of the New Testament is its own testimony. Sometimes the word means
simply to allow: "Suffer me to bury my father." [21] But more often it
means what we mean as we use the word: the follower of Christ is to
suffer with him, not only in patient endurance of the ills that "flesh is

190

heir to," but because if a man holds to the faith the world will oppose and persecute him. It is a temptation to quote passage after passage, but that would be to little purpose, for each quotation would be out of context, and a list even from the Scriptures is as dull—as a list. But consider this strange item: In a world which always asks the reason for pain, Christ tells his followers that to follow him means pain, for they will be misunderstood, slandered, and ill-treated in a world which is under the temporary sway of the devil. Thus Paul: "Henceforth let no man trouble me [try to put his branding-iron on me] for I bear on my body the marks of Jesus." [22] Men of the Faith must *welcome* this pain, for by their witness in an alien world the Cross is lifted high above our proud and rebellious culture. Thus pain in the New Testament is no longer dark judgment or dark mystery: it is vocation and testimony.

This public witness in our time is in three main areas—the issue of peace and war, the issue of poverty (the few "haves" and the million "have-nots"), and the issue of color and race. On the issue of peace the church has always talked pietistically about the Prince of Peace, especially at Christmastime, but has always been silent or "patriotically" conformist with each new war. On the issue of poverty the church has "refrained from political activities" and has been even less willing to become a voluntary sharer of the poverty. On the issue of race the church has finally found a fairly clear voice but only after yielding the vanguard to baseball and the theater. Those who in the church have made their witness for Christ have been persecuted even in the church. Thus rich men in the church have withheld their contributions, not alone in the southern states, when pastors have spoken a brave word for civil rights. They have starved their pastors and plotted against them. The administrative officers of the various denominations have wobbled, when they should have invited these critics to leave the church and to take their wretched money with them.

The above paragraph is neither politics nor economics. Christ offered no political or economic nostrums. Ideologies are never ideologies. That is to say, it is not given to our minds to draw a blueprint of the common life for all men for all time. All social patterns dissolve and re-form, and the church serves no transient system. Its concern is for each person in each person's true life—the life which God has created and for which

Christ died. Furthermore the witness for Christ is never an undue optimism. The faithful witness does not pretend that he will thus conjure up a new heaven and a new earth in our finite world. He does not pose as architect of a streamlined paradise. His job lies between him and God, the God who has found him in Jesus; and then between him and his neighbor, in a world of persons whom Jesus the Christ has redeemed. The *result* of the witness is not in his hands, for that is God's business. What a man calls success is usually anything but success, and what he calls failure may prove a triumph in disguise. All he knows is that the faith will lead to accepted pain: "Indeed all who desire to live a godly life in Christ Jesus will be persecuted, while evil men and impostors will go from bad to worse, deceivers and deceived." [23] Our current culture is sharply reflected in that mirror!

But if this vocation of pain through witness is not a false optimism or the pride that would try to ape Atlas, neither is it a pessimism. "But even if you do suffer for righteousness' sake, you will be blessed. Have no fear of them, nor be troubled, but in your hearts reverence Christ as Lord." [24] Why "blessed"? Why "have no fear"? Because the decisive blow has been struck: the weapon of love prevailed on Calvary because God raised Christ from the dead. The devil may continue his chess game, with men as pawns and empires as stakes, but checkmate has already been called—by a hidden Hand and by Eyes that miss no move. White judges and juries who exonerate white men's crimes and punish with death smaller crimes by Negroes are already judged. Yes, we should be indignant to the pitch of flashing anger, but not with any "eye-for-an-eye" vengeance, for such men are already judged. Almost we should pity them, for this little chapter of life which we call earth is just that: one chapter. The Hand writes on in worlds on worlds, and therefore we make our witness at cost, in the midst of many a joy, for the sake of Christ. Strength flows into the witness: "For this slight momentary affliction is preparing . . . an eternal weight of glory." [25] Indeed, the very witness is a carried signboard of the triumph: "But thanks be to God, who in Christ always leads us in triumph." [26] The context makes clear this picture: Christ leads captive his glad followers. They testify to his gracious power. Their sacrifice is fragrance which deals death to all cruelty and life to the coming Kingdom.

192

III

Thus we come to the deepest dimension of pain as vocation: *pain accepted for the sake of Christ becomes redemptive,* for it is gathered into his redeeming pains on Calvary and is raised in triumph with him. The Old Testament keeps asking *"Why* is there pain in our world?" Except for such gleams as those in Isaiah quoted above, the answer is: "The why is judgment and mystery." The New Testament answer is: "Don't ask *why:* grasp pain in Christ as your glad vocation!" Therefore this book has proposed that the ancient question is now transformed: we no longer agonize to *solve* the insoluble *engima* of pain, for we can now *enter* into pain's creative *purpose.* That is why pain is *constitutional:* that no man shall be cheated of the bright secret joy that lies just beyond pain's dark door! This reward awaits any kind of pain if it is borne in love for our neighbors under the sign of Christ. Any pain: the pain of natural calamity, even the pain of sin's crippledness and shame if the sin is forgiven, the pain of human estrangement through human misunderstanding, the pain of sorrow, the pain of persecuted witness, and that secret pain by which every man must bear:

> That blessed mood,
> In which the burthen of the mystery,
> In which the heavy and the weary weight
> Of all this unintelligible world,
> Is lightened.[27]

The key word about accepted pain as redemptive vocation is this: "Now I rejoice in my sufferings for your sake, and in my flesh I complete what is lacking in Christ's afflictions." [28]

That word is crucial. It should be read in full in a Letter in which every sentence is a little cosmos. The New Testament is sheer excitement to those who search its pages, for it goes high enough to "trouble the gold gateways of the stars," [29] and deep enough to explore the land which lies beneath the seas. Paul's "rejoice" means just that: a joy far more to be coveted than a million pleasures. His "in my flesh" means both physical handicaps and lacerations from persecution. When he writes "what is lacking" in the sufferings of Christ, he knows that nothing is lacking, for there was nothing lacking in the grace which arrested him

193

and transformed him on the Damascus Road: he means that the grace is so gracious that it gathers in our pain and grants us to be companions in a redemptive purpose. The words which follow, namely, "for the sake of his body, that is, the church," [30] mean not that his sufferings are locked within a limited fellowship in a limited loyalty, but that the church's vocation is to identify itself in pain (gathered into Christ's redemption) with all the pain of the world. This whole movement, he writes, is "to make the word of God fully known, the mystery hidden for ages and generations but now made manifest to" and through "his saints" [31]: in short, Calvary and Easter are not a patch on a blunder: they are our earth's destiny. Pain was purposed at the dawn of time to be a friendly enemy, and the devil from the first day of creation was God's lackey. The "saints" are simply the forgiven folk in Christ who know they can accept in joy the redemptive vocation of pain.

Thus we see the church's deepest failure: it does not offer its own pain to God's for his redemptive use, and it does not deliberately seek out and share the world's pain for the same deep purpose. It is easy to know which part of town is skid row: the Salvation Army is there, though the Army sometimes fails to understand the profound theology of the above-quoted Colossians passage. In many an instance the stated church is *not* there: it has "gone native" in the suburban culture. When the church *does* stay in the centers of sharpest need, it is not always clear about its task, for it tries to "convert" people by "evangelism." Those two words are precious for the church. But "convert" to what? To a rigid theology, or to the same deep joy of a pain shared for Christ's sake? As for "evangelism," it means in the Greek original "the Gladness." What gladness? The dubious gladness of singing, "O that will be glory for me," [32] or the strange gladness of identification in Christ with the world's sorrows? Maybe the first-century church would never have dreamed of establishing a "department of evangelism": that church at its best *was* evangelism. The church in our time has not utterly failed. Books which castigate the church, such as *God's Frozen People*[33] or *Honest to God*,[34] or *The Suburban Captivity of the Churches*,[35] or *The Secular City*[36] have come from the life of the church through the energizing of Christ's present Spirit; and the church is now moving back into the blighted areas of great cities and into the midst of racial conflict. Soon the church may once more become aware that its central vocation is the sharing of the world's pain—without condemnation: "For God sent the Son into the world, not to condemn the world, but that the world might be saved through him." [37]

Thus the church will recover both power and joy. In a collection of three-minute plays, each play having three characters, Thornton Wilder vividly pictures the scene at the Pool of Healing.[38] The Angel has just troubled the waters. It is then that they give healing. A cripple who has waited there as many years as the Israelites were in the wilderness moves toward the Pool only to find that a "Newcomer," a physician with swifter than a cripple's limbs is beating him to the chance. Then the Angel bars the physician. He protests: surely angels should know the secret nets in which human wings are caught! But the Angel is adamant. He bids the physician stand back: the healing is not for him. "Without your wound where would your power be?" Was the "net" some secret sin or dark memory? We are not told. What we are told is that what we ordinarily call power proves powerless, and that Christ's kind of power—the powerless sharing of a neighbor's pain—is ultimately the only power because ultimately the cliché is true, though with a truth a shallow world has not glimpsed: "Love Makes the World Go Round." [39]

Have you wondered why our world does not explode? Think of the gangsterism which holds great cities in an evil conspiracy. Think of the money-itch which disfigures business: much of our advertising ("Get rid of all your bills in one loan": rate of interest not mentioned, nor the subsequent "pressures") really means, "I want your money." Think of the tissues of lies, black, white, and gray, in which our speech is held: "You can't trust everything you hear." Think of multiplied marital infidelities. Think of the cruel or ignorant parenthood which abuses children by coercion or bullying or pride or neglect. Think of the slaughter on our roads, and the worse slaughter of our wars. Think of the so-called politics which preys on the public mind by specious slogans and perpetuates wars age on age. Have you ever wondered? Faith in Christ has the astonishing answer, the only answer that offsets the vastness of the threat: God has not forsaken us, for he has shown us in Christ that it is his nature and work to enter redemptively the pain of the world and by sharing it and bearing it to redeem it. Thus the Cross is at the center of all history. The further answer is that the followers of Christ are *called* to the central vocation of sharing the pain of the world that they may "complete what is lacking in the sufferings of Christ for the sake of his body, that is, the Church," [40] though nothing is lacking.

We repeat: Any pain borne in the light of the Christ-Event, even though the bearer may not own the Christian faith, fulfills this vocation: the pain of a surgical operation, the pain of human estrangement, the pain of sorrow standing at a graveside, the pain of lifting a lonely voice against war's madness, the pain of standing with the Negro in Mississippi or on Chicago's south side, the pain of remembering youthful follies and carrying the marks of them, the pain of the struggle with poverty: any pain, even the pain of sin, for only the pain of sin and of sin forgiven can testify to God's forgiving grace. No, pain will not vanish. It is not meant to vanish. The devil still stalks his prey: "Your adversary the devil prowls around like a roaring lion, seeking some one to devour" [41]; the devil is God's servant, and we are destined to the pain of resisting the devil. That pain also can be "offered" as an oblation, for the redemption of the world, though only as Christ is *our* Savior in whose redemption nothing is "lacking." Our deepest vocation is that we "take up" our cross. Burdens are thrust on us: we are conscripts then, even though we can learn to be willing conscripts. But in taking up a cross[42] we are volunteers: a cross is someone else's burden.

We now have ground for a reinterpretation of the doctrine of "the merits of the saints." Neither thoughtful Roman Catholics nor thoughtful Protestants can accept the doctrine in the angular and almost repellent form in which it has sometimes been offered. A real saint cannot claim that he has any merit, for in that case he would not be a saint. We cannot believe that any man's "righteousness" is funded in a world bank, with ecclesiastical bankers in monopolistic control, so that for the price of a Mass they can transfer funds to the credit of somebody in purgatory. The church is not that kind or any kind of mortgage company. The notion would be repugnant even of a loan association. Men are men, even though they be priests, and God is God. Men may not usurp the prerogatives of God, and God could not engage in such dubious and arbitrary transactions.

But Protestants have been in worse case, for in many an instance they have had *no* doctrine of "the merits of the saints." The New Testament doctrine is this: No man has any ultimate "merit," for he is a creature. Every "merit" is the bestowal of God. Besides, all men are held in "the power of the evil one," except for God's grace. "There is none righteous, no, not one." [43] Therefore only God can cleanse the world. "The saints" in the Old Testament are the poor and needy who know their need, and who therefore look to God constantly for his deliverance. "The saints" in the New Testament are never "righteous" in their own account: they would be hopeless in the awareness of their unworthiness if they had not been found of God's mercy in Christ. Thus Paul to the church at Philippi concerning the church in Rome: "Greet every saint in Christ Jesus. All the saints greet you, especially those of Caesar's household" [44]— the slaves in the imperial palace. The "saints" are the good folk in Christ. Their only "merit" is that they are granted, though only as his living instruments, to take on themselves in love the sufferings of mankind, and "complete what is lacking" (though nothing is lacking) "in the sufferings of Christ." [45] Both Catholic and Protestant thought now moves in a new ecumenicity towards that understanding. Catholic thought in one particular has more grip: it understands that living and "dead" are bound in one "communion of the saints."

IV

Well, there it is, as well as I can presently write it: the astonishing transformation of pain in the New Testament. It was judgment: now it is mercy. It was prison: now it is an open door. It was dark enigma: now it is cleansing, vocation, and apocalypse. The agonized "why?" is silenced: the word now is, Jesus the Christ has shown us the saving purpose of pain. Some there be in our time who follow Christ without wearing his badge, and some wear his badge who do not follow. Of those who follow without the badge he himself would surely say again in love: "He that is not against us is for us." [46] Of those who wear the badge and do not follow, he says: "He who is not with me is against me, and he who does not gather with me scatters." [47] But even though Christ is unacknowledged or unknown, he is present in Spirit, and he is in the climate of the world.

Ideals do not move us, for they soon fade into the light of common day. When trouble comes they flee like ghosts. They have power only when we see them in a face, and when they touch us with a hand on our hand. They must become incarnate: enfleshed. If we would explain true patriotism grandiose words are no help: we point to Lincoln and Lee. Even Marxism, with all its resolve to remain a system free from "the cult of personality," makes a shrine of the grave of Lenin. The understanding of the vocation of pain will dissolve under "the acids of modernity" if Christ be forgotten. So the story of the man called "The Pair" is not sentimentalism. There were two chairs at table, two glasses, two plates, two portions of food—one for the man, and the other for the first beggar who came down the road. Why? Because Christ said: "Truly, I say to you, as you did it to one of the least of these my brethren, you did it to me." [48] The man should have been called "The Three," because life for him was in another kind of triangle: Christ, the neighbor, and himself; except that at death he held out his hand to One unseen, for at death no beggar or rich man could help him: he trusted then only to One who was raised from the dead.

We have written nothing of the blessing that falls on a man who answers the calling of pain—the vocation of pain in faith held fast, in a witness which spells pain in an alien world, and in the pain of the world voluntarily shared. The man is now caught in vital life, and is careless of his fee. When we gaze on a field of daffodils we do not ask, "What do I get out of this?" Still less do we ask it of a genuine friendship: the question then is, "What can I give?" not "What can I get?" Still less could we ever ask it of the mercy of Christ: then we are "lost in wonder, love, and praise." [49] Yet there is an amazing paragraph in the New Testament about the surety which comes to a man who has answered Christ in the vocation of pain. To trust Christ seems a tenuous affair: he lived long ago, and can we be sure of an unseen Presence? But this man says that the devil has brought down every sharp axe on the seemingly frail cable between a man and his Lord, and every stroke is in vain: "For I am sure that neither death nor life [life being sometimes a worse threat than death], nor angels, nor principalities [malignities in upper space: we might say the id, the subconscious, and the bomb!], nor things present, nor things to come [the fears of today and whatever enmity the future may bring], nor powers [another reference to unseen

foes above the earth or below the threshold], nor height, nor depth
[sputnik or volcano], nor anything else in all creation, will be able to
separate us from the love of God in Christ Jesus our Lord." [50] Such
writing, and such faith unsurpassed, is treasure found only in the New
Testament.

13. Pain as Insight

If pain were only cleansing, our house might be "swept and put in order," but empty; and the emptiness might then invite seven other devils, so that the last state of life might become "worse than the first."[1] Jesus said that such a fate would befall his generation. It has already befallen ours, for we get rid (occasionally) of corrupt politics but cannot find men with true conviction about the *polis* (the city) to fill the empty posts of leadership. Perhaps psychiatry is under the same threat, for what use to scrape clean every sinew of the hidden self, getting rid of every complex (with accompanying loss of a rightful reticence), if there is no faith to fill the gap? Actually the cleansing of which we have written is under the Event of Christ: he fills the gap. Even so, cleansing would not be enough.

Likewise if pain were only vocation, and the vocation led life into darkness, life would still be bereft. We do well to turn our faces from any faith which deals centrally in rewards and punishments, and specifically from that interpretation of faith in Christ which would make him centrally the salesman of a sugary heaven or the doomster of a fiery hell. Yet we already know in this life the foretaste of both heaven and hell, and the truth could hardly be truth if its issue were evil and death.

This chapter therefore proposes that pain within the resurrection-cross of Christ leads through cleansing and vocation to a new understanding of life.

I

We repeat: *Pain of itself* cannot grant illumination, for of itself it is incipient death. It evokes the double cry: "I am mortal. Where is my salvation?" Of itself it may point us beyond itself, but the beyond must then lay hands on us. To the faith of the church those hands are the hands of Jesus the Christ. So we are writing of pain under the catalyst of his Event and his Presence. But we must keep saying that pain of itself, far from granting us new and piercing sight, is likelier to lead us to an unlit prison. Death *in itself* would drag us off into the jungle to die in loneliness, like the animals. Even a toothache *of itself* shuts us in: we may become surly, and "take it out" on our neighbors. But the startling change written on every page of the New Testament is this: Pain has become cleansing, a sought-after vocation, and—illumination. Thus Paul could say of his sufferings in prison, and say it without any pretense but in full realism, "Yes, and I shall rejoice." [2] Why? Because he now had insight into the meaning of life: "For to me to live is Christ, and to die is gain" [3] (of Christ).

Actually pain is never completely of itself. Always it is linked with the mystery of birth and death, especially when we are on a surgeon's table and the anesthetist says, "Now breathe normally." As if we could! That moment is not a normal moment. Tragedy, as when once I worked in vain to restore breath to a body taken from a lake, brings catharsis. That is to say, even pain with no meaning and no exit has this cleansing power. This implies that tragedy is never fully "closed": it has a thin aperture on the Mystery. Our "clay-shuttered doors" [4] are opened—on a world beyond our clay. Our "estranged faces" are taken between unseen Hands and made to look into the Abyss. But the pain of tragedy is still barren, and may even become a self-indulgence moving in successive steps toward death, unless the Abyss speaks in the language of our life, yes, and of our best love and bids us follow. "See the Christ stand!" [5]

Even without the catalyst of Christ we know that the slow movement from Beethoven's *Seventh Symphony* is profounder music than the gay

"Country Gardens." [6] I know: a dear friend asked in the faith that the slow movement be played at his funeral! Death as death, even without the faith, grants *some* measure of illumination, for when a near neighbor dies we no longer stress his failings, even though we are clearly aware of them: a gentler mood, far removed from sentimentalism, comes on us, so that we cherish with a smile his idiosyncrasies and that truth in him which he (like the rest of us) was never able to speak. But tragedy without the catalyst of Christ gives no glad certitude. The mists unsettle and resettle. The gleam in the sky fades again, like the "false dawns" in the Arctic after the long night. But there at last the sun breaks through, and that is the precise symbol of the Event in the New Testament: "For it is the God who said, 'Let light shine out of darkness,' who has shone in our hearts to give the light of the knowledge of the glory of God in the face of Christ." [7] The faith through pain and its catharsis grants us understanding which a bland and painless life could never give.

II

Pain under the Event of Christ gives us a new understanding of the natural world. We see the work of God's hand in nature. *We* did not make the cosmos. We brag about "the conquest of space," but we cannot go a step beyond our little planet without a hundred contrivances to reproduce the warmth, food, and air by which we daily live. Nor can we take liberties with the planet, for it is not ours: we must plow along the contour lines of the hills or the soil will run away from us down a dozen hillside streams. We must replant forests or the moisture cannot be kept against the roots, and duststorms will devastate our fields. There is fidelity in nature. Seedtime and harvest do *not* fail: the promise of Noah's rainbow has been kept. [8] Harvests may fail here, but they are abundant there—to teach us a decent sharing in the human family. Nature, like our human life, is basically joy, though with punctuations of storm and drought.

There are other signs of the Presence and the Power. An ocean sunset almost speaks about another world

> beyond the sunset, and the baths
> Of all the western stars. [9]

202

The Psalms are not trapped in nature worship, but they find the handiwork of God in nature:

> When I look at thy heavens, the work of thy fingers,
> the moon and the stars which thou hast established.[10]

The Bible does not deduce God from nature: it knows God in man's
nature (the Uncreated over against our creaturehood, the Eternal confronting our time-bound years), and thus and then finds his handiwork in
the cosmos.[11] The Psalms would have been even more sure had they
known the astronomical truth about the moon:

> The innocent moon, that nothing does but shine,
> Moves all the labouring surges of the world.[12]

Had they seen or known about the *aurora borealis,* electrically charged
particles emitted by the sun entering the deflecting action of the earth's
magnetic field, they would have said: "With a hundred mile sky as his
canvas!" They find God in the small as well as the vast in the cosmos,
and would have agreed with Francis Thompson that one blade of grass
is revelation:

> Epitomized in thee
> Was the mystery
> Which shakes the spheres conjoint—
> God focussed to a point.[13]

It need not surprise us that men have worshiped nature, even to finding
a god in every tree, river, and mountain.

(a)

But pain enters to give pause, and if pain finds its meaning in Christ
the pause gives the right understanding of nature. For nature is far from
idyllic. Tornadoes cut careless swathes of destruction. Flooded rivers carry
away whole streets of homes. Earthquakes with their aftermath of tidal
waves toss people around as if they were sand and stones. Snakes hide
in the grass, and bugs do not need to hide for they are invisible in the

air we breathe; and our bodies, part of the natural order, are invaded by cancer without our knowing either the time or the manner of the demonic invasion. In each such instance we see the *devil* "focused to a point." Then it is merely captious to prate about "natural law." We may rightly judge nature under patterns (which are still nature's *and ours*) for our scientific learning, but there is still a wild freedom in nature which our "laws" cannot tame. Pain leads us beyond pantheism, unless we wish to spoof ourselves into believing that evil is good.

Garden clubs enlist our gratitude, but garden club theology should be suspect. Jesus the Christ was betrayed in a garden. The summer conferences of the churches are not free from unrealism. As they front the sunset seen through pine trees they may become blind to nature's cruel ambiguities. Worship indoors fronting a crudely built cross might be nearer truth. The Chautauqua Hymn cannot rightly be our only food:

> Day is dying in the west;
> Heaven is touching earth with rest. . . .
> Holy, holy, holy, Lord God of hosts!
> Heaven and earth are full of thee!
> Heaven and earth are praising thee,
>   O Lord Most High! [14]

Is Pompeii suddenly obliterated by volcanic lava "full of thee"? Was Anchorage after the earthquake a choir of angels "praising thee"? But Chautauqua with its four loyalties never was realistic.[15] How can life be lived under four equal loyalties?

(b)

Nature seen under the Christ-catalyst in our pain becomes a parable of God—and of his servant the devil. So Christ taught us, or would teach us if we would listen. He reminded us that God in his gifts of sun and rain blesses equally the good men and the bad men,[16] but he was not being naïve: he was choosing an instance in nature which typifies the Grace which "shows no partiality." [17] He knew that the sun can scorch the fields, and that sudden rain can become a destructive spate: "and the floods came, and . . . beat against that house, and it fell; and great was the fall of it." [18] Nature then was symbolic of the folly that would trust

204

nature—or human nature. Christ spoke again of the beneficence of nature: a seed sown, and thus meeting the accordant mercy of soil and sky, sprouts by a miracle, for the farmer "knows not how" [19]; and the growth of the kingdom hidden in our world is like wonder. But Christ was not sentimental about soil and seed, for the seed can fall on hard ground, stony ground, and thorn-infested ground, and thus come to nought.[20] Besides, there are fields cluttered with weeds, and men cannot completely get rid of the weeds. If men should try, they will uproot the wheat with the weeds. As to the weeds, "an *enemy* has done" it! [21] But there is a coming judgment! How could we ever have believed that Jesus is naïve about the natural order?

Our pain convinces us that nature is "a mixed blessing," and Christ shows us in what opposite ways nature is a parable. If we try to worship God in nature, we shall again and again be obliged to exclaim: "God? This is not God, but the Adversary!" We by our poor human power cannot get rid of the weeds, but by his Spirit we can help sow wheat. Yet we need not fear to make nature our temporary home, since manifest evil is still in Gods' power, and the devil is still his servant, for in the Cross and the conquered grave God has shown that his love in Christ has overcome evil and turned it to his redemptive purpose. The decisive blow has been struck. Even if storms should sweep away those we love, and we are left sorrowing, we need not fear, even though in the burden of our creaturehood we shall still sorrow, for God has overcome death. Thus C. S. Lewis in his tribute to Charles Williams, who had as keen an understanding of the faith as most men in our time, tells us that when the idea of death and the idea of Williams met in his mind, "it was the idea of death that was changed." [22]

III

Pain in the Event of Christ gives insight into human nature. In man we see God at work. We understand his word through the prophet: "all souls are mine." [23] A contemporary swirl in theology, which has been a minor motif in theology since the Psalms, holds that "God is dead," actually dead, or that we must find a new name for God because that name has been so traduced as to be an untruth.[24] Of course if God is actually dead, he never lived. The worshiping ages, as in the Twenty-

third Psalm, were a colossal blunder, and Jesus himself in his constant
talk about God mistook a word for reality. Thus the spokesmen for the
swirl are hardly modest. Wisdom has *not* been born in *The Secular City*
—over which Jesus wept! Man has *not* suddenly "come of age" [25] in a
world in which men can find no better way to settle a quarrel than to
kill one another off like flies. Man "has no need for God"? [26] No, he can
make mock of justice in Alabama without God's help!

But the finite bounds of life oblige us to acknowledge the Mystery beyond the bounds. Yes, we shall continue to speak of God as "beyond,"
despite the strictures of John A. T. Robinson in his *Honest to God*,[27]
in which he proposes that we speak of the God within. For the God
within is just as geographical as the God beyond, and more vulnerable
to our self-idolatries. As to finding a new name for God, that proposal
has its share of wisdom, for Mississippi segregationists also profess to
honor "God." But it is not easy to find new names for central loyalties.
"Bread" has become a Western selfishness in a hungry world, but how to
find a new name? "Mother" points often to moralistic parenthood, but
how to find a new name? Harvey Cox rightly reminds us that the Old
Testament has many names for God.[28] But it keeps returning to the old
names under new revelation. Actually we ourselves fashion new names,
as witness T. S. Eliot's "The Stranger," [29] and W. H. Auden's "The
Father-Abyss." [30] These new names may help us honor the old name with
clearer truth.

(a)

The above-written paragraphs are only partly digression. They are
written to underline the fact that we see God in man's life, for man did
not make himself. Theology which deems man to be nothing because
God is everything hardly squares with what Jesus said. Jesus himself
found God in *The Secular City*. Thus Harvey Cox has his warrant.
Religious people come off badly in Christ's parables: the modern swirl
has its fine measure of truth. The religious people, Jesus says, professed
obedience to God and with due reverence: "I go, sir." [31] But they did not
go, for they despised the godless who also were God's children. The
godless on the other hand were curt in their refusal: "I go not." But they
changed their minds and went, in daily kindness without ulterior

hankerings. So God is found in *The Secular City*. That our scientific and technological culture is God's new word is yet in doubt. The spokesmen of the swirl are astonishingly optimistic. They hold that machines will bring the leisure in which men will creatively fashion a new society,[32] in the freedom which God (or life) has given, God being content to serve as silent and inactive partner. But men such as Jacques Ellul take the opposite tack.[33] They fear that our technic with its insistent cult of know-how and its multiplied machines is now compulsive, like alcoholism: we cannot stop—until creative thought is choked, or nuclear war gives our race a new start or obliterates all human life, or God intervenes in some new turn in history. Who knows? Nobody knows. It is not given to men to read the future. But some of us are not so enamored of metropolis. We appreciate its blessings but refuse to canonize it: it is almost the vortex of present crime and sadness, as well as of opportunity.

But the new-old swirl has left us in debt in its belief that the secular world is the locale of God's self-manifestation. Of course: "It is he that made us, and we are his." [34] The works of man's hands in a towering United Nations building testify to "the Godward side of our heredity." [35] Art at its best is not secular only, but a witness to another Realm, and the church should not try to print its pietisms on the artist's proper categories. Modern music is true in its percussions and dissonances to the time in which we live: there is a new world aborning. The compassion of the so-called godless is precisely not godless. Not soon shall I forget how, toward the close of a worship service in an Eastern college, a student came forward in response to the chaplain's, "Has anyone here a concern to express?" The student (they told me that he is not of the faith) sang to his guitar a plaintive song about the death of a "seven-year-old child." Killed in Vietnam North or South? The singer and such as he may be unsure of God, but God is sure of them, and the song is heard: "Therefore God is not ashamed to be called their God, for he has prepared for them a city." [36]

(b)

But we have written enough in the paragraphs above to give warning that man is not the object of our trust, for human nature is no more trustworthy than nature. Pain gives sharper warning. Even if men were genuinely good men (who among us could claim that adjective?), they die, from what we call "natural causes": they are subject to the contingencies of the flawed world. Even if men were genuinely wise men (the state of society makes mock of the supposition), there is a mental institution near every sizeable city: the mind easily becomes unhinged. Actually men are neither good nor wise. They rationalize, sauve followers of a suave Belial:

> His tongue
> Dropp'd manna, and could make the worse appear
> The better reason.[37]

Sermons as well as political campaign speeches open the door to this mixed deceit and self-deceit. Men even when staunchly rational are prey to irrational moods. Besides, men are outrightly wicked, not merely victims of natural and historical evil. They—meaning you and I—knowingly pervert any system, such as a chamber of commerce or a labor union, and deliberately misuse any invention. Surely none of us could dispute the change. An electric drill is the dentist's tool to safeguard health, but burglars also use it to open locked doors. Need we continue the drear indictment? The front page of any newspaper is evidence. Some papers feed on crime for the sake of circulation, and so become party to the guilt.

No, we need not continue the bill of particulars, provided we have honestly confronted it. Emerson's essay on "Self-Reliance," a favored item on the high-school educational menu, hardly stands scrutiny. It is filled with glittering sentences (which contradict one another on almost every page), but it has neither horizons of mystery nor ground-plan of realistic faith. Mortal dust posing as self-reliant might be only comic, but wicked dust in such a pose is tragic. Man has not "come of age" [38]: Bonhoeffer in that phrase could not have meant that we have reached maturity, for *bombs* threatened his *Nazi* prison while he wrote. Man is not "getting along without God." [39] Bonhoeffer's own prayers show that he intended no baldly literal meaning in that word. It would be truer to say that man is still stumbling along like a child, from dark crisis to dark crisis, every crisis invited in measure by his own egocentricities. Human nature killed Christ, because human nature is still vulnerable to the devil. The base of human nature is good, for God made man in his own image, but the reality of evil in our world cannot be gainsaid. Pain is for witness.

(c)

Thus once more we turn to the realism of the parables of Jesus. There and elsewhere he spoke of men more than of nature. He portrayed us not simply as "good guys" and "bad guys," but as guys who are strangely mixed in motive, good-bad guys. The priest and the Levite in the story of the good Samaritan [40] were not totally bad men. They were not callous: they were on their way to church. They deeply wished to worship, and would be defiled, that is, barred from worship, if they touched a dying man. A high school lad, when recently I spoke thus of them, made the perceptive though irreverent comment: "Doc, you mean they were too damned religious?" That is what the new-old swirl in theology is saying: they were not "secular" enough. They lacked Bonhoeffer's "holy worldliness." [41] But they were not wrong to give central place to worship, for our hope is neither in nature nor in man. Maybe the Samaritan in the story had not yet found that Sky by which all our times and spaces are measured. Maybe he left no place for worship. But as to that we are not told. We *are* told that human nature, even human nature intent to worship, can never be our compass and our North Star. Just as evil in nature rules out naturalism, so evil and sin in human nature rule out humanism, unless we wish to kid ourselves that two world wars were only passing clouds bringing their refreshing showers. What evil may be in the perspectives of another world we do not know, but in this world evil is evil.

Jesus in his parables spoke more about man than about nature, and more about God than about man. Dietrich Bonhoeffer rightly describes Jesus as "the Man for others," [42] and rightly reminds us that Jesus spent much of his time in *The Secular City*, with traitors and the "Godless." Bonhoeffer is again our wise mentor and friend when he warns the church that its members are called to live out their Faith in the workaday world, without censoriousness, false righteousness or proselyting. [43] Modern man has certainly "come of age" [44] in the sense that he will no longer be spoon-fed by the church's all-too-glib platitudes. He has "come of age" in another sense: he knows that God is not God if he expects us to consult him before we speak any word, and not God if he thrusts himself on us at every turn of the road. The new-old swirl is right to remind us that God has given us a certain liberty and intends and expects us to use it in liberty. But that title, "the Man for others," [45] could still mislead us. In *what way* "for others"? Not *our* way, for our very kindness has often a hidden grasping or a self-congratulatory eye.

"For others" as God in Christ is "for others"! That is what Bonhoeffer meant in life and in that martyrdom by which our easy path is put to shame. So God is always main Actor in the parables: Actor, not sleeping Partner. He goes "on a journey," leaving us meanwhile to the exercise of freedom, but always he returns and asks an accounting. He is the Father who waits for the prodigal's sad-glad homeward trek, and who then does not wait, but runs in welcome while the prodigal is yet "a great way off." He is the Shepherd who never waits, but goes at risk to seek and find the lost sheep. He is not content to live on the other side of the sky: he comes by a secret stair into our history, the Word made flesh. How do we know that we cannot live for nature? By our pain! How do we know that we cannot trust human nature? By the pain of our folly and other men's folly: by the pain we inflict and the pain we suffer! How do we know that God acts? By Christ's pain on Calvary—in the light of the Resurrection! Would we know God if we suffered no pain? Not so far as we can understand. Thus our pain becomes insight into both nature and human nature, and the spur which thrusts us toward God by faith.

IV

Therefore our pain within the light of Christ gives us *the deepest insight, a road to the understanding of the nature of God.* We still do not know why earth is destined to pain, or why God should employ so strange a servant as the devil, but that ignorance is itself insight: God's thoughts are not our thoughts, and his ways are not our ways.[46] Pain traces as with a dagger the line between two dimensions of life: "I am mortal! Where is my salvation?" Thus the initial insight is this: *We live in Mystery.* Human wisdom is quite impressive until the shadow of death appears, and that shadow appears whenever pain strikes. Think of all the knowledge in the university down the street: it is wonderful, until . . . until we are on a hospital bed, not at all sure that we shall leave the hospital alive. Similarly human skill, as in a jet plane or a nuclear submarine, seems almost godlike until . . . until pain strikes. Then we know that even the best medical skill is finally defeated, for the doctor loses every patient at last, and the patient loses every doctor.

No faith has truth which does not confront Mystery and acknowledge that all merely human wisdom and skill are but the whistling of children in the night. Consider what science now calls cosmic evolution, vast explosions of hydrogen in the far incredible reaches of space, with new galaxies emerging from the flaming vortex. Are there other races better than ours, or even worse with worse wars than our wars? Is all this the work of a Personal Hand? Where is he? Beyond space and time? But we cannot comprehend "beyond space and time." In us? Yes, or we would not worship, and could not worship without Mystery. Yet not merely within us, dying as we die? No. Then where and how? Pain drives us into that unknown, away from our safe shore; and we have no choice:

> Darest thou now, O Soul,
> Walk out with me toward the Unknown Region,
> Where neither ground is for the feet,
>   nor any path to follow?
>
> No map there, nor guide,
> No voice sounding, nor touch of human hand,
> Nor face with blooming flesh, nor lips nor
>   eyes are in that land.[47]

But the question is not if we may "dare": we *have to* make that journey. Maybe there *is* a Guide, better than a "human voice." But the Mystery still is Mystery.

(a)

Pain gives this further insight: God, the Mystery from whom we come, to whom we go, is not chiefly concerned with our length of days in this world. In India hundreds of thousands of children die in infancy. Yes, our skill, if we had love enough, could stop that loss, yet not completely stop it: children die in our land. In the wild devilishness of nature people are wiped out wholesale by storm or drought, and God does nothing. Maybe we are not meant to live an earthbound life. Maybe our true loyalty is above that line ("I am mortal! Where is my salvation?") which pain always traces. Maybe our job is sacrament—to make of earth while we are here "the outward and visible sign" of "an inward and spiritual grace." [48]

If that were true (is it not true?), we might be well rid of our word "progress," with its current earthiness and its cowardly refusal to confront the facts of transience and death. "Progress" could give place to the better word "sacrament," which then could point us to a better "progress," namely, any place where the unseen dimension of our life is honored, and thus invades redeemingly the world in which meanwhile we must live. We hardly know what to say to one another when pain strikes. Our words are banal, and sometimes untrue. "It isn't a serious operation" (but, of course, it might be!). "I'm sure you're going to get well" (*are* we sure, can we ever be sure?). "You're not dead yet!" (but, of course, you soon will be). When shall we learn to be honest with each other? Henri Perryve spoke an honest word to Charles Perraud in Perraud's trouble: "You, by the will of God, are passing through a desolate region, because your soul must not rest in mediocrity." [49] Love of this world is always mediocrity, but pain breaks that love.

(b)

But, more importantly, pain under the catalyst of Christ shows us that love (the "hard love" which we see in him) is the burning heart of the Mystery. Could we ever have known the love of God without his pain— and without our pain as we answer the question, "Were you there when they crucified my Lord?" [50] We have earlier mentioned the Old Testament story of a king walking the streets of his city in the time of a siege so merciless in its encircling power that food was almost gone. A woman demanded that he help in the extremity of famine. She, the subject, presumed to lay hands on the king! Why? Because she had made a bargain with her neighbor: they would eat "my" child today, and the neighbor's child tomorrow. But the neighbor had hidden her child! Now the king tore open the royal robe, now as he walked with the defenders on the wall, "and the people looked, and behold, he had sackcloth beneath upon his body." [51] They knew then that he shared their sorrow.

But the king could not lift the siege. It *was* lifted, but not by man's power. There was strange turn of events in a world in which every event has an aura of mystery. The story is parable: at Calvary our human race saw the royal robe of God's nature, his mystery, his majesty of aeons and galaxies, torn open, and underneath, next to his heart, the sackcloth of all our pains. He *could* and did lift the siege, first by sharing it to tell us that he is in this crux of life with us, and then by raising Christ from the dead. We may not or should not ask for scientific proof, for this Event is unveiling, not time-space measurement, but the revelation of the deeps of the Mystery. Could we ever have known this "burning heart of the Abyss" [52] without the siege? The question is conjecture, and so cannot be answered. Let us be content to say that it is by the siege that we *do* know. The siege is lifted, and our feet, even in this present time, are on an open path beyond the city walls.

> The incarnate Word, Truth-in-Event, is this:
> Love is the burning heart of the Abyss. [53]

(c)

It follows from this central insight into God's nature and purpose that he intends us to live with one another in that selfsame love. This intention is reiterated in the New Testament. The inimitable thirteenth chapter of the First Letter to Corinth is a poem in three stanzas not about our human love, though I have heard sermons to that effect with Hollywood touches added, but about God's love poured into our history through Jesus the Christ. Thus stanza one (vss. 1-3): eloquence, prophetic gift, faith, and philanthropy are all of them vain without this love. Stanza two (vss. 4-7): love is a homey everyday affair ("very patient, very kind") which does not strut, or get angry, or grow tired. Stanza three (vss. 8-13): many human gifts fail, and our knowledge is always fragmentary, but this Love never fails. Life droops in our time in many a broken home because "I am not loved," and that attrition comes because the "I" has not learned to love; and that lack arises because human beings, created and contingent, have lost the main contact of a great Faith. No lamp burns on earth except by gift of the sun. "Beloved, if God so loved us, we also ought to love one another." [54] Not Hollywood fashion, but "so," in the same way and by the same Power. This love has a worldwide sweep but keeps its homey gait. A wise psychiatrist, when his coed patient told him that her greatest wish was to live in the love of God, replied: "As Joan of Arc, or as being patient with your room-mate?"

Pain interpreted under the Event of Christ underscores this insight into God's purpose: we are on this planet for only one work—to love one another as God in Christ has loved us. We are not here to live long years, for a picture cannot be painted on a mile-long canvas or a piano concerto played on a mile-long keyboard: death delineates life, and thus makes possible the *art* of goodwill. Likewise we are not here to be self-reliant: a planet filled with self-reliant people might be a new ice age, and we had better curb our computers because a planet filled with robots would be steely death in an ice age. Joy is the base of life, but we are not here to be always smiling (Miss Diesel Engine or Miss Slaughterhouse or Miss Sewage Pipe is not more attractive because of that fixed inane smile), for joy is a far more precious commodity than pleasure or even happiness. Why does the photographer always bid us "Smile"? Or "Laugh!" as if we were a pack of hyenas? Jesus said, "Blessed are those who mourn," [55] thus pointing us to God's central purpose for bringing us into this world—that we shall love him and our neighbors in sorrow and pain, as well as in joy. We are not here to gather wealth, for, had that been the intention, God might have made us squirrels with an un-limited supply of nuts and a hole (the corner bank) in every tree. "This is my commandment, that you love one another as I have loved you." [56] Is there any other sufficient reason why we should have been born? Pain draws a red line under that command. It is better than command: it can be obeyed in love because it was written in love.

V

If God likes our technologies we cannot yet know. He has let us set foot on that straight unswerving road and is willing that we walk it for a distance yet to be determined. The road has one undeniable grace: It is drawing us together, almost obliging us to walk in step. One man may carve and set wooden type, but only a thousand men acting as one man can make and use a modern printing machine. Technology may rob us of a rightful solitude. The endless prying of newspaper men, listening devices hidden in every corner, and the ubiquitous camera plus microphone may yet cheat us of that personhood which comes from wise alternation between the noisy city and the silent fields. But it is clear that our planet is becoming one culture. Machines draw the ends of the earth to the end of every street. The radio gives a man the chance to be heard by all men. Too bad that the dubious gift has come when we have almost nothing to say. That first Tel-Star program: did it not feature a program from a Paris nightclub? But God has given us to walk down a road which gathers all men. Is it not clear beyond cavil that our wars solve no issue? Far from stopping communism, they bring the poverty and hopelessness, the fear and bitterness which invite communism. This fact we know, secretly and behind our eyes; and we fight wars now only because we do not know what else to do, and to "save face" even though a proud and angry face is not worth saving. What other word now makes sense except the word of Christ worked out patiently, sufferingly, from one partial gain to another? This insight comes from pain, our pain and God's pain: "This is my commandment, that you love one another as I have loved you." [57]

Even so, we must not seek pain except as we seek to share our neighbor's pain in love, except as we deliberately make that brave witness which we know will bring pain. We must not seek pain for its own sake, for pain of itself leads on to death. Self-inflicted pain has no virtue, for the man who plays his own providence finds anything but provision. The writer to the church at Colossae speaks of self-inflicted rigors with the unfailing workaday common sense of the New Testament: "These have indeed an appearance of wisdom in promoting rigor of devotion and self-abasement and severity to the body, but they are of no value in checking indulgence of the flesh." [58] They are still locked in an ascetic cult of the flesh! But the fact that men in the New Testament were tempted to make their own pain is tribute twistedly to a change in climate: pain is now cleansing, vocation even, and insight. The enigma of pain is still enigma. Or, rather, it would be except that the enigma has become God's strange but joyous purpose.

215

14. Pain, Death, and the Resurrection

If death is death, what happens? Nothing *happens:* there is no event. All we have written, all anybody has suffered and wrought, goes down the drain. No, worse, for a drain leads somewhere. There is not even a drain if death is death: everything disappears in total night. In a *Reader's Digest* article printed six years ago (its all-too-easy "wisdom" helped provoke this poor book) the author says: "And, most important of all, suffering is God's way of improving the world." [1] Same old unrealism, same old "improvement"! *Has* the incredible suffering of two world wars "improved" our world? And what of a God who would choose that method of improvement? Maybe he *has* chosen it or allowed it (via the work of the devil), but he is himself a dubious God unless he gives us some sure sign by which we can believe in him. Moreover, what if the "improved" world is itself, with all the proud bedraggled, yearning pageant of men clinging to its cliffs, condemned to go down the drain, without even a drain?

The author of the article quotes from Cyrus Bartol, though not before he has told us that if people, wicked and good alike, do not "slip and fall" and suffer "contagious diseases" this planet "would be an unscientific and unpredictable place in which to live." How chummy! The planet is unpredictable in any event, isn't it? Moreover, a completely scientific world would be a nightmare, wouldn't it? And is God more concerned about science and predictability than about people? But now for the quotation: "What pains and tears the slightest steps of man's progress have cost! . . . Humanity has reached blessing after blessing of all its vast achievement for good, with bleeding feet." Same old "progress"! The feet have bled all right. There is "blessing after blessing" all right, though it is doubtful if we have "achieved" them: basic joy is God's gift, not man's contrivance. But is our world thus "blessed" by human skill? We do not know, because the measuring-rod is not in our hands, but our eyes gazing across our present chaos find no instant and radiant conviction. Suppose evil is constitutional in this planet. In any event, what if all "improvement," all "progress," all "blessing" go down the drain? What if all "bleeding feet" walk to the same black doom? What if there isn't even a drain?

You, most patient reader, may now begin to understand the contention which at first may have seemed a bigotry, that the resurrection of Christ is the crucial Event in human story, crucial in very literal sense, crucial through the Cross. This morning's paper [2] tells how a fine college girl, lovely enough to be a beauty queen, yesterday fell from a mountain cliff and was killed. She leaned over too far because she wished to see the wonderful view. Was she killed in order that we may live in a "predictable world"? Science *cannot* predict such an event. Science always draws its too-neat patterns, its semisynthetic "laws," *after* the event. Moreover its very discoveries spring in measure from the mysterious deeps of the subconscious. What are we to say about that fine girl's death? Another clipping from some years ago quotes with apparent approval from Sigmund Freud. [3] The article agrees with Nicolas Berdyaev that "the fundamental and most serious question of human existence" is "how is one to triumph over suffering." But it does not dwell on Berdyaev's answer. It concludes with Freud: "As for the great necessities of fate, against which there is no remedy, these (man) will simply learn to endure with resignation." But love, even our poor human love, is never "resigned" to pain and death. It may be baffled and torn, it may live with pain in a dull persistent ache, hoping against all visible hope, but it is not resigned. Maybe any attempt to turn the psyche into a science makes us partly insensitive to man's existential pain.

Modern psychiatry dwells more on frustration than on sin as the reason for "antisocial conduct," which actually is anticreation conduct. It admits human blame, however reluctantly, as when in its examination of a criminal it reports to the law court that he was "responsible" for his actions. But it dwells more on "frustration," caused, for example, by parental coercion or neglect, or by the public indifference which eventuates in a ghetto. This approach raises some nice questions, such as these: Are the parents responsible, and all of us who comprise the public indifference? Are *their* parents also responsible and people who came before us? If so, isn't psychiatry giving us its own drearier doctrine of original sin without any doctrine of our origin in God? But psychiatry prefers the word "frustration," and our main concern now is to learn what can be learned, not to pick a quarrel. All right: death is the final, inescapable frustration. Is our race thereby forever doomed to "mental maladjustment" and "hostile behavior"? "Don't fence me in," [4] the modern song abjures us. If the ghetto fences a man in there are riots, as witness Los Angeles. But if death fences us in, will there not, must there not, always be violence and hate?

There is no doubt about the fencing in, for death is the ultimate pain. Anesthesia has largely overcome the physical suffering. But not the pain of contemplation: "Soon there will be another funeral procession, and it will be mine." Not the pain of separation: "Soon I must leave my home, my wife, my children and grandchildren, my friends, and this little planet in which I have known such joys." Not the pain of discontinuity: "The ancients were right when they pictured death as a shadowed figure holding the shears that cut the vital thread of life." Not the pain of the unknown: "What will happen in *that* moment?" Not the pain of judgment: "How have I lived my life? For toys instead of costly love?" An ancient prayer of the church has far more depth than Freud. It acknowledges the Mystery which our very finitude implies and pleads, "Suffer us not by any pains of death to fall from thee." So any realistic book on pain must confront "the pains of death."

218

I

It is no disparagement of any faith, least of all faith in Christ, that it lives in hope, for life without hope is "hopeless": nothing can be done. We say, "While there's life there's hope," but we could as rightly add, "While there's hope there's life." If we lack memory we are cut off from the backward range; if we lack hope we are cut off from the forward range. The present without past and future is a tiny prison called "Now" with no light through the narrow bars. Isn't it strange that our current jibe, "Pie in the sky by and by," should miss so plain a fact? If there is no kind of "pie" ahead of us we starve to death. "Hope deferred makes the heart sick," [5] but hope fulfilled without any new hope would deliver the heart to the morgue. Thus the seeming childishness but actual profundity of the New Testament: "For in this hope" (a world in which all suffering is redeemed) "we were saved. Now hope that is seen [fulfilled] is not hope. For who hopes for what he sees?" [6] Robert Louis Stevenson wrote, "To travel hopefully is a better thing than to arrive." [7] But we cannot accept that word at face value, for it leaves hope forever "deferred," and the "heart" therefore always ailing. When our life is creative it is a pilgrimage in which some worthy hope *is* fulfilled to provide an inn where we rest awhile, but with some new hope always beckoning us to the next exciting stage of the journey.

Do we not so travel? As little children we hope for birthdays and the time when "we shall soon go to school." In grade school we anticipate high school days when we shall be "almost grown up." Then the freedom of college "away from home" brightens on the horizon. Those four years, plus perchance added years in graduate school, seem endless in prospect, but a swift flight in retrospect. The pilgrim may not tarry: he then or earlier falls in love, and his new hope is marriage, home, and children. Only a sour mind, or a poet enamored of lovely gloaming, could have written:

> The Worldly Hope men set their Hearts upon
> Turns Ashes.[8]

The hope is not altogether worldly, for it has "bright shoots of ever-lastingness," [9] and the fulfillment is gift from life's basic joy. But after home and children "worldly hope" is not so sure and clear: competence

219

in business or profession, items of honor by which our friends acknowledge our ability and their trust, happy marriage for our children and
the arrival of grandchildren, a less arduous life in the sunset of our
years. And then?

Then the moment of truth! On the pilgrimage we have welcomed
false hopes which have laughed in our face, and many a good hope has
been broken by catastrophe and egocentricity and pain. Death has
snatched away some answers while they were in bud. But there has been
genuine joy. Then suddenly the word of the psalm strikes home: "The
years of our life are three score and ten." [10] What if we have passed that
mark, as I who write these words? Are we then living on borrowed
time? The lovely lines may be true after all:

> The Worldly Hope men set their Hearts upon
> Turns Ashes—or it prospers; and anon,
>   Like Snow upon the Desert's dusty Face,
> Lighting a little Hour or two—is gone.[11]

Even when we pass the "three score years and ten" we do not dwell very
often on the thought of death. Why, or why not? Our motives are
mixed, for they are always mixed. Maybe it is because we shy away
from the moment of truth. But we need not utterly traduce ourselves, for
maybe it is because we secretly know that we are held in that Life without which we could not know death. Maybe our jokes about death, as
when Dorothy Parker proposed for her epitaph, "Excuse my dust," [12]
are token of Grace dimly understood, but holding us nevertheless in its
power. But how can such a hope be validated and fulfilled?

II

It is interesting to speculate how men lived when they had no clear
hope of personal resurrection. Always it would seem, if we can pierce
the mists of antiquity, men have believed in some life after death. The
Greeks, Romans, and Hebrews alike foresaw a dim realm hereafter,
inhabited by the thin wraiths of those who once lived on earth. The
prospect was not attractive: better a slave among the living than a king
among the dead.[13] But always there was some hope, clearer and brighter
in ancient Egypt than in any other land perhaps, for Egyptian tombs

almost lead us to guess that to men in that time life-in-death was more vivid than life-in-life. How *did* men live cheerfully with half a hope? We can only surmise. Maybe they did not live very cheerfully: the Old Testament has no such rapture as we find in the New Testament. Maybe they had so strong a sense of community, especially in the covenant people of Israel, that they were sure their individual life would continue in the life of the people of God. Maybe they were providentially "tuned" to half a hope as we are "tuned" in different keys and registers to pre-puberty, after puberty, and beyond puberty, and for the approach of death. Always the half hope was not enough: they strained toward a better hope. For though at first they said:

> Sheol cannot thank thee,
>   death cannot praise thee;
> those who go down to the pit cannot hope
>   for thy faithfulness.[14]

they learned to cry:

> For thou dost not give me up to Sheol,
>   or let thy godly one see the Pit.[15]

How that change came, how men first believed in personal resurrection rather than in poor wraithlike continuance, is a fascinating study, but not on the main track of this book. So let us check off capsule fashion, with much inevitably omitted from the capsule, the main factors. Greek thought brought its contribution. Time's forms break and vanish, they said, but the eternal forms, without which we could not know that earth is earth, always abide. The soul or psyche moves objects: the objects may disappear, for they can be moved, but the mover persists. For these proposals and convictions the reader is referred to Plato's *Phaedo*. But soul was not uniquely personal to the Greeks as in our present conviction: all souls were alike, mind rays from some central Logos, to be gathered back at last (and lost) in that central sun. But Greek thought in the traffic of minds across the ancient world contributed its light. The mystery religions brought their gift. In the ecstasy of the Dionysian ritual, to take but one example, men were carried beyond themselves: that is the very meaning of the word "ecstasy." They were for a time "out of

221

this world." They were *en theos,* in the god: our word "enthusiasm." The Orphic mysteries held that the soul is "fallen" into our world of flesh, but can be released from "the wheel of birth" (almost the Indian notion of the circle of reincarnations) by the rapture of Orphic worship. These breakthroughs can partly be explained by outward factors, for the mystery religions were all celebrations of nature's cycle with its life springing from seeming death. But they were also mutations, and thus beyond our neat tracing.

As for the doctrine of resurrection in the Bible, the prophets of Israel were centrally concerned with the covenant and the covenant community, but they stressed individual responsibility, and that stress opened the door for belief in individual worth. Then the ecstasy of the apocalyptic writings pushed the door further open: rapture carried them "out of this world" into another world—of rapture:

> Thy dead shall live, their bodies shall rise.
> O dwellers in the dust, awake and sing
> for joy! [16]

This passage is hard to date: perhaps it comes from the third century B.C. The following is even sharper in its personal hope: "And many of those who sleep in the dust of the earth shall awake, some to everlasting life, and some to shame and everlasting contempt." [17] Thus the foregleam of our doctrines of heaven and hell. Those words can perhaps be more surely dated—from the second century B.C. Yes, there were outer "causes" for the change in faith, chiefly the frustration of worldly hopes, just as the outer conditions of Egyptian life (the preservative powers of Egyptian sand, for instance) helped the Egyptian belief in life after death. But there were also secret instigations. The "leaps" in human story, the mutations in any area of study, are beyond man's power either to contrive or explain. Thus the way was prepared for what we have called the great Breakthrough in Christ Jesus and his conquest of death.

The modern cynicism about life after death is not impressive. It goes counter to the immemorial and unfolding hopes of mankind, and thus makes mock of the journeying generations. By what credentials? By no more than the sight of the eyes, together with the iconoclastic mood of our distraught culture. The faith is condemned as selfish. But when was it selfish to hope that millions of children dying in infancy and millions of men killed in war shall have their share of vital life? It would be selfish or even callous not to hope. The faith in an eternal world is condemned again as being blind to present duty and irresponsible in the area of social concern. It can become blind, as any endeavor (such as skepticism itself) can become blind, but the faith at its characteristic best and in multiplied instances has lived in dangerous goodwill with more abandon than is found in other men precisely because it has been unafraid of death. The faith has been condemned again as "projection" and wishful thinking. But what kind of thinking is not "projection," and what faith or unfaith escapes a man's wishes? Corliss Lamont in his, *The Illusion of Immortality*,[18] claims that death is "intelligible." He means intelligible to science, science being for him the main highroad to truth. Yes, death can be described in terms of chemical change. But a personal word is in order: one summer the young wife in the cottage to the south was drowned, and a few summers later the young wife in the cottage to the north was flung against a telephone pole in an automobile accident, her body almost severed, and her baby killed in her arms; and if Corliss Lamont had told me then that "death is intelligible," I would not have wasted words, for biochemistry, if made total truth, can be worse than crass: I would have left him in silence, hoping that silence might somehow fertilize his appalling barrenness of mind.

A further protest is in order. If the modern cynicism is true, there is no justice either in God (if that faith is granted any cogency) or in the world. For a person, every person, is unique even in his fingerprint, and if he is snuffed out at death like a cheap candle

> The pillar'd firmament is rott'nness,
> And earth's base built on stubble.[19]

The basic injustice and the modern cynicism then invite *our* injustice: our present chaos is the child of four centuries of skepticism in which the faith has been held in increasing derision. If love disappears in a final blackness, earth's joys take on the irony of that grotesque last meal before the electric chair. You say that we shall still go on loving our children? Then the cynicism is not true to life. These words are not written to coerce a man's acceptance of the faith. No worthy faith can be forced, and I have no least wish to make the shabby attempt. On the contrary I would defend a man's right to doubt, not least because I myself have walked that shadowed road. But the implications of cynicism should be faced. If it is honest, it will be sad, not clever. Meanwhile we shall bring flowers on a casket, weep at a graveside, and call the cemetery "God's acre." Even Robert Ingersoll could not escape the hope, for at his brother's grave he said: "We cry aloud—and the only answer is the echo of our wailing cry. From the voiceless lips of the unreplying dead there comes no word. But in the night of Death Hope sees a star, and listening love can hear the rustle of a wing." [20]

III

So we come once again to what we have named the Breakthrough, taking due note of the fact that it is sequel to earlier preparatory breakthroughs across our world and strikingly in Israel. That is to say, Christ is in the midst of history. He is not an isolated figure standing apart from life like a statue which we can analyze so as to measure in the clay the proportions of "human" and "divine." Truth is an Event set in the nexus and continuance of events. Truth does not wear the philosopher's cap and gown, or the scientist's laboratory coat, or the theologian's surplice and stole, though all these men may be servants of the Truth. Truth is the disclosure through the happenings of history of the God who acts. The resurrection of Christ is not unrelated to what happened before him: it is climax to the succession of breakthroughs which we have traced. If his resurrection seems to us "simply impossible," it is because it is "impossible" only to philosophic and scientific norms which we try to deify, and because we have misconceived the very nature of truth. Any event is a carrier of both mystery and light. The Event of Christ carries the Mystery and the most piercing light. It gathers and interprets all events, and by its light we can and should judge the events of our own tumultuous time. How could Truth ever be as innocuous as a system of thought, or as neutral as a chemical formula? The idea is absurd when we risk bringing it to the challenge. Truth to be Truth must lay hands on us in actualities.

Christ did not originate the hope of personal life after death. It is potentially in every man, from the day when God said, "Let us make man in our image." [21] We would not know that our years are transient if we were not natively aware of eternity. What Christ did was to bring to focus a hope that is in all of us inchoately, and which was slowly gathering toward some center before his day in history. He "abolished death and brought life and immortality to light through the gospel." [22] Thus one commentator has rightly and finely said that Christ illuminated the whole area of our mortal pilgrimage "as with a flare, demonstrating through his resurrection [our] essentially immortal and incorruptible nature, [and] its sovereignty over the temporal world of change and death." [23] The same great passage of Scripture tells us that this was God's purpose "ages ago," [24] which purpose was now made sharply manifest through Christ's "appearing." That last word means the very opposite of mere appearance, namely, an Event in flesh and history, yet originating in the hiddenness of the Eternal purpose. Earlier breakthroughs led on to this Breakthrough, so that now "in him all things hold together." [25] Thus the tremendous range and depth of biblical thought. The other books keep their distance because they cannot even "come close," and they should veil their faces. Christ has split history by his resurrection. That is why we measure time, plan our calendars, and date our occasions by his coming.

It should be noted further that in his expressed convictions, in what we call his teaching, he clearly and deliberately lined up with those in his land who believed in personal resurrection. There was a sharp debate in that time between the Sadducees and the Pharisees on this very belief. The Sadducees accepted only the literal word of the Pentateuch, and therefore foresaw nothing beyond death except Sheol, the "Pit" inhabited by shadowy ghosts of those who had once lived on earth. The Pharisees conversely accepted such hope-filled passages as quoted above [26] which pictured life-after-death as a personal and heightened vitality. The Sadducees meanwhile poured scorn on such doctrine. Suppose, they said, a woman should be widowed again and again, and should thus marry seven brothers in turn, "In the resurrection, therefore, to which of the seven shall she be wife?" The answer of Jesus was categorical.[27] It has three prongs. *First,* their own faith echoed and echoed with the word of God: "I am the God of Abraham, and the God of Isaac, and the God of Jacob." The word is "am," not "was." The patriarchs are not a mist of memory or a heap of burial dust, and God is not a tinpot God ruling only an ever-expanding graveyard: "He is not the God of the dead, but of the living." *Second,* the resurrection is not a dull continuance of life on earth or any dreary Sheol: "For in the resurrection they neither marry, nor are given in marriage, but are like angels in heaven." This means not that love fades, but the very opposite: it glows in a new dimension and with undreamed-of joy. *Third,* if men knew that God is God, they would know, even if only by deduction from the disfigurement of earth, the deeps and vistas of God's creative might: "You are wrong because you know neither the scriptures nor the power of God." Other words from his lips shine with resurrection-light, the parable of the rich man and the beggar for an instance,[28] with its act one on earth and its act two in heaven. Such teaching cannot be discounted. We cannot accept from his lips what pleases our culture, and dismiss the rest as if it did not matter. The utterance of Christ is seamless. We may not rend it, keeping what pleases us, and consigning the remainder to the rag bag. Christ believed in personal resurrection.

But the teaching might have no joyous certitude except for *his* resurrection. That Event is the Breakthrough. By it we know that God on the Cross has borne our pains, both of sin and of death, and conquered them, so that death itself is now dead. Still we are asked to "prove it to me." But how is an event proved? Not by philosophy, for that deals in theories, and in events only at secondhand; and not by science, for that deals with events only as "objects," whereas life must deal with events as personal. How, then? By their impact, by their circles in the pool of life. These we have traced.[29] What are they? The Resurrection accounts themselves. They are lowly: fiction could hardly have resisted the temptation to blow trumpets. They are caught in rapture and surprise: it would be folly to try to "reconcile" raptures. They are fear-striken: "trembling and astonishment had come upon them . . . for they were afraid"[30]; and well they might be, for they had been led to the mouth of the mortal cave, and shown a world "that never was, on sea or land,"[31] and thus were required to live in a new dimension. The disciples themselves suddenly knew the grace of sins forgiven and how to laugh in face of death. Gladly they bore testimony to Christ, and persecution was as gladly accepted. Then came the birth of the church, and its persistence while governments rise and fall. Then came the New Testament, much of it composed of "occasional" pastoral letters, which became Holy Scripture by the "power of his resurrection." [32] We try to ignore these circles in the pool of history. We pretend that they are caused by pebbles called "projection" or "illusion." This could be honest, but, honest or mistaken, it could be grievous hurt, or in itself credulity. Yet, we hasten to add, no event is true except by the venture of a responsive faith.

Such faith knows in our own time the impact of the Christ-Event, because those who look on Christ in the Gospels, and then try to answer him in life, "are being changed into his likeness. . . . this comes from the Lord who is the Spirit." [33] Such an experience eludes words, yet for some of us he is "the light of the world," in whom we have "the light of life." [34] The great hearts of our race are not dead, any more than Abraham, Isaac, and Jacob. But they do not speak the sharp, incisive word; they do not flood the mind with light.

> But, O pilgrims, who
> Throng Holburn and Fifth Avenue,
> May you not meet, in spite of death,
> A Traveler form Nazareth? [35]

In his light our world so changes that each purpose shrinks or grows into its true proportion. Large homes in rich suburbs are no longer large, and the suburbs are no longer rich. The small home of the man who, lowly and content, will not provoke his neighbors to envy, is no longer small. Politicians who say nothing, but say it in organ tones, are comic figures cut out of cardboard. Suddenly in this light no man is better than his neighbor, for all are held in the divine grace, some facing the light, the others walking in their own shadow. Our clutchings are forgotten, our self-entanglements are unraveled, because the light shines. One thing matters, that Christ shall be "all, and in all." [36] If someone says, "Prove it," we laugh, for who could prove light? If someone else says, "Sentimentalism!" we can only answer: "Sentimentalism? It is Light, stern demand with joy hidden at its heart."

IV

What, then, is the meaning of the Resurrection? That pain is transitory, parasitic, and doomed. It is transitory because we and our world are in time, but also because eternity has stooped to time in Jesus Christ. It is parasitic, though real, because we could not know pain except for prior joy, but also because in the Cross it has been changed so that now it is God's agent in redemption. It is doomed because of that transformation. That is why the New Testament says with gladness: "God himself . . . will wipe away every tear from their eyes, and death shall be no more, neither shall there be mourning nor crying nor pain any more." [37] So the New Testament says likewise, "and the sea was no more," [38] the sea being for the Jewish mind the symbol of dark mystery and separation. Pliny, governor of Bithynia during the persecutions of Trojan, was amazed at the courage of a Christian prisoner. The magistrate speaks first, and the prisoner answers:

> M. "I will banish thee."
> P. "Thou canst not, for the world is my Father's house."
> M. "I will slay thee."
> P. "Thou canst not, for my life is hid with Christ in God."
> M. "I will take away thy treasures."
> P. "Thou canst not, for my treasure is in heaven."
> M. "I will drive thee away from man, and thou shalt have no friend left."
> P. "Thou canst not, for I have a friend from whom no man can separate me." [39]

What to do with such a faith? The early followers of Christ were known as "witnesses of the Resurrection." That magistrate's court that day heard a witness!

What is the further meaning? That the devil (or evil, if the reader prefers to omit the d) is God's servant. To our broken human sight the devil's acts are devilish, and we do not know why God should employ such a blackguard. But God by raising Christ has not only manifested his power over all evil, even the evil that nailed Christ to the cross, but has turned all blackguardly acts to his own purpose. The "why?" is unanswered, for the mind's questionings receive no neat explanation. But the Cross and the Resurrection are together better by far than any textbook demonstration, for they have turned the very question to cleansing, vocation, and insight. The blackguardly face is a mask: behind it is the face of a friend. All of which does *not* mean that we can ever parley with the devil. It means that Death Valley is like Death Valley in our far west, where no rain fell for a stretch of years, until one day there was a turn in the weather. Rain fell copiously, and men then found that birds had dropped seeds, for overnight the Valley rejoiced and blossomed "as the rose." [40] The Cross-and-Resurrection are the copious rain in the midst of our desert of pain and death.

Books on the problem of suffering have sought answers where none can be found. There are gleams of light across a mystery, and they are worth tracing, but all gleams fade if we bring to the inquiry no more than human wisdom. For then (let it be said bluntly) there is no answer. Then the latest tragedy, as that in today's paper of a deranged parent killing her four children, confounds all our wisdom. Least of all can answer be found by our prating about natural law, as if God cared more for that (which science itself now doubts) than for persons. The books have failed because they treat Christ and his resurrection as afterthoughts, important afterthoughts indeed, but yet only the coping stone to man's quest for truth. The claim of this book is that pain and death are events, and that therefore they cannot be answered either by a formula in science or a theory in philosophy, but only by an Event. In the New Testament pain and death are suddenly in a new climate. Nay, they take on a new nature. They are no longer a negative judgment or a dark enigma: they are a positive deliverance and a chosen pathway to joy. Through Christ our pain-stricken world enters a new age. Thus the persecuted church can say: "Beloved, do not be surprised at the fiery ordeal which comes upon you to prove you, as though something strange were happening to you. [God has this seeming darkness in his power from the foundation of the world!] But rejoice in so far as you share Christ's sufferings [in witness and in daily love], that you may also rejoice and be glad when his glory is revealed." [41] Such is the new word of the New Testament. It is incredible, not because it is untrue, but precisely because it is true. It is incredible in theory, but true in the Christ-Deed and the Christ-Fact.

V

But faith in this victory is still a faith. Doubts still afflict us, and we shall not be free of pain and evil. So far as our eyes can judge, suffering and death are constitutional in this planet. The dear friend who has died will not return from the dead: sorrow must accept separation and the final silence. Some people will still go through life almost frustrate, the music in them almost unsung. Other people will feel the lash of racial contempt. Storms, such as the hurricanes which sweep in from the Atlantic in the fall, will cut wide swathes of destruction. Planes will crash on land or sink in the sea carrying with them their human cargo. As long as blind anger and stubborn pride persist, which means as long as men abuse their veritable measure of freedom, there will be wars and rumors of war. The devil will pursue his devilish course turning means of blessings into the tools of curse, as when a telephone is used for anonymous threats or government becomes a path to the pork barrel. Flood, plague, and famine will ravage mankind. Meanwhile *we* have not seen Jesus either in the flesh or after his resurrection, and denial of the whole affair is always an open option. We walk by faith in response to an Event which is "proved" only by circles in the pool of history and by the intangible Presence. Jesus does not pity us: "Blessed are those who have not seen and yet believe." [42] We are not blinded by our eyes or deafened by our ears. But the "problem" (which is actual, not theoretical) is always with us.

It is worth remembering, of course, that all men walk by some faith. There are no invincible certainties, though there are certitudes. In fact, most faiths betray their worshipers, while faith in Christ turns suffering into cleansing, vocation, and light. What of faith in education? It dares not ask, "What kind?" So it dwindles into a cafeteria of information, or an idolatry of learning which bids fair to become a new titanism. What of faith in democracy, presently vulnerable to cells on the left plotting violence and cells on the right plotting fear-stricken slander, not to mention hosts of people careless not only of the ballot, but of human well-being? What of faith in science, its prime categories suddenly beset by erosion, and its catastrophic powers delivered into the hands of politicians, while science remains in many a place the prisoner of the laboratory? What of faith in an unexamined "progress"? All men live by faith of some kind. In the conflict of faiths our faith in Christ need not fawn or cringe.

Faith in Christ is realistic: it does not kid itself that our skill or dubious goodness can rid the planet of "the mystery of lawlessness," [43] or that our minds can pierce the mystery. Faith in Christ seeks no escape from pain, not even in the fortitude of stoicism which hopes against hope to find the answer by barring doors and windows against the question. Faith in Christ is creative in the man who dares to hold the faith, but it is not selfish, for the man chooses pain as a beckoning vocation. By the pain of witness he must needs

> Set up a mark of everlasting light,
> Above the howling senses' ebb and flow.[44]

Meanwhile by the voluntary sharing of other men's pain he tempers pain with love. Faith in Christ is not captive in time and space, not trapped in any humanistic cage: it looks in hope to life beyond life. Faith in Christ cares not that it is not "popular"; truth is neither found nor determined by any Gallup Poll. Faith in Christ is not an easy path, but the path itself was blazed by Christ and is held in the Hands that raised him from the dead. Denis de Rougement has the story of an Irish missionary preaching in an Alpine valley. The Swiss shepherds were a clear and simple folk. So when the saint told them that the sacrifice of Christ wins men, and that the blood of the martyrs is the seed of the church, they felt that they should take him at his word. So they quietly killed him, and—here is the marvelous twist to the story—it worked! They became followers of the Cross.[45]

VI

Have we dispelled the mystery of pain? No, we have deepened it, if there are degrees in mystery, for the conviction that God is good makes more baffling the persistence of suffering and evil.

> Be our joys three-parts pain!
> Strive, and hold cheap the strain![46]

May be. But the trouble is that the world seems to hold more agony than is needed for our nurture. A lad has just been killed, cleaning a shotgun that he thought was unloaded. Do the parents need that shock for their salvation? A doctor dies of a brain tumor. Do his patients need

231

that death for their cleansing? What of the millions of skulls of those slaughtered by some Timor? Or the other millions caught in a thousand Pompeiis by nature's grotesque and wanton cruelty? Let the reader testify that this book has not offered cheap answers, least of all any prating about "natural law" as if "law" were dear to God and children do not matter. Yet this fact remains: The man who whines does not win us; and the man who rebels, though we like him better, strikes at last a discordant note; while the man who dares to bow his head with, "thy will be done," [47] sets stars in the sky. Surely a glory stirs in that man before he dies.

There is no "explanation" of pain. How could there be? An explanation is in the realm of theory, while the pain itself is in the realm of event. We do not say to a man stricken with cancer, "Read this textbook in biochemistry." The only explanation of an event is another Event. That is what faith in Christ offers us, from the very depths of pain and evil, plus the victory of the Resurrection. We cannot long deny God, even though we may know that he dwells "in light unsearchable."

> If the Sun and Moon should doubt,
> They'd immediately go out.[48]

Perhaps complete knowledge of God's ways would as effectively write *finis* to our mortal life, for we would be blinded "with excess of light." [49] At long last we must offer our pain before the Unseen Eyes, yet not without cause: the Cross has issued in triumph; yet not without the final venture of faith. Have you ever thought deeply about the offering of the first fruits in ancient Israel? A tenth of the scanty harvest, an unblemished lamb from the meager flock, to be burned on an altar while men half-starve? The godless, living for practicalities, must have cursed the godly! A deeper hint is found in the story of David. In his thirst and delirium he dreamed of his boyhood and longed to drink of the water of "the well of Bethlehem which is by the gate," but when men won their way at risk of life to reach the well, there and back through the enemy lines, and brought David a flagon of that very water, he poured it out on the ground as libation: he offered it to God: "shall I drink the blood of the men who went at the risk of their lives?"[50] That act is nonsense, isn't it? Yet without it our comfortable eating and drinking might become an animal gluttony.

When that "offering" is not made we come on chaos. If trade is only trade, with profit as the sole concern, it breaks of its own internal injury. If art ceases (under its own rightful categories) to speak the eternal word, it becomes a mere copy or a corruption, as when a group of literary men, forsaking Adoration, write beer ads and pocket the cash. If philosophy ceases to be what the word implies, the love of Wisdom, it sells out to science and logic, the one a fractional mind intent on a fractional world, and the other despite itself the child of accepted axioms; and so sinks into mere empiricism or semantics. What happens when pain is not "offered"? Lethargy or bitterness, stoicism or rebellion. At best this response becomes prisoner of its own armor. But suppose a man should worship, though in darkness: "Verily thou art a God that hidest thyself, . . . [yet] the judgments of the Lord are true and righteous altogether."[51] That man may not instantly find peace, but the rest of us know him to be noble. Berdyaev, exiled for his cleaving to truth, received this word from a friend as he left, she quoting from Musset: "In life nothing is beautiful except to love, nothing is true except to suffer."[52] Yes, but the words stand only in the courage of a great faith. There is no "sense" to Christ's being killed by the petty ambition of a Caiaphas, plus the shuffling of a Pilate, plus the callousness or whipped-up fury of the crowd. Then why do we remember him? No, we do not have final and logical "proof" of his resurrection. But we have enough circles in history and awareness of his presence to hear his summons to a brave faith. Would we wish more evidence until courage were canceled?

VII

There are questions which are not within the central province of this book. What of those who came before Christ? Are they condemned by their date in history to no better destiny than some forsaken Sheol? No, the God who stooped to mankind in the cross of Christ and pierced our cloudy sky by the sun-break of the Resurrection, is not slave of the calendar or the prisoner of time. Plato with his *Phaedo* and the writer of the Twenty-third Psalm will not be far from the throne in the hereafter. Indeed, the New Testament foresees the gathering of all the musical phrases and all the movements of history's symphony in one great Amen. Then are all men finally saved? We simply do not know. If life hereafter is "as the angels," [53] that is to say, in a dimension that we cannot presently conceive, why should we try to print on that unknown country the too-sure judgments of our present earth? Men born blind may not dogmatize about our visible world, or men born deaf be cocksure about Beethoven's *Ninth Symphony.* Yes, we can surmise that if a man is free hereafter in any real freedom, he can close his eyes there as here to the light; and we can surmise that if God loses that man at last God is not God but only a defeated God; and we can thus confront an antinomy, an unresolvable. Jesus spoke the final word to minds thus curious about a world which we have no skills to explore: "Strive to enter by the narrow door." [54] He added a warning to those who, overcurious about the hereafter, failed to see in mortal life a once-for-all encounter: "For many, I tell you, will seek to enter and will not be able." [55] Any universalism is thus a presumption, and the doctrine of an irrevocable fiery hell is worse presumption. If we insist on choosing, even though we have no faculties to make the choice, God—is God.

Those who have "offered" their pain—pain of baffled mind, pain of witness to Christ in an alien world, shared pain of neighbors—are the noblest of our race. Paul with his, "I am now ready to be offered," [56] or Captain Oates seeing his white and lonely death (as he walked out into the Antarctic wilderness lest he be a burden to his comrades and threaten their safety [57]) as part of the great scheme of the Almighty, bear their testimony to One who, seeing nothing but human hands raised in malediction, yet cried: "Father, into thy hands I commit my spirit." [58] They speak a finer word than those who rebelliously propose that the world is "absurd," and that suicide may be the only intelligent option. The saints help us understand why

> Every countenance
> That warms and lights the heart of the beholder
> Shews, clear and true, the signature of pain.[59]

Joy is the ground of life, for without joy we could not know the sharp punctuations of pain. The devil is God's servant: we do not know why that blackguard should find any post in the economy of heaven, but by the Resurrection he has been relegated to the proper place: he is not Gabriel with his horn. Christ is the Breakthrough of our human pilgrimage. For his sake we accept pain. To his name we bear witness at cost of pain which we might otherwise sidestep. In his love we share our neighbor's pain which also we could evade if he had not found us. In his light we look for the life everlasting. If doubts come, as they do, we remember that we could not doubt nothing: we doubt only our faith. Is there not a legend [60] that only those may sing in the heavenly choir who have first gone to a little gray lake fed by all the tears of earth? The lake is itself in heaven, and one of heaven's treasures. There some angels bathe their eyes. Then *they* sing in the celestial choir. There they sing, men and angels, lowly folk whose pilgrimage is ended "still choiring to the young-eyed cherubim." [61] There they sing to the music of "harpers harping with their harps." [62] They sing the new song of "Moses . . . and the Lamb," [63] the old covenant of Moses become the new covenant of Christ. They sing, forever worshiping in the joy of pain overcome, greater joy than if there had been no pain, "Thou art worthy . . . for thou wast slain, and hast redeemed us to God by thy blood . . . and has made us unto our God kings and priests." [64] To Christ be glory for ever!

But you and I must not escape into any rapture, even though faith in Christ sometimes opens on rapture. This word is often all we have:

> Good News: but if you ask me what it is, I know not.
> It is a track of feet in the snow.
> It is a lantern showing a path
> It is a door set open.[65]

But we do know what it is: the Word made flesh. We must still walk through the snow, yet One has gone before us and we see his footprints. We must still journey through the darkness of pain, but there is a lantern: he is "the light of the world." [66] We must knock on the door, sometimes with bleeding knuckles from much knocking, but the door is not locked: it is half open, and we can half see a table spread and a bright hearthstone. Yet we must journey. Brave traveling to you!

Notes

Soundings

1. Jean-Paul Sartre, *Being and Nothingness,* Hazel E. Barnes, tr. (New York: Philosophical Library, 1956), especially Part 1, chap. 1, "The Problem of Nothingness."
2. Job 5:7.
3. Job 5:6-7.
4. "Solomon on the Vanity of the World," Book III, line 240.
5. Robert Burns, "Man Was Made to Mourn," stanza 7.
6. A Nazi concentration camp during World War II.
7. Reported in the *Chicago Daily News,* Sept. 3, 1958.
8. Percy Bysshe Shelley, "To a Skylark," stanza 18.
9. Title of a book by the Spanish Mystic, St. John of the Cross. Also see Evelyn Underhill, *Mysticism* (London: Methuen and Co., 1912), chap. IX, "The Dark Night of the Soul."
10. See Eleanor H. Porter, *Pollyanna* (Boston: The Page Company, 1914).
11. Louis Lavelle in *Evil and Suffering,* Bernard Murchland, tr. (New York: The Macmillan Company, 1963), pp. 61-64, proposes that we keep the word "pain" for ills of the body and "suffering" for ills of the mind. But how can we? That distinction is too artificial and too late.
12. Rachel Louise Carson (Boston: Houghton Mifflin Company, 1962).
13. I Cor. 1:20.
14. Shelley, "Adonais," stanza LII.
15. *Being and Nothingness.*

16. See *Emmett Kelly with F. Beverly Kelley* (Englewood Cliffs: Prentice-Hall, 1954).
17. James 1:2.
18. (Boston: Houghton Mifflin Company, 1958).
19. (New York: The Macmillan Company, 1948), argument of the Introduction.
20. *Suffering Human and Divine* (New York: The Macmillan Company, 1939), p. 224.
21. Henrik Ibsen, *Peer Gynt,* William and Charles Archer, tr. (New York: Brentano's, n.d.), Act V, scene v.
22. P. 10.
23. Heb. 12:2.
24. "Auguries of Innocence," line 55.

2. Some Answers Fall Short

1. See Arthur Koestler, *The Act of Creation* (New York: The Macmillan Company, 1964), especially Part Two.
2. I Kings 18:17-46.
3. The German mystic—see Henry Suso, *The Life of the Servant,* James M. Clark, tr. (London: James Clarke and Company, 1952), chap. XV, p. 46.
4. See *Dictionary of Christian Literature and Biography* (Boston: Little, Brown and Company, 1911), p. 904.
5. Gen. 1:10, 12, 18.
6. Charles F. D'Arcy, "Love and Omnipotence," in *God and the Struggle for Existence,* Lily Dougall and B. H. Streeter, eds. (New York: Association Press, 1919), p. 27.
7. I have resolved not to clutter these pages with Hebrew and Greek words. I am writing for the average thoughtful reader who is here referred to the *Interpreter's Dictionary of the Bible,* IV (Nashville: Abingdon Press, 1962), 450.
8. Rev. 21:3-4.
9. I have resisted for kindness' sake including in the text a limerick quoted by John Whale, *The Christian Answer to the Problem of Evil* (New York: Abingdon Press, 1936), p. 21. I cannot forbear here to include it:

> "There was a faith-healer of Deal
> Who said, 'Although pain isn't real,
> When I sit on a pin,
> And it punctures my skin,
> I dislike what I fancy I feel.' "

10. Burns, "Man Was Made to Mourn."

11. See chap. 5.

12. "A Creed," *Collected Poems* (New York: The Macmillan Company, 1921), p. 101.

13. Lord Tweedsmuir, *Pilgrim's Way* (Boston: Houghton Mifflin Company, 1940), pp. 117-18.

14. *Dream and Reality* (New York: The Macmillan Company, 1951), p. 173.

15. William Wordsworth, "Ode on Intimations of Immortality," stanza 5.

16. Exod. 20:5; Deut. 5:9.

17. I did not wish here to carry the argument further, but it is worth adding as a footnote that, when I argue the freedom of the will, I make the will an *object*, and that an object by definition is never free. Meanwhile the will remains *subject: I* am free to conduct the argument.

18. *The Freedom of the Will* (London: Adam and Charles Black, 1958), pp. 42-43.

19. Job 2:9.

20. Job 13:15. The RSV says: "Yet I will defend my ways to his face," and it is right, despite the preciousness of the KJV, so my translation.

21. Executed April 9, 1945. See Memoir by G. Leibholz, *The Cost of Discipleship* (Rev. ed.; New York: The Macmillan Company, 1963).

22. Ps. 37:35.

23. John Milton, *Paradise Lost*, Book I, line 1.

24. John 9:3.

25. Luke 13:4-5.

26. See "All God's Chillun Got Wings," *Nine Plays* (New York: Random House, 1932), Act II, scene 3, where Jim says: "Maybe He can forgive what you've done to me; and maybe He can forgive what I've done to you; but I don't see how He's going to forgive—Himself."

27. See chap. 4.

28. William Shakespeare, *Merchant of Venice*, Act IV, scene i.

29. See Job 38:1 ff.; 42:1 ff.

30. Milton, *Paradise Lost*, the argument of Book I.

31. Mark 3:1-6; Luke 6:6-11; 13:14; John 16:33.

32. Matt. 23:35.

33. See *The Great Texts of the Bible*, James Hastings, ed., XVI (New York: Charles Scribner's Sons, 1913), 8-9. This account from Myers' mother's diary is attributed to A. C. Benson, *The Leaves of the Tree*, p. 165.

34. *Letters and Papers from Prison*, Eberhard Bethge, ed., Reginald H. Fuller, tr. (New York: The Macmillan Company, 1953), pp. 237-38.

35. Shakespeare, *Macbeth*, Act V, scene viii.

3. On Natural Evil

1. Gen. 3:16-18.
2. Gen. 3:19 KJV.
3. Isa. 35:1, 5.
4. Rom. 8:22, 23.
5. Job 1:13-19.
6. Job 2:7.
7. Job 1:1.
8. John 9:1 ff.
9. Gen. 8:22.
10. Edna St. Vincent Millay, "God's World," *Poems* (London: Martin Secker, 1923), p. 22.
11. Gen. 1:10, 12, 18, 21, 25, 31.
12. *Chicago Daily News,* Sept. 3, 1958.
13. "The Hound of Heaven," *The Works of Francis Thompson,* I: Poems (London: Burns, Oates and Washbourne, 1925), 112.
14. Gen. 3:1-5.
15. (New York: Coward McCann, 1955).
16. Justin O'Brien, tr. (New York: Alfred A. Knopf, 1957).
17. *Brother to Dragons* (New York: Random House, 1953), p. 24.
18. Ps. 18:13.
19. Rev. 6:12.
20. Isa. 45:4, 5.
21. Matt. 7:11.
22. On April 15, 1912.
23. John 8:44.
24. I Cor. 14:33.
25. Echoing Isa. 63:9.
26. In Extracts from Bentham's "Commonplace Book," *Works,* X (Edinburgh: William Tait, 1843), 142.
27. John 14:27.
28. Matt. 5:3-11.
29. *Does God Send Trouble?* (Boston: Houghton Mifflin and Company, 1898), p. 19.
30. "Love and Omnipotence," p. 27.
31. *The Christian Answer to the Problem of Evil,* pp. 28 and 31.
32. "The Defeat of Pain," in *God and the Struggle for Existence,* p. 165.
33. *Prayer* (Apex ed.; Nashville: Abingdon Press, 1942), Part II, chap. VI.
34. George Santayana, "O World, Thou Choosest Not the Better Part," *Poems* (New York: Charles Scribner's Sons, 1923), Sonnet iii.

35. "God and Causality," in *Religion and Culture, Essays in Honor of Paul Tillich,* Walter Leibrecht, ed. (New York: Harper & Brothers, 1959), pp. 212-13.

36. *Systematic Theology,* I (Chicago: University of Chicago Press, 1951), 184-86.

37. *Suffering Human and Divine,* p. 112.

38. *Ibid.,* p. 113.

39. John Donne, "An Anatomie of the World," The Second Anniversary, line 288.

40. Milton, *Paradise Lost,* Book IV, line 110.

41. *Mr. Britling Sees It Through* (New York: The Macmillan Company, 1916), p. 406.

42. *Memories and Studies* (London: Longmans, Green and Company, 1917), p. 212.

43. Dr. Coit was a passenger on the rescue ship, "Carpathia," and wrote of the experience in *The Outlook,* C (April 27, 1912), 894-95.

44. Quoted by Paul Scherer, *Event in Eternity* (New York: Harper & Brothers, 1945), p. 168.

45. Katharine Day Little, *François de Fénelon* (New York: Harper & Brothers, 1951), p. 207.

46. Shakespeare, *Macbeth,* Act V, scene v.

47. Elizabeth Barrett Browning, "Aurora Leigh," II, 952-54.

48. Ps. 34:6.

49. Luke 16:9.

50. Matt. 5:45.

51. John 4:7-15.

52. Matt. 7:24-27; Luke 6:47-49.

4. On Historical Evil

1. Gen. 3:13 ff.

2. Shakespeare, *As You Like It,* Act II, scene vii.

3. Heb. 11:38.

4. John 4:38.

5. Quoted by James A. Lindsay in "Religion under Repair," *Nineteenth Century,* October, 1917, 801.

6. *Dream and Reality,* p. 225.

7. A letter written Sept. 17, 1919, in *Letters from Baron Friedrich Von Hügel to a Niece,* Gwendolen Greene, ed. (Chicago: Henry Regnery Company, 1955), p. 122.

8. James Anthony Froude, *Thomas Carlyle, 1834-1881,* I (New York: Charles Scribner's Sons, 1884), 35.

9. I John 5:19.

10. Sir John Hawkins, *Life of Samuel Johnson* (2nd ed.; London, 1787), p. 563.

11. Shakespeare, *Hamlet,* Act III, scene i.

12. Mark 7:14-15; Matt. 15:10-11.

13. Mark 7:21-23; Matt. 15:19-20*a*.

14. *Providence and Suffering in the Old and New Testaments* (London: Thomas Nelson and Sons, 1953), p. 45.

15. *Ibid.,* p. 47.

16. Jean Kerr (Collins), (Garden City: Doubleday & Company, 1960).

17. *Good and Evil* (New York: Fleming H. Revell Company, 1918), p. 32. There is also an almost identical sentence in Albert Camus, *The Plague* (New York: Alfred A. Knopf, 1948), p. 120. "The evil that is in the world always comes of ignorance."

18. *New Introductory Lectures on Psycho-Analysis* (New York: W. W. Norton and Company, 1933), in a lecture on "A Philosophy of Life," p. 229. Also quoted by John Wisdom in an essay, "The Modes of Thought and the Logic of God," in *The Existence of God,* John Hick, ed. (New York: The Macmillan Company, 1964), p. 292.

19. *The Rubáiyát of Omar Khayyam,* Edward Fitzgerald, tr., stanza lviii.

20. John 8:44.

21. II Thess. 2:7.

22. Gen. 6:2.

23. Phil. 2:6-7.

24. John 8:44.

25. Matt. 4:1.

26. Matt. 13:38*b*-39.

27. John 13:2.

28. C. S. Lewis (New York: The Macmillan Company, 1954).

29. Jerold Rosenberg (New York: Random House, 1956).

30. George Axelrod (New York: Random House, 1956).

31. Rom. 7:15.

32. Matt. 6:13.

33. Eph. 6:16 (italics mine).

34. Eph. 2:2.

35. Gen. 3:1-2.

36. I Peter 5:8.

37. I Peter 5:10-11.

38. I John 4:3.
39. I John 4:4.
40. Robert Browning, "Pippa Passes."
41. Rom. 2:15.
42. I Cor. 15:24-26.
43. Matt. 13:35.
44. Matt. 12:24.
45. Robert Browning, "Abt Vogler," stanza ix.
46. *Evil and the Christian Faith* (New York: Harper & Brothers, 1947), p. 8.
47. What we write here shall continue to be not philosophical, but existential in the sense of cleaving to the concreteness of the Bible and to what we know in the bones of our existence.
48. *The Rubáiyát,* stanza xxvii.
49. Matt. 7:11; Luke 11:13 (italics mine).
50. Luke 11:50.
51. Luke 13:33.
52. John 16:2.
53. John 12:31-32.
54. Adapted from Carlyle, *Heroes and Hero Worship,* Lec. 4, describing Luther.
55. John 13:7.
56. Heb. 11:39-40.
57. I Peter 5:11.

5. On Personal Evil

1. *Descent into Hell* (New York: Pellegrini and Cudahy, 1949), pp. 21-23, referring to Pauline Anstruther.
2. See chap. 2, p. 31-34.
3. Alfred Tennyson, "Vastness," stanza ii.
4. II Thess. 2:7.
5. Exod. 20:17.
6. E.g., Exod. 19:5; 20:2; 34:10.
7. Ps. 106:2; 145:4, 6, 12; 150:2.
8. The five famous arguments in the *Summa Theologica* of Thomas Aquinas.
9. Ps. 51:4.
10. Prayer for the Confession of Sins, *The Book of Common Worship* of The United Presbyterian Church, U.S.A.
11. Prov. 14:9 KJV. The RSV "God scorns the wicked" rightly says that the Hebrew is obscure, but the KJV is not untrue to life.

12. Rom. 7:15.
13. Deut. 30:19.
14. "Love and Omnipotence," p. 23.
15. *Ibid.,* p. 26.
16. *The Rubáiyát,* stanza lxxiii.
17. *Ibid.,* stanza lvii.
18. Ps. 139:18 KJV.
19. Burns, "Man Was Made to Mourn," stanza 7.
20. Austin Farrer, *Love Almighty and Ills Unlimited* (Garden City: Doubleday & Company, 1961).
21. Rom. 6:23.
22. Alfred Tennyson, "In Memoriam," Introduction, vs. iii.
23. Josh. 7:1, 18-26.
24. *The Journals of André Gide,* Justin O'Brien, tr., II (New York: Alfred A. Knopf, 1948), 189. Many references in this volume show clearly that, during these years, Gide was struggling with an awareness of evil and the actuality of the devil.
25. I John 5:19.
26. There is an interesting discussion of law and pain, though from a different angle, in Leslie Kingsbury, *The Way of Suffering* (London: Longmans, Green and Company, 1948), pp. 39-52.
27. Lev. 11:44.
28. II Cor. 3:3.
29. *The Little Flowers of St. Francis,* T. W. Arnold, tr. (New York: Frederick A. Stokes Company, 1925), pp. 226-30.

6. Dawn Watch

1. I John 5:19.
2. Ps. 106:2; 145:4, 6, 12; 150:2.
3. Thomas Hobbes, *The Leviathan* (New York: E. P. Dutton and Company, n.d.), Part I, chap. xiii.
4. In *Essays and Addresses on the Philosophy of Religion,* Second Series (London: J. M. Dent and Sons, 1926), pp. 167-213.
5. *Ibid.,* pp. 174-83, and especially p. 178.
6. Robert Browning, "Abt Vogler," stanza ix.
7. Mark 12:37.
8. "Suffering and God," pp. 183-86.
9. Zech. 9:13.
10. Isa. 57:15.

11. "Suffering and God," p. 185.
12. Isa. 55:9.
13. Ps. 2:4.
14. "Suffering and God," pp. 187-88.
15. This may be the better translation of the first phrase of the Lord's Prayer.
16. Matt. 5:35.
17. Jude 25.
18. "Suffering and God," pp. 188 ff.
19. *Ibid.*, pp. 199-200.
20. *Ibid.*, pp. 200-202.
21. Isaac Watts, "Before Jehovah's Awful Throne," vs. 1.
22. "Suffering and God," pp. 202-4.
23. *Ibid.*, pp. 204-5.
24. *Ibid.*, pp. 205-10.
25. Matt. 5:48.
26. In theological terms, which we have deliberately avoided whenever possible, the doctrine of a "limited" God is called personalism. See e.g., Edgar Sheffield Brightman, *The Problem of God* (New York: Abingdon Press, 1930).
27. II Kings 6:30.
28. "Suffering and God," p. 195.
29. Luke 22:42.
30. *The Mystery of Pain* (London: Hodder and Stoughton, 1866), pp. 57-58. Found also in Hügel's much longer quotation, "Suffering and God," pp. 168-72.
31. *Atonement in Literature and Life* (Boston and New York: Houghton Mifflin and Company, 1906), Part II, chap. IV, p. 232, found also in "Suffering and God," pp. 172-73.
32. In an essay on "The Divinity of Christ" in *Foundations*, a statement of Christian Belief by Seven Oxford Men (London: Macmillan Company, 1920), p. 222, mentioned by Hügel, "Suffering and God," p. 173.
33. II Cor. 5:19.
34. Fourth Ecumenical Council, A.D. 451. For the text of the Chalcedon Formula see Arthur Cushman McGiffert, *A History of Christian Thought,* I (New York: Charles Scribner's Sons, 1932), 285.
35. "Suffering and God," p. 205.
36. Bishop of Rome about A.D. 180. See *Anti-Nycene Fathers,* Book IX, chap. V.
37. John Milton, "Lycidas," line 71.

38. In May, 1921.

39. Notably in Emmanuel Kant, *The Critique of Pure Reason,* Book II, chap. I, "Antinomy."

40. See pp. 42-44, 50.

41. *Dogmatics in Outline* (Torchbook ed.; New York: Harper & Row, 1959), p. 57.

42. George Santayana, "O World, Thou Choosest Not the Better Part," *Poems* (New York: Charles Scribner's Sons, 1923).

43. *Dogmatics in Outline,* p. 57.

44. *Systematic Theology* (Chicago, University of Chicago Press, Vol. I, 1951; Vol. II, 1957). See Index references.

45. See p. 29.

46. McGiffert, *A History of Christian Thought,* I, 285.

47. "Suffering and God," p. 191.

48. Owen Meredith, Earl of Lytton, *Lucile,* a novel in verse, Part I, canto III, sec. 2.

49. *Religio Medici* (London: J. M. Dent and Sons, Everyman's Library), p. 10. My translation of the actual phrase "O altitudo!"

50. *Mere Christianity* (New York: The Macmillan Company, 1960), Book II, chap. 2, p. 47.

51. "The Hound of Heaven," lines 90, 95-96.

52. "A Fallen Yew," stanzas 18 and 23.

53. *No Exit and Three other Plays* (New York: Vintage Books, 1955), p. 47.

54. See Edward D. McKinney and W. R. Anderson, *Music in History* (New York: American Book Company, 1940), p. 480.

55. Arthur Miller (New York: The Viking Press, 1949).

56. *Suffering Human and Divine,* pp. 195-199; four pages summarized in a few lines!

57. Rowland Taylor, Vicar of Hadleigh, England. See John R. Green, *History of the English People,* II, 257-58.

58. Rev. 13:8 KJV.

59. Rom. 8:22-24.

60. I Cor. 13:12.

61. II Cor. 5:19.

62. "Suffering and God" pp. 199 ff.

63. Dinsmore, *Atonement in Literature and Life,* p. 232.

64. Acts 26:8 KJV.

7. Breakthrough: The Event

1. John 1:11.

2. John 1:46.

3. Matt. 3:13-17; Mark 1:9-11; Luke 3:21-22; John 1:29-34.
4. Mark 3:14-19; Matt. 10:1-4; Luke 6:13-16.
5. Matt. 26:52.
6. Luke 18:10-14.
7. Matt. 22:37, 39 KJV.
8. Matt. 5:35; Isa. 66:1.
9. Matt. 10:28.
10. See chap. 6, note 15.
11. Mark 3:29. My translation is, I think, a better one.
12. Luke 6:20.
13. John 16:8.
14. Matt. 13:3-9; Mark 4:3-9; Luke 8:5-8.
15. See issue of Dec. 14, 1962; and also *New York Herald-Tribune*, Dec. 2, 1960.
16. John 21:3.
17. Matt. 28:10.
18. John 20:19.
19. Mark 12:24; Matt. 22:29.
20. *Kerygma and Myth*, Hans Werner Bartsch, ed. (Torchbook ed.; New York: Harper & Row, 1961), p. 42.
21. Title of a book by C. S. Lewis (New York: Harcourt, Brace and World, 1956).
22. Acts 2:24 KJV.
23. Acts 1:22.
24. Acts 3:15; Acts 2:32.
25. I Cor. 15:14-15.
26. I Cor. 15:29-30.
27. The quotation from which these words are drawn reads "Glory to the Almighty, the sun has risen in the west!" It is attributed to an oriental poet by Joseph Fort Newton in *If I Had Only One Sermon to Preach on Immortality*, William L. Stidger, ed. (New York: Harper & Brothers, 1929), p. 191.
28. Isa. chaps. 40–56, especially chap. 53.
29. Isa. 53:3.
30. I Cor. 15:45-47.
31. Matt. 13:35; Matt. 25:34; Luke 11:50; John 17:24; Eph. 1:4; Heb. 4:3.
32. I Cor. 15:45.
33. Heb. 10:20.

34. Gal. 4:26.
35. At the Battle of Marathon. See Robert Browning, "Echetlos,"

> "Care for no name at all!
> Say but just this: 'We praise one helpful whom
>   we call
> The Holder of the Ploughshare!' The great deed
> ne'er grows small."

36. John 16:33.
37. Luke 23:34.
38. Matt. 20:28.
39. Phil. 2:8.
40. Charles Rand Kennedy (New York: Harper & Brothers, 1908).
41. Rom. 4:25.
42. John 1:29.
43. George Stewart (New York: George H. Doran Company, 1927).
44. John 1:14.
45. I Cor. 11:24. See also Matt. 26:26; Mark 14:22; Luke 22:19.
46. William Wordsworth, "Ode on Intimations of Immortality," stanza ix, line 148.
47. E.g., Franklin L. Baumer, *Religion and the Rise of Scepticism* (New York: Harcourt, Brace and World, 1960)—a book better in its diagnosis than in its proposed therapy—see chap. 4 entitled "The Age of Longing."
48. Samuel Alexander (New York: Humanities Press, 1950).
49. Tr. Arthur Mitchell (New York: Henry Holt and Company, 1911).
50. William Barrett (Anchor Books; Garden City: Doubleday & Company, 1958).
51. See Descartes' *Discourse on the Method of Rightly Conducting the Reason and Seeking Truth in the Sciences* (Edinburgh: Sutherland and Knox, 1850), p. 75.
52. *Ethics,* Eberhard Bethge, ed. (New York: The Macmillan Company, 1955), pp. 58-59.
53. "We Have Seen the Anguish of Vietnam," Sunday, August 1, 1965.
54. My wife and I visited the village and dedicated the new plot of land in December, 1951.
55. John 1:3.
56. Father Cuthbert, *Life of St. Francis of Assisi* (London: Longmans, Green and Company, 1921), p. 267.
57. Rev. 3:1.

58. *G. F. Watts* (Chicago: Rand McNally & Company, n.d.), p. 49.

59. Rom. 8:24, 25.

8. Breakthrough: The Faith

1. Gal. 1:15.

2. *Concluding Unscientific Postscript,* David F. Swenson and Walter Lowrie, tr. (Princeton: Princeton University Press, 1941), p. 275.

3. Williams, p. 80.

4. Luke 2:1. The RSV says, "Now the birth of Jesus took place in this way" (Matt. 1:18).

5. John 1:14 KJV.

6. Rev. 3:20.

7. Isa. 53:5.

8. Luke 2:25.

9. Isa. 9:5.

10. Luke 24:21.

11. Acts 2:23-24.

12. John 20:29.

13. II Tim. 1:12.

14. II Cor. 12:10.

15. Shakespeare, *Hamlet,* Act III, scene i, lines 62 and 70.

16. Matt. 27:33; Mark 15:22; Luke 23:32; John 19:17.

17. John 1:1.

18. Gen. 1:3. The Hebrew could almost as well be translated, "God spoke light, and there was light."

19. John 1:2-3.

20. Gen. 2:17.

21. John 1:14 KJV.

22. See chap. 5, note 7.

23. John 12:20.

24. John 12:23-24.

25. Luke 13:33.

26. Matt. 17:1-9; Mark 9:2-9; Luke 9:28-36.

27. II Kings 2:11.

28. Mark 15:13; Luke 23:21; John 19:15; Matt. 27:22-23.

29. John 16:33.

30. Rev. 11:15 (italics mine).

31. Luke 23:34.

32. Luke 10:18.

33. Luke 15:24, 23.
34. Luke 22:53.
35. John 1:14 KJV.
36. Acts 16:31.
37. Eph. 2:8.
38. Matt. 13:24-30.
39. (New York: Brentano's, 1924), Epilogue, p. 154.
40. Masefield, "Biography," a few lines before the end of the poem.
41. Described in a poem, "The Triumph of Life," especially lines 85-200. The vision described is not necessarily a personal experience although Shelley was so subject.
42. Tr. by the author (New York: Grove Press, 1954), p. 34.

9. The Way of Suffering: Dead End

1. *Dream and Reality,* p. 40.
2. Mark 9:24 KJV.; John 9:38.
3. See *The Myth of Sisyphus and Other Essays,* Justin O'Brien, tr. (New York: Alfred A. Knopf, 1955), especially "An Absurd Reasoning."
4. Title of a book by Dale Carnegie (New York: Pocket Books, 1952).
5. Quoted by William James, *The Will to Believe* (London: Longmans, Green and Company, 1911), p. 62.
6. See chap. 8, note 16.
7. *A Kierkegaard Anthology,* Robert Bretall, ed. (Princeton: Princeton University Press, 1946), pp. 97-108, "The Equilibrium between the Aesthetical and the Ethical in the Composition of Personality."
8. This is my wording of his argument. See *The Principles of Psychology,* II (New York: Henry Holt and Company, 1904), 450.
9. Acts 17:27-28. See *The Interpreter's Bible,* IX, 236.
10. "Eagle Sonnet VII," Clement Wood.
11. Charles Kingsley, "The Three Fishers," stanza 3.
12. Shakespeare, Act IV, scene vi, line 75.
13. Louise Driscoll, "God's Pity."
14. *Ad Marciam,* XII, 5, also quoted in Merrill Proudfoot, *Suffering: A Christian Understanding* (Philadelphia: The Westminster Press, 1964), p. 54.
15. See Proudfoot, *ibid.,* p. 55, in a chapter on "Paul and Epictetus."
16. *Dogmatics in Outline,* p. 117.
17. Job 13:15.

18. John 13:4.
19. Job 13:7, 9.
20. Job 2:9.
21. Job 9:32, 33.
22. "The Guest," *The Atlantic Monthly,* December, 1957, p. 51.
23. *The Fall*, pp. 112-13.
24. Ps. 35:17.
25. Ps. 82:2-3.
26. Ps. 89:46-47.
27. Scherer, *Event in Eternity*, p. 168.
28. Ps. 8:4.
29. Job 7:18—my own free translation which gathers in the mood as well as the meaning. I have changed "visit" to "inspect" and have added adverbs.
30. Job 7:16.
31. *Leaves of Grass* (New York: Grosset and Dunlap, 1850-81), pp. 40-41, in a poem entitled "Walt Whitman," sometimes known as "The Song of Myself."
32. Scherer, *Event in Eternity*, p. 168.
33. Jer. 37:17.
34. Becket.
35. See Martin Esslin, *The Theatre of the Absurd* (Anchor Books; Garden City: Doubleday & Company, 1961), p. 12.
36. *The Myth of Sisyphus and Other Essays.*
37. Camus.
38. "Go, Bitter Christ," *Redemption, An Anthology of the Cross*, George Stewart, ed. (New York: George H. Doran, 1927), p. 307.
39. Thompson, "The Hound of Heaven," line 153.
40. Jer. 22:16, capital mine.
41. Matt. 25:40.
42. State worker of the NAACP, killed June 21, 1963, in Jackson, Mississippi —see *Life,* June 21, 1963.
43. Luke 9:51.

10. The Way of Suffering: Breakthrough

1. See John 14:6.
2. Luke 22:31 NEB.
3. John 1:3.
4. Matt. 13:35.

5. Nicholas Vachel Lindsay, "The Chinese Nightingale," *Collected Poems,* (Rev. ed.; New York: The Macmillan Company, 1959), stanza 5.
6. Rev. 15:2.
7. II Cor. 4:17.
8. II Cor. 5:5.
9. John 4:34.
10. See *The Courage to Be* (New Haven: Yale University Press, 1952), chap. VI, "The Courage to Accept Acceptance."
11. Eph. 3:17.
12. "Biography," last four lines.
13. *Suffering Human and Divine,* p. 204. Dr. Robinson's translation reads: "Weeping may come in to lodge at even, but at morn there is a ringing cry of joy."
14. Ps. 30:5.
15. *Ibid.*
16. Matt. 21:12-13; Mark 11:15-17; Luke 19:45-46; John 2:13-17.
17. "A Hymn," *The Collected Poems of G. K. Chesterton* (New York: Dodd, Mead & Company, 1940), pp. 136-37.
18. (Boston: Little, Brown and Company, 1951), pp. 181-82.
19. Matt. 13:30.
20. Matt. 9:38.
21. Alfred Tennyson, "In Memoriam," canto xxxii, stanza 4.
22. Exod. 15:22-25.
23. Shelley, "Adonais," stanza lii.
24. *and Other Stories* (New York: Review of Reviews Corporation, 1923).
25. Phil. 3:10 KJV.
26. Matt. 25:35-36.
27. Matt. 25:34.
28. James H. Leigh Hunt, "Abou Ben Adhem."
29. *Dream and Reality,* p. 40.
30. Thompson, "The Hound of Heaven."
31. Mal. 3:2.
32. Luke 23:34.
33. Camus, *The Plague,* p. 205.
34. Ps. 73:15-17.
35. I John 4:19.
36. Luke 23:46.
37. Written by the Rev. Martin Rinkart (1586-1649) parish minister of Eilenburg, where 8,000 persons died during the famine and pestilence of 1637.

38. Vss. 4-5.
39. Vs. 6.
40. Ps. 119:165.
41. II Tim. 4:6 KJV.
42. II Tim. 4:8.
43. II Cor. 12:10.

11. Pain as Cleansing

1. John 13:34.
2. Austin Farrer, *The Freedom of the Will;* and M. C. D'Arcy, S.J., *The Pain of This World and the Providence of God* (London: Longmans, Green and Company, 1935).
3. G. Chappell (New York: G. P. Putnam's Sons, 1921).
4. A Sophocles drama. For an excellent discussion of the *Antigone* see H. D. F. Kitto, *Greek Tragedy: A Literary Study* (Anchor Books; Garden City: Doubleday & Company, 1954), pp. 129-35.
5. I John 4:11.
6. See chap. 9, note 42.
7. Matt. 27:46; Mark 15:34.
8. Matthew Arnold, "Empedocles on Etna," stanza 34.
9. Burns, "Man Was Made to Mourn."
10. Shaw, *Saint Joan,* scene V, p. 136.
11. Ps. 51:4.
12. Acts 26:5 KJV.
13. I Tim. 1:15 KJV. The RSV says, "I am the foremost of sinners."
14. Luke 15:11-32.
15. William Herbert Carruth, "Each in His Own Tongue."
16. Thomas Edward Brown, "My Garden."
17. I John 2:15.
18. Children of a professor friend.
19. I John 4:19.
20. Shakespeare, *King Lear,* Act III, scene iv, line 27.
21. Luke 6:46.
22. See Boswell's *Life of Samuel Johnson,* Journal entry for Saturday, July 30, 1763.
23. Luke 10:29-37.
24. Eph. 4:12; I Cor. 12:27.
25. John 3:16.

26. See *Descent of the Dove* (Living Age Book; New York: Meridian Books, 1956), "Postscript," pp. 234-36; and *The Image of the City* and other essays, sel. Anne Ridler (London: Oxford University Press, 1958), Introduction, p. xl. The theme runs through several of the novels, in particular Williams' *Descent into Hell*, pp. 103-4 and p. 189.
27. Quoted by Barrett, *Irrational Man*, p. 227.
28. Edmund Burke, from a speech at Bristol, Sept. 9, 1780.
29. *Heroes and Hero Worship*, chap. 1, "The Hero as Divinity," p. 10.
30. I John 2:17.
31. Quoted by Ian Macpherson, as reported in *Treasury of the Christian World*, compiled by A. Gordon Nasby (New York: Harper & Row, 1953), p. 228.
32. Luke 15:19.
33. II Cor. 5:13.
34. Matt. 10:39.
35. II Cor. 12:4.
36. Phil. 3:10.
37. Widely used in the civil rights demonstrations of the present time.
38. C. H. Gabriel, "When All My Labors and Trials Are O'er."
39. D'Arcy, *The Pain of This World and the Providence of God.*
40. *Ibid.*, p. 129.
41. *Ibid.*, p. 135.
42. Matt. 13:35.
43. See *Holy Week*, Ronald A. Knox, tr. (New York: Sheed and Ward, 1951), p. 253, in "Holy Saturday," a prayer for "The Blessing of the Paschal Candle," "O happy fault that won so holy and so high a Redeemer."
44. Rom. 6:1.
45. Rom. 6:2*a* KJV, which here seems more true to the force of the exclamation, though RSV, with its "By no means," is literally more accurate.
46. Rom. 6:2*b*.
47. Owen Davis (New York: Samuel French, 1941), Act I, scene 1, p. 14.
48. Knox, *Holy Week*, p. 253.
49. I Cor. 1:25.

12. Pain as Vocation

1. (New York: The Macmillan Company, 1965).
2. Isa. 53:4-5.
3. Phil. 1:29.

4. John 1:14, my translation.
5. I Sam. 5:2-5.
6. Heb. 12:24.
7. Rom. 8:16-17.
8. Ted Koehler, "I've Got the World on a String."
9. See chap. 8, note 2.
10. Job 2:9.
11. Phil. 4:1.
12. I John 5:19.
13. In *Chantecler,* 1910. Edmond Rostand is a French dramatist.
14. Matt. 26:39; Mark 14:36; Luke 22:42.
15. Carnegie, *How to Win Friends and Influence People.*
16. Luke 14:27.
17. John 16:33.
18. Mark 13:9-13.
19. See Matt. 25:31-46.
20. Rom. 12:2.
21. Matt. 8:21 KJV; Luke 9:59 KJV.
22. Gal. 6:17.
23. II Tim. 3:12-13.
24. I Peter 3:14.
25. II Cor. 4:17.
26. II Cor. 2:14.
27. Wordsworth, "Lines Composed a Few Miles Above Tintern Abbey," lines 37 ff.
28. Col. 1:24.
29. Thompson, "The Hound of Heaven," stanza 2.
30. Col. 1:24.
31. Col. 1:25-26.
32. Gabriel, "When All My Labors and Trials Are O'er."
33. Mark Gibbs and T. Ralph Morton (Philadelphia: The Westminster Press, 1965). A book for and about ordinary Christians.
34. John A. T. Robinson (Philadelphia: The Westminster Press, 1963).
35. Gibson Winter (Garden City: Doubleday & Company, 1961).
36. Cox.
37. John 3:17.
38. *The Angel That Troubled the Waters* (New York: Coward McCann, 1928), p. 145. See also John 5:2-9.
39. Theme song of the musical, "Carnival," 1961. Words and music by Bob Merrill.

40. Col. 1:24.
41. I Peter 5:8.
42. Luke 14:27.
43. Rom. 3:10 KJV; Ps. 14:3 KJV; Ps. 53:3 KJV.
44. Phil. 4:21-22.
45. Col. 1:24.
46. Mark 9:40.
47. Luke 11:23.
48. Matt. 25:40.
49. Charles Wesley, "Love Divine, All Loves Excelling."
50. Rom. 8:38-39.

13. Pain as Insight

1. Matt. 12:43-45; Luke 11:24-26.
2. Phil. 1:19.
3. Phil. 1:21.
4. Phrases from Francis Thompson, "The Kingdom of God."
5. Robert Browning, "Saul," canto xviii.
6. Percy Grainger.
7. II Cor. 4:6.
8. Gen. 8:20-22; 9:12-17.
9. Alfred Tennyson, "Ulysses," line 60.
10. Ps. 8:3.
11. The classic proofs of God could be shown to "beg the question," but they thus give more than "proof": they testify to the presence of God within the life and mind that seek "proof."
12. Francis Thompson, "Sister Songs," part the second.
13. "All Flesh," Vol. III, stanza iii.
14. Mary A. Lathbury.
15. Education, Religion, Music, Art; on the Monument of the Four Muses in the central plaza.
16. Matt. 5:45.
17. Acts 10:34.
18. Matt. 7:27; Luke 6:49.
19. Mark 4:27.
20. Matt. 13:3-9; Mark 4:1-9; Luke 8:5-8.
21. Matt. 13:24-30.
22. Quoted in *The Image of the City,* Introduction, p. xxx.
23. Ezek. 18:4.

24. See for example, Harvey Cox, *The Secular City;* Paul Van Buren, *The Secular Meaning of the Gospel* (New York: The Macmillan Company, 1963). *Deus absconditus* (the absence of God) has been a recurrent theme in the history of Christian thought.

25. This phrase is quoted from Dietrich Bonhoeffer, *Letters and Papers from Prison,* pp. 194 ff. and p. 208. *Letters from Prison* is almost the textbook of the new school. It is doubtful if his followers remember sufficiently his devotion to the Bible and the church. He himself, martyred for the faith in a Nazi prison, had no chance to clarify his new thrust in thought.

26. *Ibid.,* pp. 195-200; pp. 211 ff.; pp. 218-19.

27. See chap. III, "The Ground of Our Being."

28. *The Secular City,* see especially Part IV, "God and the Secular Man," chap. 11.

29. "Choruses from 'The Rock,'" *Collected Poems* (New York: Harcourt, Brace and World, 1936), p. 181.

30. "For the Time Being," *The Collected Poetry of W. H. Auden* (New York: Random House, 1945), p. 411.

31. Matt. 21:28-30. Jesus did not speak in aphorisms. He spoke sharply to the then current scene.

32. See William Hamilton in *The Christian Century,* October 6, 1965, p. 1221, who says, "A new feeling of hope and optimism in American life today . . . a decisive halt should be called to the persuasive "modern" hostility to technology, speed, urbanization."

33. *The Technological Society,* John Wilkinson, tr. (New York: Alfred A. Knopf, 1964), particularly author's introduction to the American edition and "Total Integration," pp. 412 ff.

34. Ps. 100:3.

35. J. B. Phillips, *Letters to Young Churches* (New York: The Macmillan Company, 1955), p. 218, his translation of the last phrase of I John 3:1.

36. Heb. 11:16.

37. Milton, *Paradise Lost,* Book II, line 112.

38. Bonhoeffer, *Letters from Prison.*

39. *Ibid.*

40. Luke 10:29-37.

41. *Letters from Prison,* pp. 222-23, 225-27.

42. *Ibid.*

43. *The Cost of Discipleship,* pp. 277 ff.; chapter on "The Visible Community"; and *Letters from Prison,* pp. 239-40.

44. Bonhoeffer, *Letters from Prison.*

45. Bonhoeffer.

46. See Isa. 55:8.
47. Whitman, *Leaves of Grass*, p. 448.
48. See "A Catechism," *The Book of Common Prayer*, in the answer to the meaning of the word "Sacrament."
49. From *Lettres de l'Abbé Perreyve* (ed. 1903), and quoted *The Expositor's Dictionary of Texts*, II (New York: George H. Doran Company, 1910), 593.
50. Negro spiritual.
51. II Kings 6:24-31.
52. From an unpublished "Christmas Sonnet Sequence" of my own, kept under wraps because it is not strong enough to trot out on the field.
53. *Ibid.*
54. I John 4:11.
55. Matt. 5:4.
56. John 15:12.
57. *Ibid.*
58. Col. 2:23.

14. Pain, Death, and the Resurrection

1. Robert W. Youngs, "Why Do Good People Suffer?" Sept., 1959.
2. *Chicago Tribune*, October 12, 1965.
3. Mortimer Adler, "How to Endure Suffering," *Chicago Sun-Times*, October 22, 1961.
4. Cole Porter.
5. Prov. 13:12.
6. Rom. 8:24.
7. Last paragraph in "El Dorado," *Virginibus Puerisque* (London: Chatto and Windus, 1913).
8. *The Rubáiyát*, stanza XIV.
9. Henry Vaughan, "The Retreat."
10. Ps. 90:10.
11. *The Rubáiyát*, stanza XIV.
12. C. 1930, quoted by Burton Stevenson in *The Home Book of Proverbs, Maxims, and Familiar Phrases* (New York: The Macmillan Company, 1948), p. 646.
13. The reply of Achilles to Ulysses in the 11th book of Homer's *Odyssey*, William Cowper, tr., line 593, "I had rather live the servile hind for hire, and eat the bread of some man scantily himself sustain'd, than sovereign empire hold o'er all the shades.

14. Isa. 38:18.
15. Ps. 16:10.
16. Isa. 26:19.
17. Dan. 12:2.
18. (2nd ed.; New York: Philosophical Library, 1950), pp. 194 ff.
19. John Milton, "A Mask Presented at Ludlow Castle, 1634," line 5.
20. In June, 1879. See C. H. Cramer, *Royal Bob, The Life of Robert G. Inger-sol* (Indianapolis: The Bobbs-Merrill Company, 1926), pp. 151 and 263.
21. Gen. 1:26.
22. II Tim. 1:10.
23. Fred D. Gealy, *The Interpreter's Bible,* XI, 469.
24. II Tim. 1:9.
25. Col. 1:17.
26. See pp. 221-22.
27. Matt. 22:23-33; Mark 12:18-27; Luke 20:27-40.
28. Luke 16:19-31.
29. See pp. 105-6, 121-22.
30. Mark 16:8.
31. William Wordsworth, "Elegiac Stanzas Suggested by a Picture of Peele Castle in a Storm," line 15.
32. Phil. 3:10.
33. II Cor. 3:18.
34. John 8:12.
35. John Drinkwater, "To and Fro About the City," in *Seeds of Time* (New York: Houghton Mifflin Company, 1922).
36. Col. 3:11.
37. Rev. 21:4.
38. Rev. 21:1.
39. Quoted by Eric O. A. Brampton, *Treasury of the Christian World,* p. 126. See also Pliny's letter to Emperor Trajan reporting his method of arrest and punishment of Christians in his province, M. Lincoln Schuster, *The World's Great Letters* (New York: Simon and Schuster, 1940), p. 23.
40. Isa. 35:1 KJV (the RSV says "crocus").
41. 1 Peter 4:12-13.
42. John 20:29.
43. II Thess. 2:7.
44. Matthew Arnold, "East London."
45. *The Devil's Share* (New York: Pantheon Books, 1944), Introduction, p. 11.
46. Robert Browning, "Rabbi Ben Ezra," stanza vi.
47. Matt. 6:10.

48. William Blake, "Auguries of Innocence," line 109.
49. Thomas Gray, "The Progress of Poesy," III, 2.
50. II Sam. 23:13-17.
51. Isa. 45:15; Ps. 19:9 KJV.
52. *Dream and Reality,* p. 121. Actual words: "Dans la vie rien n'est beau que d'aimer, rien n'est vrai que de souffrir."
53. Matt. 24:36.
54. Luke 13:24*a*.
55. Luke 13:24*b*.
56. II Tim. 4:6 KJV.
57. A member of Captain Robert F. Scott's last and ill-fated expedition to the South Pole (1912). See Leonard Huxley, *Scott's Last Expedition* (New York: Dodd, Mead and Company, 1913), I, 408; II, 238.
58. Luke 23:46.
59. Alan Porter, "The Signature of Pain," *The Signature of Pain and Other Poems* (New York: The John Day Company, 1931), last three lines.
60. Fiona Macleod (William Sharp), *Pharais and the Mountain Lovers* (New York: Duffield and Company, 1909), pp. 168-69.
61. Shakespeare, *Merchant of Venice,* Act V, scene i, line 54.
62. Rev. 14:2 KJV.
63. Rev. 15:3.
64. Rev. 5:9-10 KJV.
65. See Maisie Ward, *Gilbert Keith Chesterton* (New York: Sheed and Ward, 1943), chap. 5, "The Notebook," p. 65.
66. John 8:12.

Index of Scripture

261

Index of Names and Subjects